*The Journal of*
# Margaret Hazlitt

MARGARET
A portrait on ivory by John Hazlitt

# The Journal of
# Margaret Hazlitt

*Recollections of England, Ireland,
and America*

*Edited and Annotated by Ernest J. Moyne*

*The University of Kansas Press
Lawrence, 1967*

828

HH295

PR 4769
.H9 Z5

*For*

**Kathleen and Elizabeth**

# Preface

The research for this annotated edition of Margaret Hazlitt's journal has been done at the University of Delaware Library, the Historical Society of Delaware, the Widener and Houghton Libraries at Harvard, the Massachusetts Historical Society, the Library of the American Unitarian-Universalist Association in Boston, the New York Public Library, the Historical Society of Pennsylvania, the American Philosophical Society, the Presbyterian Historical Society, the Enoch Pratt Library in Baltimore, the Maryland Historical Society, the Library of Congress, the Maidstone Museum and Art Gallery in Maidstone, England, and the National Library in Dublin, Ireland. I am indebted to many members of the staffs of these institutions for their courteous cooperation. I am also indebted to Mrs. Nina Fletcher Little for permission to quote from her *American Decorative Wall Painting, 1700-1850*. Quotations from the Adams Papers are from the microfilm edition, by permission of the Massachusetts Historical Society. Special thanks are due officials of the following institutions for permission to quote from manuscripts in their collections: the Historical Society of Pennsylvania, the Maryland Historical Society, and the Maidstone Museum and Art Gallery in Maidstone, England. The portraits of the Hazlitt family in this book are all from the W. Carew Hazlitt Collection in the Maidstone Museum and Art Gallery and have been reproduced here by permission of the Curator, Mr. A. Grove, whose kindness and assistance I very much appreciate.

I am grateful for the help given me by Mr. Norman A. Hersey and Mr. Mason Foley, of Hingham, Massachusetts; Dr. Lyman H. Butterfield, Editor of the Adams Papers; Mr. Wendell D. Garrett, Managing Editor of *Antiques;* Professor A. R. Dunlap, of the University of Delaware, and Dr. John M. Dawson, Director of Libraries at the University of Delaware; and Mr. A. Russell Slagle, of Baltimore, a descendant of one branch of the Hazlitt family in America. I am also particularly grateful to the staff of the University of Kansas Press for helpful suggestions.

I wish to thank the University of Delaware for summer research grants which greatly aided the progress of my work, and also the Winterthur Program in Early American Culture at the University of Delaware for a travel grant and for assistance in getting my manuscript typed.

University of Delaware                    E. J. M.

# Contents

**Preface**                                                       vii

# Introduction                                                   3
THE FATHER, WILLIAM HAZLITT, 1737-1820          4
THE MOTHER, GRACE LOFTUS HAZLITT,
 1746-1837                                                       14
THE SONS, JOHN THE ARTIST, 1767-1837,
 AND WILLIAM THE ESSAYIST, 1778-1830          15
THE DAUGHTER AND AUTHOR, MARGARET,
 1770-1841                                                       22
THE AUTOBIOGRAPHICAL JOURNAL: ITS
 COMPOSITION AND HISTORY                            25

# Margaret Hazlitt's Journal
DEDICATION                                                      30
THE ORIGIN OF THE HAZLITTS AND THEIR
 EXPERIENCES IN ENGLAND AND IRELAND          31
THE HAZLITTS IN AMERICA                              48
THE HAZLITTS AFTER THEIR RETURN
 TO ENGLAND                                                   99

# Appendices

"An Account of the State of Rational
    Religion in America"    113
The Shronell Hazlitts    123

# Notes
126

# Index
167

# Illustrations

Margaret    ii
The Rev. William Hazlitt    7
Grace Loftus Hazlitt    8
John and William    17
Margaret    18

# Introduction

# Introduction

Between the years 1835 and 1838, Margaret Hazlitt (1770-1841)—the only surviving daughter of the Rev. William Hazlitt (1737-1820), and sister of John Hazlitt (1767-1837), portrait and miniature painter, and of William Hazlitt (1778-1830), essayist and critic—compiled from family papers and her own recollections, as well as those of her mother, a very remarkable diary. Written expressly for the information and instruction of her nephew William, the son of her brother the essayist, this journal is full of interest both for its account of the origin and history of the Hazlitt family, with their experiences in Ireland and England, and for its detailed and vivid description of the visit of the Rev. William Hazlitt and his wife and children to North America from 1783 to 1787. Not only is Margaret's journal the sole source of material concerning her brother William's earliest years, but it is also a valuable record of conditions in the United States immediately after the American Revolution.

On April 18, 1835, the ninety-eighth anniversary of

her father's birth, Margaret began to write her long-planned account of her father's life, devoted as it was to the cause of liberty and truth. Margaret's mother was still alive and was known and loved by her grandson William. But William had been born too late to remember his grandfather very well, so that Margaret's main purpose in writing was to acquaint William with the stirring events in the Rev. Mr. Hazlitt's long and full life as one of the founders of Unitarianism. Although her recollections focus on her father, Margaret does of course bring into her narrative the rest of the family as well.

The origin and descent of the Hazlitt family have of necessity remained obscure. Margaret's account goes back only as far as the generation of her own grandfather and grandmother, John and Margaret Hazlitt of Shrone Hill, or Shronell, in the County of Tipperary, Ireland. Her references to earlier generations and collateral branches of the Hazlitt family are general, and so too are her references to kin encountered in America, which often leave the reader wishing she had been more explicit in defining the exact relationship between the American Hazlitts and the British.

# I

## THE FATHER, WILLIAM HAZLITT, 1737-1820

The Rev. William Hazlitt was born at Shronell in 1737. At the age of nineteen he went to the University of Glasgow, where he remained for four years and took his master's degree in 1760. Although he was brought up to believe in orthodox principles, he gradually imbibed rational views of religion and at the time of his leaving the university he possessed general Unitarian sentiments. His first settlement was with the Presbyterian congregation at Wisbeach, in the Isle of Ely, in 1764. At the end of his two-year stay in Wisbeach, he married Grace Loftus, the daughter of an ironmonger of that town. From Wisbeach he moved to Marshfield, in Gloucestershire, and thence to Maidstone, in Kent, where he remained for ten years, from 1770 to 1780. During this time he enjoyed the friendship of such eminent men as Dr. Priestley, Dr. Price, and Dr. Kippis, and at the home of his friend Mr. Viny, of Tenterden, he frequently met Benjamin Franklin. It was during his sojourn in Maidstone that the Rev. Mr. Hazlitt began contributing articles to Priestley's *Theological Repository* under the *noms de plume* "Rationalis" and "Philalethes" and published anonymously *An Essay on the Justice of God,* London, 1773, and two sermons on *Human Authority in Matters of Faith,* London, 1774. From Maidstone he removed, in 1780, to the charge of a congregation at Bandon, in the County of Cork, in Ireland, where he remained for three years. At Bandon he exerted himself in behalf of American prisoners of war confined at Kinsale, and his exposure, in the newspapers, of the cruelties exercised towards them by the British soldiers, considerably alleviated their condition.[1]

On April 3, 1783, the Rev. William Hazlitt and his wife and family left Ireland for America. They landed in New York on May 26, and, after a few days there, proceeded to Philadelphia. On the way to that city, Mr. Hazlitt preached, by special invitation, before the Assembly of New Jersey, then meeting in Burlington. In Philadelphia the Hazlitts lived for fifteen months, and besides preaching occasionally in various places of worship there, Mr. Hazlitt also preached in New London, Pennsylvania. At the recommendation of his warm supporter, Dr. John Ewing, pastor of the First Presbyterian Church in Philadelphia and provost of the University of Pennsylvania, Mr. Hazlitt was considered for a vacancy in the Presbyterian Church in Carlisle, Pennsylvania, and also for the presidency of Dickinson College, which was just being founded. Dr. Benjamin Rush, however, saw to it that the candidate of his personal enemy, Dr. Ewing, was not appointed to either position.[2] In the late fall of 1783 Mr. Hazlitt went to Centreville, Maryland, to preach, but there he was rebuffed as a dissenter. During the winter of 1783-1784, he delivered a course of lectures entitled "Evidences of the Truth of the Christian Religion" in the Common Hall of the University of Pennsylvania, and in May, 1784, just before leaving Philadelphia, he republished some of Priestley's Unitarian tracts, to which he prefixed short addresses of his own.

From Philadelphia the Rev. Mr. Hazlitt went, by invitation, to preach at the Brattle Street Church in Boston, but a report of his heterodox principles which preceded him and his own frank admission of his beliefs prevented his being permanently settled there. After staying in Boston and Lower Dorchester for a few months, the Hazlitt family moved to Weymouth, where they lived for a year and eight months, and then to Upper Dorchester, where they lived for one year.

During his residence in and near Boston, the Rev. Mr. Hazlitt preached repeatedly to various congregations in Boston, and early in 1785 he gave in Boston the same course of lectures that he had given at the University of Pennsylvania. He also preached at Dorchester, Jamaica Plain, Weymouth, Marshfield, Scituate, Prov-

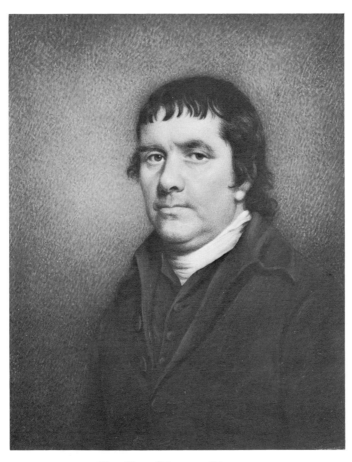

THE REV. WILLIAM HAZLITT

GRACE LOFTUS HAZLITT

idence, Hingham, and Salem. In Hingham, where
the venerable Rev. Ebenezer Gay was the pastor, he
preached more than forty times. In Salem he preached
to three large congregations which generally heard liberal ministers with acceptance. Mr. Hazlitt made many
friends in almost every place he visited, but the majority
were never in his favor. For example, even though he
preached in Hallowell, Maine, for four months as a candidate for settlement in the work of the ministry there,
he was finally rejected.

Unable to find the means of supporting his family in
America, Mr. Hazlitt sailed for England late in 1786,
and his wife and children followed him during the summer of 1787. Mr. Hazlitt's stay of three and a half years
in the newly created republic was not in vain, however,
for he succeeded in laying the foundation of Unitarianism in this country. He did this by leaving behind him
warm friends to the cause wherever he went; by the publication of Dr. Priestley's works and his own sermons: *A
Discourse on the Apostle Paul's Mystery of Godliness
Being Made Manifest in the Flesh* (Falmouth, 1786) and
*A Thanksgiving Discourse, Preached at Hallowell, 15
December, 1785* (Boston, 1786); and by being instrumental in the formation of the first Unitarian Church in
Boston.

In September, 1782, almost two years before the Rev.
Mr. Hazlitt came to Massachusetts, James Freeman, a
graduate of Harvard in 1777, became lay reader at King's
Chapel in Boston, one of the oldest Episcopal churches
in New England. Freeman's background was Congrega-
tionalist, but the Wardens of King's Chapel invited him
to serve as lay reader because they had no prospect of se-
curing a candidate with episcopal orders. They author-

ized Freeman to use the Athanasian Creed or not, as he wished, and he accepted their offer by discarding the Creed. Freeman's congregation wished to have him receive episcopal ordination, but when Freeman refused to subscribe to the Thirty-nine Articles, the American bishops would not ordain him, even though Freeman would have gladly acceded to ordination on his own terms.[3]

On May 15, 1784, the day on which the Rev. Mr. Hazlitt arrived in Boston, he was taken by the Rev. John Eliot to a meeting of the Boston Association of Ministers at the home of Dr. Charles Chauncy; there he first met James Freeman. The conversation at the ministers' meeting turning to the subject of ordination, Mr. Hazlitt expressed his opinion "that the people, or the congregation, who chose any man to be their minister, were his proper ordainers." Freeman, who was still unordained, jumped up from his seat in a kind of transport, saying, "I wish you could prove that, Sir." Mr. Hazlitt answered that "few things could admit of an easier proof," and from that moment Freeman and Hazlitt were good friends.[4] Mr. Hazlitt then proceeded to publish several letters, under various pseudonyms, supporting the cause of Freeman. In the October, 1784, issue of the *Boston Magazine,* under the pseudonym of "A New Testament Christian," he published a collection of all the New Testament benedictions and doxologies, which he recommended as replacements for the orthodox benedictory form and doxology. In the November issue of the same magazine, the Rev. Samuel Parker, of Trinity Church in Boston, using the pseudonym "Elakistoteros," answered Hazlitt's article by asserting the twofold nature of Jesus Christ. When the *Boston Magazine* declined to print Hazlitt's reply, as it was part of a theological controversy, he sent it to the *American Herald,* which published it in the January 3 and 10 (1785) numbers. "Elakistoteros" replied in the January 31 issue, and Mr. Hazlitt brought the controversy to a close in the issue of February 21. In the meanwhile, readers of the newspaper had sent in their comments on the theological battle.

At the solicitation of Freeman, Hazlitt published a scriptural confutation of the Thirty-nine Articles in the November 1, 1784, issue of the *American Herald* under the pseudonym of "Philalethes." Notice having been circulated that this publication would appear on November 1, the printer, apprised of the circumstances, ran off a hundred papers beyond his usual number, and all the papers were sold out by noon. This publication, Mr. Hazlitt believed, in its consequences converted Freeman's congregation into a Unitarian church. A committee was appointed to reform the Book of Common Prayer and to strike out all those passages which savored of Trinitarian worship.[5] Mr. Hazlitt assisted Freeman in this work, providing him with a copy of the Prayer Book revised by Theophilus Lindsey according to a plan of Dr. Samuel Clarke. On June 19, 1785, the proprietors of King's Chapel voted, 20 to 7, "that the [Book of] Common Prayer, as it now stands amended, be adopted by this church as the form of prayer to be used in future by this church and congregation."[6]

After all attempts to secure ordination for Freeman by the American bishops failed, the congregation decided to proceed with lay ordination. This took place on November 18, 1787.[7]

Having been influenced by the Rev. Mr. Hazlitt in the reforming of the liturgy and in accepting lay ordination, Freeman never forgot Mr. Hazlitt, and he expressed his gratitude to him on many occasions. In a letter to the Rev. Theophilus Lindsey on July 7, 1786, he wrote, "I bless the day when that honest man first landed in this country."[8] Three years later, in June, 1789, he wrote, "Before Mr. Hazlitt came to Boston, the Trinitarian doxology was almost universally used. That honest, good man prevailed upon several respectable ministers to omit it. Since his departure, the number of those who repeat only scriptural doxologies has greatly increased, so that there are now many churches in which the worship is strictly Unitarian."[9]

Like Freeman, the Rev. William Bentley of the East Church in Salem was influenced by Mr. Hazlitt, who occasionally preached for him, and soon adopted Priestley's Catechism as a substitute for the Westminster Catechism.[10] In addition, during the fall of 1787 Bentley made a spirited attack on the doctrine of the Trinity in a course of sermons upon this subject delivered in Salem.[11] Of all of Hazlitt's friends among the clergy in America, James Freeman and Freeman's college classmate William Bentley were the most receptive to Hazlitt's Socinianism.

After his return to England, the Rev. William Hazlitt settled at Wem, a small market town in Shropshire. Here he served as pastor of the dissenting congregation from 1787 to 1813, when he retired from the ministry. After leaving Wem, he and his wife and daughter lived for a time at Addlestone, in Surrey, then at Bath, and finally at Crediton, in Devonshire, where Mr. Hazlitt died on July 16, 1820, at the age of eighty-three.

The Rev. William Hazlitt deserves to be remembered as one of the founders of modern Unitarianism, as a friend to truth and liberty, as a man of humanitarian aspirations and achievements, and even as a man of culture, who enjoyed the friendship and esteem of some of his most distinguished contemporaries in the ministry and in public life. He also deserves recognition as a man of letters, not only for his published sermons but also for his letters and essays. In addition to the sermons and articles that he published early in his career in England and Ireland, and those he published in America, after his return to England he contributed articles to the *Monthly Repository* and published *Discourses for the Use of Families* (London, 1790) and *Sermons for the Use of Families* (London, 1808). His sermons on important subjects of practical religion are of moderate length, plain, serious, and judicious, and some of his non-religious writings, such as an "Anecdote of Sterne" and "The Man of Honour," in many ways anticipate the work of his son William. There is much truth in W. Carew Hazlitt's observation that the Rev. Mr. Hazlitt was "not merely the father of his son William, but the parent of his son's genius; and that the seeds, which only came to full maturity a generation later, were in that 'poor Irish lad' who left the cradle of the Hazlitts to seek a better fortune."[12] To his son William, the father bequeathed not only an interest in art and a taste for theatrical amusements and distractions but also a love of books.

In the portraits of him painted by his sons William and John, the Rev. William Hazlitt appears as a man of commanding figure and strongly marked features, his face having been scarred with the smallpox. William's tributes to his father in numerous essays are too well known to need repetition here, but the Rev. Mr. Hazlitt's own assessment of himself is worth noting. He described himself as "a plain-spoken, unreserved man, who does not possess much of the *sneaking* virtue, commonly called *discretion*. Some of his *friends* charge him with imprudence. His enemies, call him many hard names, propagate numberless lies against him, and by *orthodox,* secret, machinations, do him every possible injury, in their power. But the advocates of the best interests of men have, almost always, been treated in a similar manner."[13] But even those whom he offended by his heresy or his zealous Whiggism admitted that he was a man of good natural abilities, a man of sense, and a scholar.[14] From him William inherited his inability to hide what he felt, as well as his love of truth and his passion for individual liberty.

## II

### THE MOTHER, GRACE LOFTUS HAZLITT, 1746-1837

As noted earlier, Margaret's diary does not have much to say about her mother beyond tracing the Loftus family history and describing the young Grace Loftus as a very beautiful girl, elegant in her person and manners, and beloved by all who knew her. Her son John's portrait of her testifies that she retained something of her beauty and elegance even in her later years. Without disclosing his sources of information, W. Carew Hazlitt writes that the comely Mrs. Hazlitt was an object of more special attention on the part of the captain of the ship which took the Hazlitts to America than her husband approved of.[15] He also speaks of the aged Mr. Hazlitt's "occasional playfulness" and of his wife's resulting "little jealousies"; "of her recovery of her sight, so that she could thread Margaret's needles"; and "of her second dentition."[16] From Margaret's account and from various extant letters, we can infer that Mrs. Hazlitt, who gave birth to seven children, only three of whom grew to maturity, was a loving wife, mother, and grandmother. She lived to the age of ninety, dying on June 10, 1837, and she lies buried with her husband in Crediton.

## III

### THE SONS, JOHN THE ARTIST, 1767-1837, AND WILLIAM THE ESSAYIST, 1778-1830

The oldest of the Hazlitt children was John, who was born in Marshfield, Gloucestershire, on May 13, 1767. Apparently a self-taught artist, John grew into manhood in America and began painting portraits when he was only eighteen years old. As early as February 17, 1785, Joseph Dunckerley, a miniature painter in Boston, and John Hazlitt advertised in the *Independent Chronicle, and the Universal Advertiser* that they were going to open a drawing school in Joseph Dunckerley's house in North Square. (Today this house in Boston is known as the Paul Revere House.) In this advertisement and in one which they first ran in the *American Herald* of March 7, 1785, they also noted that they executed portraits in miniature and crayons. Three months later, in the June 14, 1785, number of the *Salem Gazette,* John Hazlitt advertised that he intended to paint portraits, in all sizes, in Salem. It was probably at this time that he painted a miniature of his father's Salem friend, the Rev. William Bentley.[17]

John also painted in Weymouth, Dorchester, and Hingham. At home he painted miniatures of his father and his brother, William. A picture of his sister, Margaret, which he had done in crayons, he gave to one of

Margaret's friends. For Mr. Samuel Vaughan he painted
a picture of two wild turkeys, which was sent to Germany. In Hingham he executed likenesses of the Rev.
Dr. Ebenezer Gay, General Benjamin Lincoln, Colonel
Nathan Rice, Dr. Joshua Barker, and others.[18] The portrait of the Rev. Dr. Gay, done in pastel, is still owned in
Hingham by his descendants, but the other portraits
seem to have disappeared. Of special interest to us is the
presentation in 1901 by Miss Susan Barker Willard of a
miniature of the Rev. William Hazlitt, by John Hazlitt,
to the Wompatuck Club in Hingham. Presumably this
miniature was originally given to Dr. Joshua Barker and
then handed down in his family until it was bequeathed
to the Wompatuck Club.[19]

In addition to painting portraits, John Hazlitt may
have ornamented some panels in two houses in Hingham
owned by the Thaxter family. Although there are a
number of sources for the attribution of these panels to
John Hazlitt,[20] perhaps the best account of these painted
panels in Hingham is given by Nina Fletcher Little.
"North of Duxbury," she writes, "in the seacoast town of
Hingham, are remains of painted decoration of particular interest and merit. These consist of a number of
panels from each of two early Thaxter houses which
stood facing one another in the center of the town. One
of these houses was owned by Elisha Leavitt, a bitter
Tory during the Revolution. It was owned later by the
Lincoln family and was torn down in 1865. The other
was purchased by the Wampatuck [*sic*] Club in 1900 and
still stands on its original site. The fireplace wall of the
principal room in each house consisted of multiple
raised panels, upon the surface of each of which was
painted a landscape scene. When the Thaxter-Lincoln

JOHN

WILLIAM

MARGARET

house was taken down a number of the panels were saved. One of these hangs in the Hingham Historical Society, several are locally owned. . . . In the Wampatuck Club the entire chimney wall incorporates seventeen panels, each decorated with a different view. . . . They are well painted in a style more competent than that of the usual travelling decorator. The subjects bear no resemblance to American scenery but might be either English or Continental. However, the British Jack flies over the turreted castle which surmounts the fireplace.

"Probably because of the foreign character of these subjects their authorship was many years ago credited to John Hazlitt, a portrait and miniature painter who lived in nearby Weymouth during the 1780's. . . . John was only eighteen years of age at this time, but he was already proficient in the media of miniature, pastel, and oil. . . . Were the Hingham panels done by Hazlitt? There appears to be no evidence to support this attribution except the facts that he was painting portraits in the town between 1784 and 1787, that he was a competent artist, that the panels are unusually well executed, and that the subject matter appears to be European rather than American. If Hazlitt did indulge in a bit of architectural painting it must have been as a sideline from his regular occupation of portrait painter."[21]

After returning to England, John Hazlitt, whose self-portrait shows him to have been a handsome man with a strong resemblance to his mother, became a famous painter in London, where he won praise from Sir Joshua Reynolds and exhibited at the Royal Academy every year from 1788 to 1819. Making the acquaintance not only of eminent artists but also of some of the leading literary men of the time, he became a member of the

circle which included Godwin, Thelwall, Holcroft, Stoddart, Coleridge, and Lamb. About the year 1793 he
married Mary Pierce, by whom he had three children.
According to the Rev. Joseph Hunter, John in his later
years was such a bear and a sot that his wife separated
from him.[22] John Hazlitt died in Stockport on May 16,
1837, at the age of seventy.

John's younger brother, William, of whom he was
always very fond, was born in Maidstone on April 10,
1778. William was only five years old when he arrived in
America with his family and nine years old when the
Hazlitts returned to England. As a result, his chief
memory of the United States, as recorded in his writings,
seems to have been the taste of barberries that hung all
winter in the New England snow. This taste he had in
his mouth even after an interval of thirty years. But
surely William could never have forgotten the times
when his father took him into the pulpit with him while
he preached at the Old Meetinghouse, widely known as
the "Old Ship" Church, in Hingham, or at the Rev.
William Bentley's East Church in Salem. The reader
can well imagine the future essayist's boyish restlessness,
sitting through a long sermon, under the eyes of a congregation which must have often numbered between five
and seven hundred people.

Margaret Hazlitt gives some charming pictures of
her younger brother in America, and mentions among
his playmates George Brewer in Philadelphia, little Maria, a chance acquaintance made on the trip from Philadelphia to Boston, and Beale Cushing in Weymouth.
John Hazlitt's miniature of his brother done in America
presents him as he then was, a little boy with grayish-
blue eyes, a placid brow, dimpled mouth, and long rich

brown hair falling over his shoulders. This was the boy who carried home a dead black snake on a stick to show his mother and, on another occasion, exhibited seven tortoises in the family parlor at Weymouth. There must have been something special about young William which endeared him to Captain Abiah Whitman, of Weymouth, who enjoyed his company, to Madam Derby, of Hingham, who doted on him and would have him indulged in every whim, and to the Rev. James Freeman, of Boston, who remembered him as a curly-headed, bright-eyed boy.[23] It was in Upper Dorchester that William began his studies under the tutelage of his brother, John, but even before this Kirk Boott, of Boston, one of the great merchants of the day, recognized young William's genius and some years later offered to bring him up as a merchant.

Young as he was, William must have sensed the bitter disappointment which the Hazlitts felt when they discovered that the United States was not the promised land of civil and religious liberty that they had anticipated. At any rate, a letter of November 12, 1786, written by eight-year-old William to his father after the Rev. Mr. Hazlitt had departed for England, seems to reflect the Hazlitts' disillusionment. William wrote: "I shall never forget that we came to america. If we had not come to america, we should not have been away from one and other, though now it can not be helped. I think for my part that it would have been a great deal better if the white people had not found it out. Let the [others] have it to themselves, for it was made for them."[24] And yet, less than four years later, in July, 1790, writing from Liverpool to his father at Wem,

William complained about English "ceremonial unsociality" and expressed a wish to be back in America.[25]

William Hazlitt's career as a struggling painter, jour-
nalist, essayist, and critic is so well known that it is un-
necessary to retrace here the familiar outlines of his later
life.

## IV

### The Daughter and Author, Margaret, 1770-1841

Margaret Hazlitt, to whom we are indebted for so
much of our knowledge of the Hazlitts, was born in
Maidstone on December 10, 1770. All the sources seem
to indicate that she, like her brothers, was a highly gifted
person and very artistic. The miniature of her painted
by John Hazlitt sometime before 1806 and praised by
Lamb as being of special excellence reveals a sweet,
gentle, and attractive girl with perhaps a touch of her
father's strength of character, and W. Carew Hazlitt
writes that Margaret, or Peggy as she was called, was "a
successful essayist in oils, and was a good painter in
landscape and of poultry and flowers."[26] Basing his
opinion on several extant examples of her work, he says
that if she had had instruction she would have made an
excellent artist. Unfortunately, she never had a chance
to develop her talents. With the exception of the four
years spent in America during her girlhood and occasional trips to London and Winterslow to visit her
brothers, her life was extremely undiversified. It is
small wonder that after half a century she looked back
on her life in the United States with great nostalgia.

Even as a girl of twelve, when the Hazlitts' Irish maid,
Honour, ran away in New York, Margaret took over the
task of cooking for the whole family. This was prophetic

of the course of events throughout her long life. As a maiden sister, she helped both of her brothers and their families in times of crisis. As a devoted daughter, she cared for her long-lived parents and even befriended strangers. While they were living near Bath, she took into the Hazlitt home Miss Catherine Emmet, the daughter of Christopher Temple Emmet, eldest brother of Robert Emmet, the Irish patriot. No doubt the tie between the two families was common Irish blood and common republican sympathies, but equally important was the addition Catherine Emmet made to the meager income that the Hazlitts derived from various church funds. In 1815 Catherine Emmet executed her will, leaving Margaret Hazlitt for her life the interest of £500.[27] In 1817 Miss Emmet, who, like Margaret, was talented and had been to America, wrote to a cousin in the United States: "Most grateful do I feel for having met with a friend such as my dear Miss Hazlitt, who can feel and allow for all my weaknesses. We are now, together with her good Father and Mother, residing on Combe Down, near the town of Bath. . . . My dear Miss Hazlitt could tell you how often our conversation is of New York. . . . As to company, we see none. Our enjoyments are totally of the domestic kind."[28] Never very strong, Catherine Emmet died in 1824.

After the death of the Rev. Mr. Hazlitt in Crediton in 1820, Margaret and her mother took into their home, as a boarder, the Rev. John Johns, who was appointed minister to the congregation of English Presbyterians in Crediton in 1821. When the Rev. Mr. Johns married in 1833, it seems likely that his wife also came to live with the Hazlitts. In 1836 Mr. Johns left Crediton to become the first minister to the poor of the Liverpool

Domestic Mission Society.[29]  When, after the death of her brother John and that of her mother within a month of each other in 1837, Margaret was left alone in the world,[30] she went to Liverpool to live with the family of the Rev. John Johns. She died there in 1841 and is buried in Liverpool.[31]

The Rev. John Johns, at whose home Margaret died on September 19, 1841, paid her the following tribute: "Margaret [Hazlitt was the] daughter and only surviving child of the late Rev. William Hazlitt, the first Apostle of Unitarianism in Boston, U. S., and the father of William Hazlitt, the distinguished essayist and critic. Miss Hazlitt's character was equally uncommon and unworldly. She had made many literary attainments, and could use the pencil and the pen with no everyday power. But her heart was her chief charm. It was not opened indiscriminately; but it was opened to those whom she loved with the meekest, the warmest, the most self-forgetting love. She had passed the four last years of her life with the friends under whose roof she peacefully died, at the age of seventy-one. Her religious sentiments were held with a rare mixture of mildness and firmness. The reading of the Bible was to her a daily duty; and,whenever her health permitted, she rejoiced to attend on the public worship of the sabbath. Holy and endeared will her memory be in the household from which she has passed away; and the members of it will have happier views of futurity than that which arises from the hope of meeting her again, where we shall know even as we are known, and where the meek will be beautified [*sic*] with salvation."[32]

## V

### THE AUTOBIOGRAPHICAL JOURNAL: ITS COMPOSITION AND HISTORY

In her journal Margaret more than once complains about the hard lot which doomed both her and her father to spend their lives in Wem, an obscure provincial town. She regretted very much that they had not settled down in America. Either she had forgotten or she never knew that her father could not get a permanent position in the United States because of his radical religious principles. In almost every instance she reports some other excuse for his failure to get himself a church in the United States. Perhaps the disappointments experienced fifty years earlier had been forgotten with the passing of time and she wanted to remember only the pleasanter aspects of her family's life in America.

With an artist's eye for beauty in nature and a historian's eye for important events and people, Margaret wrote her diary in a straightforward, unaffected style. And even though she recorded her recollections many years after the events described had occurred, her account is, on the whole, remarkably accurate and trustworthy because she used family letters and journals, some of which are still extant.

Because Margaret wrote her journal specifically for her nephew William's use, her failure to give the manuscript journal to him seems ironical, particularly since he could have drawn upon it for information in writing the sketch of his father's life prefixed to the *Literary Remains,* which he published in 1836. But one must realize that Margaret had not finished her account in 1836 and never did complete it. Dedicating it to the Rev. and

Mrs. John Johns on December 10, 1836, Margaret continued her account briefly in October, 1838, but the spirit had gone out of it. Apparently the death, in 1837, of her mother caused her to lose interest in her literary work.

Margaret Hazlitt recorded her recollections in a duodecimo volume, half roan. She filled 185 pages (plus the dedicatory page) with her even script, using 141 rectos of the volume and, then, having turned the book upside down, using 45 versos, but misnumbering pages throughout. On her death this volume passed into the hands of the Johns family. After the death of the Rev. John Johns in 1847, his wife and children returned from Liverpool to Devon, and later emigrated to Australia.[33] Presumably Margaret's diary went to Australia with them, for it did not turn up again until 1884, when a daughter of the Rev. John Johns brought it to the attention of W. Carew Hazlitt, the grandson of William Hazlitt the essayist. Then it disappeared again until the late 1940's. In 1949 it was purchased, as part of a Hazlitt collection, from a New York bookshop for the University of Delaware Library.

Although W. Carew Hazlitt published copious extracts from Margaret Hazlitt's journal in the September and October, 1884, numbers of the *Antiquary* and later reprinted the same extracts, with some additions and variations, in his *Four Generations of a Literary Family* (London, 1897) and in *The Hazlitts: An Account of Their Origin and Descent* (Edinburgh, 1911), Margaret's journal has never before been published in its entirety. This annotated edition of her whole account makes available for the first time much of interest and value that W. Carew Hazlitt did not publish, and at the same time it corrects errors made by W. Carew Hazlitt in transcribing Margaret's manuscript and in explaining some of her statements.

In preparing Margaret Hazlitt's journal for publication, I have divided her narrative into three sections and supplied titles for them. I have given her account verbatim, but I have made such changes in punctuation, capitalization, spelling, and paragraphing as seemed necessary to make it intelligible. Since by modern standards her punctuation is confusing, too many marks slowing the reader to the point of exasperation, I have simplified it. I have also changed her capitalization to conform with present-day usage. In some cases, I have changed both her punctuation and capitalization in order to join clauses and phrases which belong together in one sentence. As for spelling, I have silently corrected the few obviously misspelled words in her account and standardized the spelling of some proper names, but I have not tampered with British forms. Throughout the text I have supplied the word *and* in place of the ampersand, which Margaret Hazlitt uses often but not consistently. I have also expanded some common abbreviations and supplied italics, missing quotation marks, apostrophes, and periods where needed. For purposes of clarity, I have occasionally altered her paragraphing. Editorial additions are enclosed in square brackets.

To the possible charge that the notes are too numerous, too long, and too thorough, I need only say that I have preferred to err on the side of inclusion rather than exclusion. However, to simplify the documentation as much as possible, I have omitted specific citation of generally known and easily accessible works of reference in the notes.

# Margaret Hazlitt's
# Journal

To my good friends

MR. AND MRS. JOHNS

FROM THEIRS AFFECTIONATELY

MARGARET HAZLITT

CREDITON, DECBR. 10TH 1836[1]

# I

## The Origin of the Hazlitts and Their Experiences in England and Ireland

My dearest William,[1]

On this eighteenth of April, 1835 (being the birthday of my dear father), I begin, as I have long intended, to note down such imperfect recollections of him as I can remember or gather from old letters or other papers. And I think it will be gratifying to you to know something of your grandfather (whom you can scarcely recollect) and the events of a long life spent in unwearied labours to promote the cause of liberty and truth. Without regarding his own interest, but rather in direct opposition to it, he preferred the duty of teaching what he believed to be the truth, to every other consideration.

My father was born on the 18th of April, 1737, in, or near, Tipperary in Ireland.[2] His father (whose family had formerly been more opulent, but had lost most of their property in the Civil Wars)[3] was in but poor circumstances; and lived on a small farm, where my father passed his infancy. When I saw the picture of the Rock of Cashel in that neighbourhood,[4] I fancied to myself that it must have been the attracting spot for all his childish rambles in the happy half holidays; and the scene where, amidst the sublimity of Nature, the future champion of truth and liberty learned to despise the noise of the multitude and the false glare of wealth and power. Here he spent his early youth and attended the common grammar school of that place, where he must have made the best use of his time, as when he went, some years after, to the university, he was thought to be one of the best classics there.[5]

Of my father's family I know little, but I believe they were one of the old Scotch Presbyterian families driven away by the Civil Wars, and settled in this part of Erin.[6] My grandfather, whose name was John, was of a gloomy turn of mind and saw all things as "through a glass darkly." My grandmother (whose name I bear) was an amiable and sweet-tempered woman, of whom my father always spoke with respect and tenderness. She and my grandfather both lived to more than eighty years of age. My father was the eldest son, but his sister Elizabeth was older than he. She married very unfortunately a farmer of the name of M'Cleland.[7] She has left many children, most of whom are now in America. One of them, Jane, was a sensible girl and by her own exertions rose superior to her station in life. Her letters to my father shew both talents and elegance of mind. My Uncle John, who went to America before the Revolution and served all that war under Washington, was made a Colonel by him. He lived a few years after the war was over, but his constitution was worn out by fatigue, and he died in the prime of life, leaving no family. I have seen his name, in a history of the Revolution, mentioned together with another John Hazlitt, a cousin,[8] as behaving gallantly in the affair of Trenton or Prince Town.[9] I am not certain as to the place.

My Uncle James was educated for the ministry, but being disgusted with the austere manners of the dissenters with whom he was engaged, and they in their turn thinking him too gay, he left them and conformed to the church, a dereliction my father never could relish.[10] He was at the time we saw him, in Dublin, curate of St. Mary's Church.[11] The living of Castle Bar was afterwards given him (worth about 400£ an year). How long he lived there I forget, but his last days were harassed by the performance of his duty as a magistrate, which oft obliged him to commit to prison as rebels poor deluded wretches whom he thought it would have been a more Christian act to feed and instruct.[12] He was married three times, and left several children, of whom I have lost all knowledge. John, whom I saw, was an officer. His [James's] son Kilner you know.[13]

In the year 1758, my father was sent, as a student, to the University of Glasgow.[14] Here he remained five years, and although his attention was chiefly devoted to the study of divinity, yet he gave some time to Physic. From the pleasure with which he always spoke of Glasgow, and with which he remembered his college days, his time there must have passed very pleasantly and his annual visits home have given a keener relish to renewed study. Some certificates of his regular attendance at lecture hours, and general good behaviour, are the only notices that remain of that time.[15]

Some time after leaving college, he came to England, and spent some time in London, and preached occasionally for the different ministers who, pleased with his opening talents, were not slow in recommending him to those vacant congregations who applied to them for a pastor. For a few months he officiated as chaplain to Sir Giles Joscelyn.[16] In the year 1764 my father had an invitation to settle with a dissenting congregation at Wisbeach, in the Isle of Ely. Here he remained two years, where he first saw Miss Loftus, a very beautiful young girl, elegant in her person and manners, and beloved by all who knew her.[17] She was the daughter of an ironmonger, a most respectable and upright man. But although my father had fixed his affections on this lady, he went away, for the present, without opening his heart to the mistress of it, hoping that on some future day he might obtain a settlement which would make an offer of his hand neither a rash [n]or an imprudent step. After an absence of a year he returned, and was married to Miss Loftus on the tenth of January, 1766,[18] at Peterborough, where she was on a visit to Miss Coulson, her brother's future wife.[19] As you both know and love your grandmother, I need not say more of her here.

Her father died some time before her marriage, at the age of sixty-two. He was, I have been told, very handsome, and mild and gentle in his manners, never being moved to violent anger except when anyone told him a falsehood, a thing he never could tolerate. The father of Mr. Loftus was a watchmaker, and came from Hull in Yorkshire (with the grandfather of William Godwin, the author of *Political Justice*) to settle at Wisbeach, and I have heard Godwin speak of a watch in his possession made by the elder Loftus, a curiosity I should much like to see. Mr. Godwin, the father of William, was the minister at Wisbeach when my mother was a little girl. I have heard her speak of going, on a Saturday afternoon, to draw the still younger Godwins in their little coach. They all rejoiced to see their friend Grace, and William had not yet dreamed of *Caleb Williams*. Godwin's mother was a woman of great talents; her father's name was Hull.[20] But to return to our own ancestors. My grandfather Thomas Loftus, in the year 1725, married Miss Grace Pentlow, the daughter of a gentleman in Oxfordshire. Mr. Pentlow was once possessed of an estate of [£]400 a year, but by some unfortunate speculation he had lost it all, and was forced to accept of fifty pounds an year as an excise-officer. An hard reverse this to a gentleman! His estate was near Henley-on-Thames, and he lived some time at Banbury,[21] and afterwards at Oxford, for I have heard my grandmother tell of two yew trees, cut into the shape of giants, standing at the entrance of the Botanical Gardens there, of whom she stood in great dread, and of a sad fright she was once put in by her father pretending he would take her to prison for climbing to a cupboard to get a lump or two of sugar! She must have been very young at that time, and it shews that Mr. Pentlow had lost his patrimony early in life. And he was rather a youngish man when he died. He was twice married, and had two daughters; the eldest was all her life subject to fits brought on by a fright. One evening when Mr. Pentlow was absent, the servants ran away to a dance, leaving the two girls alone in the house. A bat getting into their room, by its fluttering about terrified her and occasioned that dreadful malady. She inherited 700 £ from her mother. My grandmother, who was the daughter of the second wife, had nothing to recommend her but good sense, prudence, a true heart, and a fair face. She was very pale, and her hair black, and her figure very good. She was eleven years old when Queen Ann[e] died. The news of her death came on a Sunday morning, and the dissenters, who were waiting in fear of having their meetings shut up, went joyfully to their prayers![22] I was very little when she told me this story, but I believe I am correct. I wish I had been more inquisitive about former times. But I knew not then that my brain was so retentive, or that I should so regard these recollections in after life.

My grandmother was twenty-two when she married Mr. Loftus and their union was a most happy one. They had four children, but my uncle[23] and mother only lived to grow up. He is still living, and four year old[er] than my mother. My father and mother, soon after their marriage, went to Marshfield in Gloucestershire. Here they lived four years with a poor but friendly people, whom they visited in a simple, old-fashioned manner, going without an invitation when they had leisure, or inclination, to take their tea at whatever house they found to be disengaged, the hour four. A more comfortable mode than the present fashionable parties.

At Marshfield almost all the people were maltsters, and found a ready sale in Bristol and Bath for their malt. Among my father's hearers there Mr. Oland, a poet, Mr. Shapland, Reed, Freeme, and Osburne were the chief.[24] Marshfield stands very high in a wild-looking country, and is very heathy. It is 8 miles from Bath, and 12 from Bristol, and while here my father became acquainted with some people in both places, and more especially with some of the Lewin's Mead congregation of Bristol. Here he was invited to preach as a candidate, and his services were acceptable, and he would have been chosen had not a few bigots raised an outcry of heresy against him. In other words, he did not think exactly as they did. This alarm put an effectual stop to his being chosen there.

Had he succeeded, how happy, as it seems to us, it would have been for him and his family, but of this we are not the best judges. But it is certain that our fate must have been different and our lives cast in another lot, and acted upon by other circumstances, would have been totally different! Even you, perhaps, might have been cast in a different mould. I must not forget to mention a Mr. Smyth and his lady, who lived at Bristol and behaved with the greatest kindness to my parents. They came one Sunday morning to Marshfield to hear my father, who was a perfect stranger to them, and were so much pleased that they sent for him and my mother to the inn to dine with them, and often invited them both to their house, where my mother often spent weeks pleasantly, my grandmother keeping house for her. Mr. Smyth was an Irishman.[25]

At Marshfield John and Loftus were born.[26] The latter died at Maidstone, in Kent, at the age of two years and an half, of a putrid sore throat and fever which first made its appearance in England that year and carried off hundreds of children. Mr. Evans, who succeeded my father at Marshfield, continued to preach there until 1817, when he died.[27] His wife kept a school at Bath.[28]

In June, 1770, my father removed to Maidstone, where he settled as the pastor of a large and respectable society there. Here as at every other place he was much esteemed as an able and judicious preacher, and he and my mother were much beloved. When I paid a visit to Maidstone, many years after we left it,[29] I was told by those who had known her when young of the admiration her beauty and the elegance of her manners obtained. Here they lived ten years and acquired the most firm and respectable friends, among whom men of the highest talents and reputation may be reckoned, as Drs. Priestley, Price, Fleming, Kippis, Mr. Lindsey, Palmer, and a host of others,[30] the brightest ornaments of a thankless age, which the Birmingham Riots but too well prove.[31]

But my father's nearest and most beloved friends were Mr. Wiche,[32] a Baptist minister, who lived at Maidstone, Mr. Viny,[33] of Tenterden, and Mr. Thomas,[34] minister of Eustace Street [Chapel], Dublin. For these three he bore the love of a brother, and no cloud of dissension ever cast a shade over their friendship.

Mr. Wiche was twenty years older than my father, and died at the age of seventy-two.[35] Mr. Viny was older also. At his house Dr. Franklin was often a visitor, and here my father used to meet him. Tenterden is 20 miles from Maidstone, a pretty little village, and stands on a rising ground. In my imagination a perfect fairy land, but I was only six years old when I saw it and may be mistaken. Yet perhaps these dreams of infancy were worth all the realities of after life. Mr. Thomas was about my father's age and died young. He and my father took different views of the politics of the times, and the American War was a fruitful source of dispute between them. But this never left behind any angry feeling. Besides these my father enjoyed the friendship of many of his hearers: Mrs. Lewis, the widow of his predecessor, and her sons;[36] Dr. Milner, a physician; [and] two brothers of the name of Jacobson, very sensible, ingenious men.[37] One of them, an excellent musician, made himself an organ, and he was the author of a clever pamphlet on the Book of Job. His infant son[38] and your father were called (for their beauty) the morning and evening star. These, alas, are all fallen asleep, waiting in the hope of an happy meeting hereafter.

Soon after my father's settlement at Maidstone I was born, and seven years afterwards, your father.[39] Here my father remained ten years and would not have left it then but for a dispute that divided the congregation into two parties, and the contention was so sharp between them that one party would not attend the meeting if the others were there. And this made it unpleasant to remain, though both parties professed the highest respect for my father and often sent for him to the vestry, saying they would abide by his decision. But as the dispute was about money matters he did not chuse to interfere.

And accordingly he removed to Bandon, near Cork, in Ireland. This society would have chosen him from the character they had heard of him, but he would not accept it without first going to preach to them. We left Maidstone in March, and spent a week in London at the house of Mr. [David] Lewis. We then went on to Chester and through Wales to Holyhead. At St. Asaph the first sight of the Welsh peasants with their flat beaver hats and blue cloaks struck us as singular. The road over Penmaenmawr I still recollect and the grand and terrific appearance of the cliff that overhung the road and the dreadful depth of the sea beneath.[40] At Holyhead we staid two days, the whole of which it rained so hard that I was forced to be content with running up and down a large kitchen and hall. We were very sick this short voyage and landed in Dublin at six in the morning. It was wet and cold, and we were obliged to wait at a little dirty ale-house until a customhouse officer had seen our baggage and a coach could be brought to take us to Mr. [Samuel] Thomas's. When we had been here a week, he and Mrs. Thomas left us in possession of their house, and one of their servants to attend on us, and went into Wales, where he had been advised to go to try the effect of his native air and to drink goat's milk. Here we staid a month. I remember but little of this city; of Stephen's Green, and a fine piece of water they called the Basin, and of the Barracks just opposite to my Uncle James's house I have an imperfect recollection.[41]

The journey to Cork was very pleasant, and the distant view of the Wicklow mountains beautiful. A garden at Rathcormac delighted John and me, but Kilkenny disappointed us. Its streets are paved with marble, and we expected to see fine slabs instead of what seemed but common stones.[42] At Bandon we were received very kindly, and Mrs. Clugston, the widow of the former minister,[43] insisted on our staying at her house until a suitable lodging was got ready for us.[44] Here we found a very large and respectable congregation,[45] and my father met with sincere and lasting friendship from many of his flock. Here began his correspondence with Mr. Wiche, Viny, and the rest of his Maidstone friends, whom I have mentioned above, which was a source of much pleasure to them and to him, and ended but with their lives. Many of these letters, which we still have, were written during the course of the American War, and shew the steady and conscientious principles by which they were actuated, both in religion and politics, and the light in which that war appeared, not only to them, but to all the liberal men in the kingdom.

At Bandon my father lived three years. But though

happily situated in many respects, some events happened at this time which served to strength[en] the wish he had long entertained of transporting himself and family across the Atlantic, and seeking an haven of rest in the Western World. The feud between Whigs and Tories ran high, and my father, who never disguised his sentiments, gave great offence by his freedom in writing and speaking at a time when the unbridled licence of the army (who took liberties in Ireland that they dared not do at home) made it dangerous to offend the haughty officers, who seemed to think wearing a sword entitled them to domineer over their fellow-subjects. The American prisoners, being considered as rebels, were most inhumanly treated, particularly in Kinsale prison, where some officers amused themselves by running their swords into the hammocks of the sick. These and similar practices my father exposed in the newspapers,[46] and he and many friends made frequent journey[s] to Kinsale to see and assist the poor prisoners. And three of them, escaping, were a long time concealed among our friends. An unfortunate circumstance created great alarm. One of the prisoners fell sick of a fever, and his death was expected. How to bury him in that case without discovery was the question, and if secretly, there was a danger of being charged with murder. These fears caused many anxious forebodings. But fortunately a good physician was one of the party concerned, and young Reed recovered. My brother John and I were trusted with this secret, young as we were. The next affair that happened was the extravagant conduct of some officers who sallied out into the street and forced some Roman Catholics to eat pork on a Good Friday, by holding the point of their swords to their throats and thus compelling them to do

an act they abhorred, besides making them walk on
their knees over the rough paved streets, and other acts
of wanton cruelty. One man died in consequence of
this abusage.[47] This my father and others took up and
the guilty would have been punished, but they found
means to intimidate or bribe the witnesses, who not
appearing, they got off. The particulars of the whole
affair and the affidavits of those concerned are [in] the
trunk with my father's other papers. This spirited conduct of my father and his friends provoked the malice of
the other party, who threatened him with assassination,
but he did not regard their threats; and when some soldiers' wives came to my mother, saying the officers would
certainly kill Mr. Hazlitt, she affected unconcern, and
said she feared them not, [for] they dared not do it.
Doubting if they came out of good will and to prevent
mischief, as they pretended, or had been sent on purpose
to terrify her. At last three officers, Gamble, King, and
Keily,[48] took an opportunity to insult my father one
Sunday in the street as he was returning home from
meeting, calling him rebel and other opprobrious
names, with threats. To which he replied, "I will report
you to the War Office." My mother was not present, but
Miss Rolt, one of his congregation, was with him, and I
was by his side. I well remember the feelings of exulta-
tion with which I looked forward to the glory of suffering in so good a cause. For my head was full of the
courage of the martyrs, and I read with admiration, and
perhaps with emulation, of their glorious deeds.

My father wrote accordingly, and soon after a Court
of Inquiry was held on the affair, which lasted two
days.[49] It rained hard all the time, yet one or other of
our friends would run up from time to time to relieve

my mother's anxiety with tidings of what was going on. Miss Rolt was his only witness and she gave her evidence with clearness. Some of them tried to put her out by sneeringly asking her of what religion she was. "Gentlemen," she answered, "I am a Protestant dissenter, and I am not ashamed of my religion." The court seemed inclined to treat the offenders severely had not Mr. Hazlitt interceded for them. When his letter was read in court, they said who could have thought a Presbyterian parson could have written such a letter.

This happened in the time of Lord Shelburne's administration, and the regiment was in consequence ordered away[50] and another sent in their place, who behaved quietly, at least while we staid; but in a year or two after, we had a letter that spoke of the soldiers being more insolent than ever, going into the market and laying about them with their swords.[51] And the writer added, "We want you here more than ever." But this would not have done long, and had my father been there in '98,[52] his life would have been sacrificed to party rage, and pretences would not have been wanting to destroy a man whose honest zeal for liberty gave so stern a rebuke to the slaves of power.

We had many friends at Bandon, people who deserved the esteem of all who knew them, and these were for the most part of my father's hearers. The names of the Kingstones and the Wheelers, of whom there were several families, must never be forgotten by us.[53] These were true men, steady to the principles they had well examined, and to these my father was closely united. Dr. Vize, a young physician, and his mother,[54] a very pleasant old lady, to whom I delighted to listen and used to bring my chair and sit close to her to catch every word of the nice stories she used to tell of other days. Miss Rolt, the lady I mentioned above, was another whose society my parents much valued. She kept a day school, and I was one of the many pupils who looked up to her with respect and love. Nor can I forget her firm but gentle manner that ensured obedience, and a reproachful look from her made a deeper impression than the harsher chidings of a sterner tutor. Besides these, we were on a friendly footing with the Pophams, Biggses, and many others too numerous to mention.[55] But I do not mean to say there were no *Black Sheep* among the flock. In truth, there were some who gave trouble, but their names are better passed over in silence.[56]

Most of the young men of our society were enrolled in the Volunteer Corps, their uniform dark green, turned up with black.[57]

At the end of three years the war with America being happily ended and the independence of the United States settled on a firm basis, my father's *enthusiastic* love of freedom, in which my mother fully participated, led them to embark for that country. It was with feelings of deep regret they left their friends at Bandon but cheered with the animating hope of a future and happy meeting in another and everlasting world.

Some friends at Cork invited us to spend a little time there. My father, mother, and William were to be at Mr. Perrot's, a worthy friend and brother minister.[58] John and I were at Mr. Bradshaw Popham's,[59] with our little Harriet and nurse. Here for the first time in my life I was taken almost every night into large fashionable parties. The splendid rooms, gay dresses of the ladies, and above all the life and spirit of the conversation opened a new scene to my wondering eyes, and I remember two pretty little girls, of seven years old, who were shewn off as prodigies and could do twenty things of which I knew nothing, yet I was five years older, and I looked on them with admiration and marvelled at my own awkwardness. After the first impression had worn off, I believe I was more dazzled than pleased with what I saw, and I looked back with regret on our comfortable and quiet visits to our dear old friends at Bandon.

We stayed at Cork a fortnight, and spent one day and (as I thought) the pleasantest at Reuben Harvey's, a rich merchant, a Quaker, and a great friend to the Americans.[60] He had ten children and a pleasant garden close to the river, where we played and watched the ships all the afternoon.

At length a summons to be ready to go on board ship took us away, and we sat [set] off to Cove.[61] It was the last week in March, and as we rode along, we looked with pleasure on the goodly rows of peas, beans, and cabbages in the neat cottage gardens, wondering to see them so forward, and sighed to think how many weeks must pass before such a sight could meet our eyes again. Between Cork and Cove we passed through Passage, a little dirty village, the resort of sailors.[62] The harbour of Cove is very beautiful, and the country round is very fine, a variety of shrubs growing on its banks down to the water's edge; primroses, violets, and other[s] mixed their mild beauties with the yellow broom. We waited here five days and had many pleasant walks round the Cove. The town is built along the shore facing the sea. Here we lodged and had a full view of all the ships in the harbour, the one destined to convey us across the wide Atlantic lying nearest. We went on board on Thursday, the 3rd of April, 1783. We sailed with a fair wind and fine weather, and with mingled feelings of hope and regret.

I had just been reading the *American Farmer*,[63] a book that gives a most delightful and romantic description of that country, and though true in the most essential points was (to say the least) too highly coloured. I had formed to myself an ideal terrestrial Paradise, and, with the love of liberty I had imbibed, looked forward to a perfect land where no tyrants were to rule, no bigots to hate and persecute their brethren, no intrigues to feed the flame of discord and fill the land with woe. Of course, all the Americans were to be good and happy, and nothing was to hurt or destroy in all that holy mountain. Full of these pleasing illusions, I bore up against seasickness and a thousand other disagreeables.

We soon found we had a most villainous captain who did everything in his power to annoy us,[64] and longed to throw us all overboard because we were the friends of liberty, which he cordially hated. Often wishing he might find the whole continent of America "in the flat sea sunk" when he arrived, not reflecting that such a catastrophe would draw both him and his good ship *Henry* after it.

Our fellow passengers were [included] Captain Gilles, an Irishman, a noble-spirited fellow and our chief defence against the wicked devices of the captain. He had crossed the Atlantic 41 times. The other inmates of our cabin were a young man called De La Motte and one Bannon, the butt of the sailors. The weather was pretty good, on the whole, but once or twice the deadlights were put up and everything rolled about the cabin to the amusement of the younger part of the family who did not know, or think of, any danger. We took a servant with us who was of little use on board and ran away as soon as she landed. After a disagreeable voyage of six weeks,[65] we were cheered with the sight of land, and sailing for two days up the river, we landed at New York on the 26[th] of May.[66] In sailing along the shore, we could not enough admire the Highlands of Never Sunk[67] and the beautiful woods of the Jerseys. I don't think at that time that I knew much of landscape beauty, but I was delighted with the sight of land and the green and beautiful trees. The fresh air and the smell of the pines seemed to revive my poor mother worn out with seasickness and the fear of the rough and boisterous ocean and the still more rough and brutish captain.

Even the goats kept their heads to windward to snuff up the grateful odour. My brother John suffered much from seasickness, my father was never sick at sea, and the children were quite well, and except the first few days, or in stormy weather, I felt no inconvenience from the motion of the ship. Before we went on shore Captain Jeffries was glad to beg pardon of the two *Philistines,* as he called Captain Gilles and my father, for his very bad behaviour through the whole voyage. If he had not, his true character would have been exposed in the public prints, and perhaps it ought to have been done. For some days we were all busy in catching mackerel. They were fine like those in London; we ate them with the greater relish after our salt fare. The sailors caught and salted up some barrels full. As soon as we cast anchor, we were visited by some of the British officers, who came on board eager to hear the news. Ours was the first ship that brought an account of the treaty of peace.[68] And then how they raved and swore, cursing both the Congress and those at home who had thus put a

stop to their ravaging with fire and sword their brothers'
land, and in this our most valiant captain most piously
joined them. So much were their American brethren
transformed in their eyes (by that little magical word,
*rebel*) into bands of lawless banditti whom it would be
meritorious to destroy. So much do those who are un-
used to think attend to words rather than to reason.

# II

## The Hazlitts in America

But to return, we landed at six in the evening, but it
was some time before we could get a lodging. This was
owing to an oversight of a friend who had given my father a letter to Mr. Tench Cox,[1] a gentleman of New
York, who was obnoxious to the Americans on account
of his favouring the British cause. And his walking
about with my father and John made us to be looked on
as refugees, and no one would take us in. I remember
my mother sitting down in the porch of some door with
me, the children, and servant to wait, with no very pleasant feeling, the return of my father with his most unlucky, though kindly intentioned, conductor. At last
the mistake was cleared up, and we were admitted into
the house of Mrs. Gregory. The next morning our
trusty Honour[2] had decamped with what few things she
could lay her hands on, and left me to make my first
essay in the art of cooking, etc. My mother was too ill to
do anything but direct me, and the people of the house
praised my attempts and called me a clever little girl,
but gave me no help. Here we staid two days in order to

receive our goods from the ship, and then set off for Philadelphia, that beautiful city of which we had heard so much. We went to Perth Amboy and next to Burlington, a very pretty township by the side of a fine river. On the opposite bank stood Bath and Bristol,[3] which looked beautiful with their green woods on either side. It was Friday when we arrived there, and on Saturday the Jersey Assembly (sitting there at that time) sent an invitation to request my father to preach to them, on the morrow, which he accordingly did.[4] By what means they knew that a minister of the Gospel and a warm friend of liberty and to them was come over to cast in his lot amongst them, I do not know. The room he preached in had no pews, but only benches to sit on, as I have seen in some Quakers' meetings. Here a house to let which had belonged to a son of Dr. Franklin (who, strange to say, had been banished as a refugee) made my mother desire to settle here.[5] And she proposed to my father to open a school here. It was an excellent plan and would have succeeded well, but it was his wish to go on. And we took our departure for Philadelphia in a stage-waggon (not unlike our long coaches) and rode two days through the Jersey woods, full of various majestic trees, mingled with the blossoms of the wild peach and apricot, and the sweet-scented yellow flowers of the locust trees perfuming the air.

We passed through many little towns where the ground was cleared away for some miles round each and made a pleasant contrast to the neighbouring forests. When we arrived at the city, we took a lodging, the first week, in Strawberry Alley. My father then hired a house in Union Street. This house had a parlour with a door opening to the street, a kitchen, two bedrooms, two attics, cupboards in every room, and a good cellar; our only pantry, a shelf on the cellar stairs, where a colony of ants devoured everything that did not stand in a pail of water. The kitchen had a door into a bit of a yard, and this with a small plot of ground that had never been dug or inclosed were the whole of our premises, and for this fifty pounds a year of their money, about thirty English, was paid.

On the 25th of June my beautiful little sister Harriet died of the croup. She was born at Bandon, and was an year and [a] half old. This was a sad stroke and was sudden and unexpected. On the first of August the same year another girl was added to the family, of whom we were soon deprived by the carelessness of a nurse who let the baby fall, which occasioned her death on the 12th of September. She was called Esther. This was another sad trial to my parents, but others awaited them, though not exactly of the same kind. I forgot to mention my brother Thomas, who was born and died at Bandon in 1780.

As we staid so long in Philadelphia, I have a perfect recollection of this fine city. It had 19 straight streets from north to south, crossed by 19 others from east to west, reaching from the Delaware to the Schuylkill.[6] They were each two miles long, but were not all finished; those between the rivers were called Water Street, Second, Third Street, and so on. The others were named after different fruits [*sic*], as Walnut, Pine Street, etc. There were only three Episcopalian churches here, but a great many of Dutch, Presbyterian, and Quakers, and some few Catholics.[7] A great part of the population of this city were Irish and German. My father dined on[e] day with the Society of the Cincinnati on the banks of the Schuylkill.[8] My father and John went to St. Peter's Church on purpose to get a sight of General Washington; it was on a week day, on some public occasion when that great and good man was present.[9]

In July my father went to preach at New London, and here he met with some of his own name and kindred,[10] some of whom we afterwards saw in Philadelphia, where also lived, with her guardians, Miss Hazlitt, a daughter of Colonel Hazlitt, to whose wedding my mother went.[11] She was a distant relation. From New London my father went to Carlisle, where he spent some time and might have been settled, with three hundred an year and a prospect of being president of a college that was erecting, if he would have subscribed the confession of faith which the orthodox insisted on, but he told them he would sooner die in a ditch than submit to human authority in matters of faith.[12]

In Philadelphia my father became acquainted with Dr. Rush,[13] Carson,[14] and Judge Dana (brother to a clergyman he afterwards knew at Salop).[15] But in one of his letters I found lately, he says, "Dr. Ewing is my firm friend; many of the gentlemen to whom I had letters were civil, but gave themselves no further trouble about me." Dr. Ewing was the pastor of a large congregation.[16] He had ten children, and we found it very agreeable to go there. Once we were to go early to breakfast, to avoid the heat, and were thought late though we sat [set] out at six! Mr. Davidson, professor at the College, was another hearty friend. He and his wife were from the north of Ireland. There was another Mr. Davidson, assistant to Dr. Ewing; he wrote a geography in rhyme for children.[17]

Some of our neighbours in Union Street were very

friendly. Mr. Gomez and his family were much interested about us; they were Jews and had lost much of their property by the war but were still rich. His family, besides his wife and mother and his sons, contained two boys and two girls, his brother's orphan children. His eldest niece, a[n] amiable girl, died of a decline soon after our arrival.[18] She was a beautiful brunette. Late in the summer Mr. Gomez returned to New York, where his property lay, and whence he had been driven by the British troops. He often enquired what were my father's sentiments and why the orthodox were so bitter against him, and he thought the Unitarian doctrine the most reasonable scheme of Christianity he had ever heard. Of course the notion of a Trinity must ever be a stumbling block in the way of Jews and Mahometans. Our next door neighbours were Captain and Mrs. Atkinson and their daughter, Mrs. Brewer.[19] She was a widow of two and twenty, very little, very pretty, and remarkable for her fine head of hair.[20] Her son George was a playfellow of our William. Her mother, a cheerful old lady, was fond of seeing young folks enjoy themselves. She once took some of us to spend the day in the country. The Gomezes, Mitchels,[21] John and I were the party. We rose to go at four in the morning; and how chilly it felt at that hour, though the heat was so great in the day. Our old lady led us through fields of corn and buck wheat until we came to the skirts of a wood on the banks of the Schuylkill, two miles from the city. She first conducted us to farmer King's to breakfast on coffee, cakes, eggs, and dried fish. Bacon, of course, was prohibited. We next went into the wood to fish in the river and gather nuts. Here I had a very narrow escape; as I was going to pick a bunch of blackberries, a sportsman pass-

ing by drew me back and without speaking shot a snake
that he saw ready to dart on me. He told us it was one
whose bite was deadly! Thus was I providentially preserved (by the accidental passing of this stranger) from a
fearful death! After having dined and had coffee, we returned home, our kind old friend as happy as any of us.
She laughed and ran and enacted the part of an hen
while we, her chickens, all ran, scampering, after her,
highly enjoying the joke.

I forgot to mention, among our friends here, Mr.
Vaughan and his two sons, English gentlemen of large
property.[22] They wished my father to take a school at
German Town, five miles from the city, and offered to
advance him any money necessary to begin with, but this
he declined, as he did not think it right to give up
preaching entirely. Mr. Vaughan, with his wife and
daughters, afterwards returned to England, but his sons
remained there some years longer, and one that we afterwards met in Boston behaved to us in a very friendly
manner. While he was in Philadelph[ia], Mr. Vaughan
assisted some English ladies to open a boarding school
there. German Town is a beautiful village, and it is
said the yellow fever never reached it,[23] so that it seems a
pity we did not settle there. But perhaps my father was
destined to remove the rubbish and to clear the way for
more fortunate Unitarians, who, coming after him, entered into his labours and reaped the fruits thereof.

Stephen Kingston, a son of our old friend at Bandon,
was settled in Philadelphia when we went there.[24] And
soon after our arrival another of our Bandon friends
came over with a cargo to sell. As soon as the ship arrived, my father went on board, and inviting him to
make his house his home, brought him with him; and

he remained with us eight months, and then returned to Bandon. This was Joseph, the son of Jonathan Wheeler.[25] He died many years ago of a fever.

Soon after the death of Esther my father was invited to preach in Maryland. It was a township (as they call their scattered villages, where a field or two intervene between every house). And here in the midst of the forests, and at a distance from the cities, on the coast, he found a respectable and polished society with whom he would have been happy to spend his days; and they were very anxious to have him for their pastor. But on the second Sunday he was seized with the fever of that country and fainted in the pulpit. Although he might himself, after so severe a seasoning, have been able to have borne the climate, he feared to take his family there, and a stop was put to our being settled with a people so very suitable in many respects. I forget the name of the place,[26] but to Mr. Earl and his family our everlasting gratitude is due.[27] At this gentleman's house he was hospitably entertained, and but for the great care and attention with which he was nursed, he must have died. Nothing could exceed the kindness with which they watched over him, even sending twenty miles for lemons and oranges for him and providing him with every comfort. Two black men sat up with him every night, and he partly ascribed his recovery to a large draught of water that he prevailed on them to let him have, which, however, had been strictly forbidden. For a long time his family were ignorant of his situation. But at last Dr. Ewing and Mr. Davidson came to break the matter to my mother, who very naturally concluded he was dead, and it was some time before they could make her believe it was not the case. At length she was convinced that he was recovering, and the next morning my brother John sat [set] off to go to him. He went alone, on horseback. He rode through woods and marshes an hundred and sixty miles, in 56 hours, over an unknown country and without a guide. He was only sixteen at that time, and how he performed so difficult an enterprise astonished every one who knew it. But he was wild with his fears for his father, and his affection for him made him regardless of every danger. He found him slowly recovering, but dreadfully weak; and after staying there some weeks, they both returned together. How they got on, I cannot think, but when they came to the door, my father could not get off his horse without help. It was November, and the snow [fell] for the first time that day. My father was very ill and weak for a long time after his return. I recollect he looked very yellow and sat by the fire, wrapped in a great coat and taking Columbia root.[28] The 23rd of this month we felt the shock of an earthquake.[29] This winter proved very severe; the snow lay many feet on the ground, and the cold was intense, and more like a New England winter than (to speak comparatively) the usually mild frosts of Pensilvania.

In the spring my father was well enough to give lectures at the College of Philadelphia on the evidences of Christianity. These lectures were well attended,[30] and were of great service to a numerous class of young men who, taking it for granted that the doctrines of Calvin were those of Christ, were ready to renounce the whole system at once. But the Unitarian doctrine, being consistent with reason and Scripture, brought many of them back to the ranks of the believers. Not but there were some few Unitarians there before my father arrived in that country. But none dare[d] avow their real senti-

ments, fearing to offend the many. And here I cannot
help remarking how strange it seems that my father,
who openly preached the doctrine of the divine Unity
from Maryland to Kennebeck, should have been so entirely overlooked and the whole work ascribed to Dr.
Priestley, who went there so many years after him.[31] But
so it is!

In the spring of 1784 my father had an invitation to
settle at Charlestown in North Carolina,[32] but this he
was obliged to decline for the same reason that prevented his staying in Maryland, as the heat there is so
great that for two months every summer the places of
public worship are shut up. Yet some of our friends
wished us to go, as they thought it would be an advantageous situation, and argued that the sea breezes, at mid-
day, made the heat tolerable. About the same time my
father had an invitation to Pittsburgh, 200 miles from
Philadelphia.[33] But this he also declined on account of
its being at that time so far back in the wilderness.[34]
But now it is a very flourishing place and by all accounts
most beautifully situated. I remember the two farmers
coming to talk the matter over with my father[35] and
thinking to myself how much I should like to go and
see those wild and beautiful forests, and even now the
sight, or even the name, of a wood has a charm for me
and seems shining with the freshness of the morning
dew. Often indeed have I wished that we had gone
there. But to my father it is now of no consequence and
will be of as little to us ere long.

In June my father went to preach at Brattle Street
meeting in Boston,[36] where he was so much liked that no
doubt was entertained by his friends of his being chosen,
and they advised him to send for his family. And we, of

course, prepared to follow him, hoping we should at last find a "resting place for the sole of our foot." But in this we were again mistaken! For the persecuting zeal of the orthodox sent one of their chosen brethren after him, and thus put a stop to his settling there.[37] But this we knew not till afterwards.

We then bid [bade] farewell to Philadelphia and to our friends there, whose kindness to us, strangers as we were, deserves remembrance, and casting [cast] a last look at this beautiful city of William Penn, where so many events had befallen us and where we left my two infant sisters sleeping in their early graves—the beloved and the beautiful! In August, 1784, having lived there 15 months, we took our departure in the stage, which brought us here the year before, and [were] riding through the same woods, now rich with wild peaches instead of blossoms, ripe grapes, and hickory and other nuts, the oak and ash raising their lofty heads above the rest. We came the first day to Burlington, and were welcomed as old acquaintance[s] by our host. And here we again admired the little towns of Bath and Bristol, shining in the morning sun, whose very names brought back to my mother many sad and pleasing recollections of former days. From Burlington we went on to Perth Amboy. This is a very large inn said to contain an hundred beds. It stands alone, and its green lawn in front gently slopes down to the river. From the rising ground, on which the house stands, there is a beautiful and extensive view, and more than one river is seen from hence. I am told that Cobbet [William Cobbett] has somewhere given a very fine description of it. But as I have never seen his book, you must be content with my imperfect recollections. Here we slept one night, my mother and

William and I in one room with a lady and her little girl. In the night I awoke and heard a snoring under the bed. I crept softly out to feel, and hoping it was only a dog, I made up my mind not to speak, but to watch till daylight, when seeing a large Newfoundland dog who was come to guard us stretched at his full length under the bed, I went quietly to sleep. Early in the morning a very large party met to breakfast on the lawn before the door. We had tea, coffee, cakes, pastry, eggs, ham, etc., for an American breakfast is like a Scotch one.

What most struck me was a puritanical old gentleman of the name of Shakespeare, on whom I looked with great reverence, thinking perhaps that with the name he [had] inherited the talents of his immortal namesake. Besides, his face bore a strong resemblance to all the prints I had seen of the great poet, of whom I had heard so much. He was dressed in a sad-coloured suit, was reserved and stately, and took his coffee with the air of a prince in disguise. All our company were curious to know who he was, some affirming that he must be a Jesuit, and others made many different conjectures! But we left him there without making any discovery.

After breakfast we went on board a little sloop to proceed to New York. But just as we came near Sandy Hook, the vessel ran aground, and we stuck fast on a sandbank for five hours. It was one of the finest days in summer, and was owing to the captain's leaving the helm to the guidance of an ignorant black boy while he slept! We had many women and children on board, and great was their fear and lamentation. The little Maria who had shared our room the night before wept in concert with our William on hearing some of the people say we shall be all drowned. At last we pacified the two little friends, and in the evening the tide set us afloat, and we got safely to New York as the sun set.

Here we parted with Maria and her mother, who resided in that city. We waited here two days for the packet going to Rhode Island, and took our lodging at a boarding house. Our old neighbours, the Jewish family, came to ask us to spend a day at their house. My mother and John went but left me to take care of William, lest we should be tempted to laugh at the odd ceremonies they use in saying grace. Mr. Gomez had some months before returned to his possessions in this city. His eldest son was at this time in a deep decline, and we heard some months after of his death.[38] This was the last time we saw these good and friendly Israelites. Of how many kind and excellent friends have we, both before and since, taken a last and sad farewell.

We left New York on Sunday in the packet for Rhode Island. Our company was large and cheerful. We had many gentlemen on board. One of [them] was called O'Connor, a pale, sickly looking man (not O'Connor of the West). He was from the vicinity of Bandon and was making the tour of the United States. Another of our shipmates was a little solitary Frenchman who, by keeping aloof from the rest, made himself the jest of the party. But he bore their saucy remarks with great good humour, and perhaps he had his reasons for being reserved. We passed through Hell Gate, a dangerous whirlpool, and over the Hog's Back safely before sunset. It was a very fine evening and pleasant sailing between the mainland and Long Island. The views on each side were very beautiful, and we remained on deck until a late hour, enjoying the moonlight and the fresh air. About noon the next day we arrived at Newport. This

[is] a pretty, neat town, but it had not at that time recovered from the devastations of the British troops, who had not left a tree on the island, and many of the floors bore the marks of their axes where they cut up the mahogany furniture of the houses for firing![39] My brother joined a party of gentlemen and ladies in riding round the island on horseback. It is twelve miles long, and made but a desolate appearance then. It had been pretty formerly, and I doubt not has since been well planted and has recovered its good looks. We staid here two days, and eat [ate] of a most delicious fish, of the size of a mackerel. They are called black fish and seem to be peculiar to these seas, as we never met with them anywhere else.[40]

Our next day's voyage brought us to Providence, a very handsome town on the banks of the river, thirty miles from its mouth.[41] The river itself and the scenery on each side, the most beautiful that ever was seen, and the clear blue sky over our heads, and sun shining in all its glory, set them off to the best advantage. Providence, though built on the continent, belongs to Rhode Island. Here we staid one night. My mother, Mrs. Enderwick, and myself got a lodging in the house of a widow; John and the gentlemen of our party were obliged to seek another shelter, as our hostess would not admit any of them under her roof. She was even absurd enough to object to William, but my mother positively refused to part with him, and said if that were the case, we must all go. At last an ungracious consent was given, and the child was admitted within the sacred walls. This affair afforded no small amusement the next day. Some of the gentlemen, finding a ball was given at the governor's house that evening,[42] got introduced there, and spent the night in dancing, and told us how happily they had passed the time in the society of angels.

At six o'clock the next morning we went on in two coaches, and this day's journey brought us to Boston. Our road lay through woods abounding with every variety of beautiful trees dressed in their most lovely foliage, majestic in stature, and tenanted by numberless tribes of the feathered race, whose matin and vesper hymns rose sweetly on the ear! At intervals we passed by many little townships, but I only remember the name of one. It was called Jamaica Plain; it was pleasant and near Boston. Here lived Dr. Gordon, who wrote an history of the War of the Revolution, and came over to London to publish it. What his fate was, I never heard.[43] But now there is not any necessity for American authors to take a voyage to this country to publish their works. On arriving at Boston, our fellow travellers took leave of us, and we saw them no more. There is always an interest attached to those who have been our companions in danger, or in a distant land, and I should like to know the fate of many that we have met at different times and places.

As soon as we got to the inn, my father, who had been anxiously expecting us, took us to his lodgings in State Street. This was a boarding house and table d'hôte kept by Mrs. Gray and her two sisters.[44] Here we staid three weeks and then went to lodge in the country, at farmer Witherington's [Ebenezer Withington's], in Lower Dorchester, five miles from Boston. He was a good old man, and his eldest son was called Mather, a name given to many out of respect to Cotton Mather, a celebrated minister.[45] An Indian who worked for the

Witheringtons we often saw. He had a good voice and sung some songs about Washington. He had a little girl who might have passed for one of our handsome brunettes. It is said those Indians that come to live among the white people are generally such as have been turned out of their own tribe, and so it proved in this instance. I do not know that I saw any other Indians, except six Cherokee chiefs that I met once in the street at Philadelphia dressed in their robes of state with feathers bound round their heads like a coronet. These were come to conclude a treaty with the Pensilvanians. At the end of seven weeks my father having an offer of a good and cheap house at Weymouth, 15 miles from Boston, we prepared to leave the worthy farmer and remove to that place. Of this we made [a] two days' journey. We passed through Milton and some other places; and about tea time reached the house of Judge Cranch,[46] at Braintree, where we had been invited to sleep. We here found a very pleasant family, and spent an agreeable evening, and they always treated us with the greatest kindness, whether drawn by a secret sympathy (for Mrs. Cranch was of the Quincy family, though we knew it not at the time) or from their natural benevolence to strangers. Braintree is very pleasant but not so fine as the country round Weymouth, from which it is distant about four or five miles. The next morning, after breakfast, I sat [set] out on foot with Mrs. Cranch's maid as a guide and to assist me in getting our new abode in some order before the arrival of my father and mother, who came with William in the one horse chaise so common there at that time. A far more sober sort of vehicle than our modern, dashing tandems and gigs, etc. It was the beginning of November, a dry and pleasant day, and I sat [set] off in

high spirits, delighted with the wild scenery, as we drew
near to Weymouth, and went on singing like one who
knew no care. Our new house I liked much, and its
situation still more. It was indeed beautiful, but of that
bye and bye. I soon set about preparing dinner. It was
a brant, a sort of wild duck, that Mrs. Cranch had provided us with. These birds are very plentiful here and
are very fine and fat, but near the sea are apt to be fishy.

Our house[47] belonged to the lady of John Adams, at
that time ambassador to England from the Congress.[48]
She was another unknown relation, yet the name of one
[of] the sons, who was called Quincy, was enough to have
informed us of it.[49] Dr. Tufts's wife, who lived at Weymouth,[50] and the lady of Governor Hancock,[51] in Boston, were of the same Quincy family, and of course our
relations. This house was divided into two habitations;
the inferior part was occupied by a tenant who took care
of the farm and had half the produce for his trouble, a
very common mode of payment in that country. Our
part was entered by a small wicket that opened into a
green lane from the grass plot before the house, whose
folding doors brought us into a small square entry. The
first object we saw here was a large and very old picture
in oil of the meeting of Esau and Jacob. The embracing
of the two brothers, the meeting of their followers on
either side, with the groups of camels and other cattle,
and the background winding up between the hills and
seeming to vanish in the air completed the enchantment.
On this picture I used to gaze with delight, and won-
dered at the skill of the artist who had made so natural
and lively a representation of the scene! But as John
never copied or said much about it, I suspect it was not
so fine a painting as I imagined. I have heard it was one

of the first attempts of Copely;[52] he was afterwards a painter of some note. He and West,[53] who were both Americans, lived chiefly in England and produced most of their works there.

A door on the left hand opened into a large parlour with a good sized closet within. It was wainscoted with polished brown oak. It had four sash windows; two looked out on the grass plot, and two facing the east overlooked the garden, whose greatest ornament was a peach tree near the window, and when in blossom was visited by the humming bird, the most beautiful and irascible of the feathered race. One of them once flew into the room, and in its rage and terror had like to have beaten itself to pieces. On the right hand a smaller parlour that we used for a kitchen, and a very large wash house, with I know not how many little windows, for window taxes were unknown there. Upstairs, a wainscoted bedroom and a small one inside, where a colony of wasps had taken up their nest, but they hurt no one, nor did we disturb them. A large back room and another with shelves that held the books. It had been the study of Mr. Smyth,[54] who had formerly been the minister here. To these add two garrets and that was the whole of our part of the house. The house stood in a most romantic spot, surrounded on three sides by very steep hills that sloped down just in sight of the windows, and were covered with locust trees. These trees grow to a great height, and their yellow blossoms (somewhat like the laburnum) perfume the air in spring. On the green before the door stood a large solitary pear tree beyond the shade of which in the hot days William was not allowed to go until four o'clock, when the sun was in some sort shaded by the neighbouring hills. On the pales that inclosed this sloping green the woodpeckers were wont to sit and make a noise with their bills like a saw. Beyond the garden and lane was a large meadow which in the summer evenings, with its myriads of fireflies, made a brilliant appearance. On a little, low hill to the eastward stood the house of prayer, and below it, Dr. [Cotton] Tufts's [house], the road to Boston passing close by them. To the north, King-Oak Hill, which in the winter, when covered with snow, reflected the golden and purple tints of the setting sun. Over this hill the road leading to Hingham was seen. How often have we stood at the window looking at my father as he went up this road with William, in his nankeen dress, marching by his side like one that could never be tired! The hills behind the house are very steep, and it was one of our childish exploits, when they were covered with ice, to climb up and write our names on the frozen snow. From the top of these hills we had a distant view of the Bay of Boston and many of its islands and the hills beyond it, with Dorchester Heights, famous for the battle of kegs,[55] [and] Bunker's Hill, where so many British officers fell in the space of five minutes, singled out by the sharp shooters of the Yankees.[56] To the south, dark and frowning woods, and nearer to us, the river, with a mill and two houses on its banks, with a variety of meadows, fields, and trees below. Here also was seen the house of Captain Whitman, a good friend of ours.[57] He was so fond of William that the boy spent half his time in going with him to the woods or to the fields to see them plough, or attending the milking of the cows, where I, too, was often present. Once William came home from the wood with a dead black snake on a stick across his shoulder, because he thought mama would like to see it, and another time he brought in seven little tortoises and, putting [them] down in the parlour, called us to see his company; and when we had looked at them, carried the little things home to their wood. We paid frequent visits to Mrs. Whitman and were always glad to see her and her niece Nelly when they came to us at three in the afternoon and brought their work with them. A bright wood fire and a clean hearth to bake the Johnny cakes on (cakes made of Indian flour, without yeast, and baked on a pewter plate before the fire) were always prepared on the occasion. Then we heard tales of the late war and sometimes curious ones. The reports of the landing of the regulars (so they called the British troops) often drove the women and children into the woods, and once an old woman who had been bed-ridden eight years rose up and went away with the rest, a remarkable instance of the powerful effects of fear.[58] General Lovell lived in Weymouth.[59] He and Captain Whitman, like many of the American officers, after the war was over, retired to their farms, which, in general, were large, cultivating them with care, and sometimes guiding the plough with their own hands, and thus not only directing their servants, but giving them an example of industry. Beale Cushing,[60] a boy who lived with Captain Whitman, was a great playfellow of our William and famous for playing on the Jew's-harp. Why is this poor little instrument so called? King David's harp was a far different one, I ween! Perhaps the contempt in which barbarism and superstition formerly held the sons of Abraham may be [the] reason of the name. General Lovell and his family were very friendly. They lived a mile and [a] half nearer to the sea, and in our visits to them, I was delighted to hear the roaring of its waves.

But my greatest pleasure was to climb the hills and to ramble from one to another, and from grove to grove, and to gaze on the boundless ocean and think how far away lay the land of my birth and the friends of my infancy. Yet, oft-times in the midst of my contemplations a sudden panic would seize me at the loneliness of the place, and then I ran swiftly down, nor stayed to look behind, until I was near home. Happy days; how many pleasing recollections occur to my mind at this moment, dear to memory, yet too trivial to note down.

Next to these rambles, my chief delight was to shut myself up in the study and read for hours, if haply I was not wanted. Many of these books, it is true, I did not quite understand; yet still it was a pleasure to read, and in the monthly reviews, of which we had a great number, I found abundant amusement. In the summer a variety of beautiful little birds flew about us, humming birds of five or six different kinds, some of them brown, others of different colours, all of them very small, with a body an inch and [a] half in length, and a bill like a coarse needle, which served them to suck the honey out of the flowers. But the most beautiful were dressed in purple, green and gold, crimson, and a mixture of white and a little black about the head. Some of this sort used to enliven us by their visits to the peach tree, and it was one of them that flew into the window to his own great discomfiture. Besides the birds common to Europe, there are many others: the bluebird, of a pale sky colour; the scarlet bird, whose name tells of her bright plumage; and the fire-hang-bird, so called from her colour and the curious way in which she hangs her nest at the end of a bough, suspended by a string of her own making.[61] This, it is said, she does to protect her young from the monkeys.[62] It is also a protection against the boys, for the bough chosen is too small to bear the least weight. This bird differs from the scarlet bird in having some black under its wings. There is also the mocking bird, who delights in imitating every note he hears; the Bob Lincoln, a very pretty singing-bird; the red linnet, the Virginia nightingale;[63] and the king bird, from whom the hawk is glad to escape; the little snow bird,[64] and many others that I forget. The swallows [are] of a brighter purple than ours. The robins are much larger, but their notes and colour [are] the same. Of its size, one that I saw stuffed, some years after, in the British Museum, convinced me I was not mistaken in thinking them twice as large as ours. We had a tame one at Weymouth, who used to go and come as he pleased, and perch on my finger to be fed. One night he did not come home to roost as usual, and I called him in vain. A gentleman had shot poor robin, for which I counted him a churl.

This winter was a very severe one, and my father spent it chiefly in going to and from Boston, where he was engaged to give lectures on the evidences of Christianity,[65] the same that he had delivered at Philadelphia the winter before. And here also they were attended with great success.[66] It was fifteen miles, and he was often obliged to walk through the snow. But he thought no labour or fatigue too much in the cause he had so much at heart. Once he and John sat [set] out to walk in a most tremendous rain. There was no conveyance, and he was expected, and I believe it was the last lecture, as the weather was breaking up. Standing at the window, we sorrowfully watched their progress up the road, which we could see for a quarter of a mile, lamenting the heavy rain and the sad colds they would get. But they were strong and healthy, and no bad consequence[s] ensued. At Braintree and at Milton (Mr. Blake's)[67] my father always had a friendly welcome, and a bed was always at his service if [he was] not disposed to perform the whole journey at once. At Milton John spent much of his time; there were several young men in the family who were fond of his society, and he enjoyed himself there. Yet I fancy their sister, who was elegance personified, was his greatest attraction.

I do not recollect my father preaching at Weymouth more than once,[68] and when he was with us on Sunday we had service at home. The congregation there was large, and they were Presbyterians of the old orthodox stamp. Calvin and the Kirk of Scotland had settled the faith of two out of three of the American churches at that period. There were but few Episcopalians, and their churches but poor building[s] and often without steeples or bells, while the popular party had both. There were many Quakers (but not so many as in Pensilvania) and here and there a very few Catholics. This winter was a severe one and when the snow and ice melted, the low lands were threatened with a deluge; but a[s] I remember no damage that ever happened from these thaws, I suppose they were properly guarded against. Here is also, about February, what they call a middle thaw, when the weather is mild for a week or two and the snow seems to have vanished. Yet to this, other and deeper snows succeed, and the frost is as sharp as ever! This winter the melted snow ran into our wash house and froze so hard that my father and John were obliged to cut it up with axes in pieces of half a foot thick and throw it out.

My father often went to Hingham to preach for Mr.

Gay,[69] a very pleasant old man above 90 years of age. He was fond of a good story, and used to tell with great glee how he cured a man of a propensity to steal. It seems this man was in the habit of making free with his pastor's hay, which, Mr. Gay suspecting, he one evening took his pipe in his mouth and, standing behind the stable door, softly shook out the ashes of his pipe on the hay the man was carrying away on his back. And as soon as he got out, the fresh air kindled it into a flame, at which the poor fellow was so much terrified that he came the next morning to confess his trespass, saying that fire came down from heaven to consume his stolen hay, and promised never to steal again, and this promise he faithfully kept. And though Mr. Gay, in compassion to his fears, kindly explained the matter to him, he never could believe but that a fire from above had fallen on him.[70]

Hingham is twenty miles from Boston, and five from Weymouth. Here my father met with society quite to his mind. Dr. Barker,[71] General Lincoln,[72] and many others were his warm friends. There was Mrs. Derby, an old lady who at the age of ninety used to superintend her household and walk over her grounds looking into everything; nothing escaped her.[73] Once my father took me to dine with her, being himself engaged elsewhere. I know not exactly why, but the respect I felt for her almost amounted to fear and made the walk home with my father much pleasanter than my visit. Yet she was kind to me, and on my brother William she quite doated and would have him indulged in every whim. There were two Mr. Shutes who often came to our house. The father was a minister in that neighbourhood, and the son a surgeon at Hingham.[74] Once when Mr. Shute was sitting with my father after dinner, a very handsome young man came to the front door, and, kicking it open, burst into the parlour and asked if we did not know Bet Collins. He staid but a short time, and we were glad to see him go out. He was a maniac who had escaped from confinement. Mr. Shute told us his name was Willard and that he had gone out of his senses for love.

My father often spoke of the number of fine-looking old men between eighty and ninety that attended that meeting and sat together before the pulpit. This congregation was very large, but in a place where there was no other church and where none but the sick or infirm absented themselves from public worship, five or seven hundred people being assembled together is nothing extraordinary.

At Boston, too, my father had many friends, [including] Dr. Chauncy, a fine old man above ninety.[75] He was very cheerful and retained all his faculties. He is the author of a book on universal salvation and one on the benevolence of the Deity. Drs. Lathrop,[76] Freeman,[77] Clarke,[78] Elliot,[79], Everrit,[80] and Howard,[81] men of learning, talents, and integrity, and besides these many others who were not clergymen. Boot,[82] Pratt,[83] Gregory,[84] and Sharp[85] were English merchants, and with these, more especially with Boot and Gregory, we were on the most friendly terms. James Lewis, the son of our old friend at Maidstone, spent one year at Boston,[86] and he paid us frequent visits at Weymouth. It was pleasant to see one of our own Maidstone people, and he was always a welcome guest, for he was good tempered and lively. He settled at New York, and his nephew James Cooper with him, as merchants, and some few years after, just as he thought to return home and had written to his mother that he hoped to eat his dinner with her at Christmas, he and James Cooper both fell victims to the yellow fever![87]

In the summer of 1785 my father often went to Salem, where he sometimes preached for Mr. Barnes, the minister of that place.[88]  But his visits were to Mr. Derby, son of the old lady at Hingham.[89]  He was a merchant and had large concerns with Russia, where some of his sons, for he had many, have since been, and have published an account of their travels, which I learned from a review.[90]  Mrs. Derby invited my mother to visit her at Salem, but she declined it.  Once it was settled that my father should take me there.  How it happened, I forget, but I did not go.  A disappointment at the time, no doubt.  William often went there, as well as to Hingham and many other places, with his father, who used often to take him into the pulpit with him when he preached!  While we remained at Weymouth, John spent a great part of his time in Hing[h]am with Dr. Barker and some others, where he painted many portraits, and perhaps some of his first pictures are to be seen there even at this present time.[91]  At Scituate and some other neighbouring places my father often preached,[92] and at one of these towns he met with two of the prisoners to whom he had been of so much service at Bandon.  They were rejoiced to see him again and expressed the warmest gratitude to him, and to those friends at Bandon, from whom they received such kindness in time of need.  And they made many enquiries about them.  I think it was at Marshfield that he met with them.[93]  At Hingham my father frequently assisted Mr. Gay.  Here he was so much liked that it was the wish of the people that Mr. Gay would resign and leave them at liberty to chuse him, but this he did not do, and six months after my father sailed for England Mr. Gay died.[94] Had he staid but until the next spring, all would have been well!

This summer my father visited Cape Cod, and staid there three weeks, but he could not make up his mind to settle in so desolate a place. It was a neat little town inhabited chiefly by fishermen,[95] but nothing was to be seen but rocks and sands and the boundless ocean. He took William with him, who, child as he was, could not help being struck with the barren and dreary look of the country and enquired if any robins or Bob Lincolns came there, and being told there were none, he said, "I suppose they do not like such an ugly place." Stepping into the boat, he dropped his shoe into the sea, which he lamented because of his silver buckle.

It was while we resided at Weymouth that my father assisted Mr. Freeman in preparing a liturgy for his church, which had been Episcopal, and furnished him with the form of prayer used by Mr. Lindsey in Essex Street Chapel, which they adapted to suit the transatlantic church.[96] He also republished many of Dr. Priestley's Unitarian tracts, and many other little pieces to the same purpose, such as the trial of Elwall, etc., besides writing much himself.[97] These things took up much of his time, and occasioned many journeys to Boston, where John often went with his father.

In the autumn of this year Mr. Sam Vaughan persuaded him to go to a new settlement on [the] Kennebec River called Hallowell, in the Province of Maine, where Mr. Vaughan had a large tract of land and much interest in settling the township.[98] This was in the midst of the woods with a few acres cleared round each farm as usual in all their new places, which by degrees are

changed from solitary woods to a fruitful land. At this
time the wolves were near neighbours, and sometimes at
night wo[u]ld come prowling about the place, making a
dismal noise with their hideous barking. And as the
doors were without locks, and my father slept on the
ground floor, he used to fasten his door by putting his
knife over the latch to prevent a visit from these wild
beasts. In this remote place he found a very respectable
society, many of them genteel people. Here he preached
a thanksgiving sermon, which was afterwards printed at
Boston.[99] It was a custom in New England to preach one
every year after harvest. He would have had no great
objection to settling with these people, but it would not
have been eligible for his sons.[100] John's profession was
not wanted in the woods, where good hunters and hus-
bandmen were more needed. He, therefore, after spending the winter there, returned to us in the spring; and he
narrowly escaped being lost in the Bay of Fundy,[101] to
which the sailors, for its frequent and dreadful tempests,
have given the name of the Devil's Cauldron. Thursday,
the day he sailed, was one of the finest of days, and
we were quite delighted to see the winter over, as we
thought; but on Saturday, the first of April, a most tremendous gale came on, with a heavy fall of snow in
which the vessel my father had embarked [on] was over-
taken. But happily they got safe into Falmouth harbour[102] before it had attained its utmost fury. And after
a few days' rest there, he came home by land. We little
suspected at the time the danger my father was in, and
were only intent on getting in what was wanted before
the snow was too deep. After the storm was over, we saw
old Uncle Aron's cot was blown down, but he and his
wife were both dug out unhurt. This old man was called

uncle by all the parish on account of his great age, for he was many years above ninety.[103]

In a week the snow was gone, and the time of the singing of birds was fully come. And soon after we began to think of moving nearer to Boston,[104] as my father and John were frequently obliged to go there. Weymouth with its sloping hills and woods, beautiful and romantic as it was, yet had its inconveniences, the greatest, the distance from the city. There was no market or butcher's shop, or any baker, in the parish, and only one shop, containing some remnants of linen, a few tapes and thread, with a small assortment of grocery.[105] Hard sea biscuits, butter, cheese, some salt beef and pork were our winter's fare. In the summer it was better as we often got a joint of fresh meat from some of the farmers who would spare us some of what they provided for their own use. This, when not wanted directly, was kept by being suspended over the well. Sometimes we had barrels of flour and made our own bread; and when the farmer's wife heated her oven, she would kindly bake our bread for us, or any [one] else. So that, on the whole, we did very well and thought not of the flesh pots of Egypt.

One day I observed the water in the well was red. I asked Mr. Beales[106] the reason. He said, "We shall have an earthquake soon; but" he added, "do not tell my wife." The next morning about seven we felt a smart shock, but not bad enough to throw anything down. Yet it made the handles of the drawers rattle. To the eastward it was worse, and, indeed, it came from the East. It was in February and the weather was very close and cloudy, and not a breath of air stirring.[107]

One evening a gentleman knocked at our door, and

as he did not answer the question, "Who is there?" we did not open it, and we heard him go round to the next door and Beales telling him, by way of excusing us, "They come from London, Sir, and are fearful." I wish they may still live in this happy security from robbers, but I fear it is not the case now. I had almost forgotten to mention our nearest neighbour, Dr. Tufts and his family; his wife was of the Quincys and handsome of course. They had one son[108] and a niece (who lived with them), Lucy Jones, a very beautiful girl.[109] She was a constant companion of mine, and we did not agree the worse for her being three years older. I fancy I see her now, in her polanese [polonaise] dress, which set off her fine figure to advantage. I think Sophia Western must have looked like her. If I have said more about Weymouth than I need have done, it is because I love to linger over every trifling recollection of times long past, and [I] must soon enter on the last year of sojourn in this land of liberty.

New England abounds more in maize, Indian corn, than wheat; and in the country it is much used, and is not unpleasant to the taste, though rather too sweet, and it is very convenient as it requires no yeast. Besides maize they have buck wheat, barley, and rye, and from the other states they have plenty of the finest wheat. With the West Indies they carry on a considerable traffic, exchanging their cattle and lumber for rum and molasses. On the southern states the West Indies chiefly depend for corn and other food, and send them in return the finest fruit, sugar, rum, pepper, etc. I once saw a cartload of pineapples that were just landed in Philadelphia market, that were sold for a half pistareen each, about nine pence.

The woods are filled with a variety of game. The number of pigeons are incredible, and the wild turkeys are very large and fine, and their colours very beautiful, and they make a grand appearance when seen standing, being from four to five feet in height. They have also plenty of wild geese, ducks, teal, and all the wild and tame fowl that we have in Europe; many kinds of parrots and the Virginia nightingale, of a bright crimson; snakes and monkeys,[110] more than enow; foxes, wolves, and bears; and the tiger cat, very fierce and strong for its size, about two feet high, I think.[111] The moose deer is peculiar to North America. Once while we were there, an animal they called a cat-a-mount made its appearance near Falmouth. It was said to be 5 feet long, besides the tail was as much more, and could mount trees, from whence its name. It was hunted by 18 dogs, [and] killed six of them and got off. It was said that only one of these animal[s] had been seen before. But no one knows what or how many unknown creatures may be concealed in those endless forests. In the southern states the birds are dressed in a richer plumage, and the snakes, too, appear in brighter colours as they increase in venom. There the trees are more majestic, and the beautiful tulip tree grows to sixty or seventy feet high. There also they have most of the fruits of the East (I have heard of an orchard of oranges, in Florida, of forty acres) and they have all their luxury and enervating heat. But the middle and northern states are happier, if not so rich in nature's gifts. The New England seas abound with the finest fish. Sturgeon, halibut, turbot, and soles are very plentiful, as well as every other kind common with us, to say nothing of their cod fishery carried on by the people of Nantucket Island and those of Cape Cod, who are also famous for their dexterity and boldness in catching whales, seals, etc.

At Weymouth I first learned to know the different trees, and an elm near Dr. Tufts's gave me my first lesson. Oaks and ash there were plenty near our dwelling. These I can still see here, but the *beautiful locust* trees I shall never, never see again. In July [1786] we took our leave of Weymou[th], where we had spent an year and eight months, and bid [bade] farewell to our good friends the Whitmans and others with whom we had begun a friendly intercourse, and left our romantic hills and groves, never to see them more, but we did not then know that it was a last farewell!

We removed to a small house in Upper Dorchester. It was pleasantly situated but not to be compared to the one we had left. It was five miles from Boston and in the high road to it. In front, on the other side of the road, were some large meadows, and beyond, at the distance of a few miles, the Blue Mountains[112] rose to our view. Covered with thick woods, they are said to be famous for rattlesnakes. It is observed that the rattlesnake is never found near the seashore. Behind, and on each side of the house, there was a very large orchard, and ascending a little way, we had a fine view of Boston, its bay, and many islands, the same we saw at Weymouth but nearer and more distinct. To the eastward, Fort William and its lighthouse,[113] and to the north, a vast extent of country. And behind the city the hill of battle[114] where so many fell in the beginning of that quarrel which in the end gave liberty and happiness to millions who still regard England as the land of Father. May ambition and despotism never enter to destroy that happy land! Our time in Dorchester passed smoothly on; we met with some friendly neighbours there, and Boston was near, if we wished to go there. Susan Butt was my favorite.[115] Once when we were drinking tea with Mrs. Tyler,[116] Dr. and Mrs. [John] Lathrop came to pay a friendly visit. Susan was from home, and Boston, their black servant,[117] was not to be found. The fire was out, and the tea kettle wanted in haste. In this dilemma I offered my services, and as a wood fire is easily kindled, we soon had tea in comfort, and cold ham and pastry were not wanting. Nor did I enjoy it the less for my share in the preparation.

On the other side of the orchard lived Captain Homans, our landlord. He had been a sailor, and in one of his voyages to England had married a Bristol lady.[118] These and a few others we visited, and once dining with Mr. Wales, we had thirteen different sorts of vegetables on the table, which shews the art of gardening was not unknown there, though not much attended to in general; the farmers, having so much land, cannot spend much time about their gardens. The green heads of Indian corn are eaten as a vegetable and are always brought to table in their season.

While we were at Dorchester, I made many visits to Boston. The first was to Dr. Lathrop's. I remember my father driving me there in the chaise that had been sent by Dr. Lathrop and the green fields and the bright sunshine that to me looked doubly bright with the pleasing anticipation of the week I was to stay. My dear father gave me some advice, on the road, how to conduct myself, and I promised to be very good, and attentive to the least hint from Mrs. Lathrop. She was the most amiable of women. Her mother and sister lived with them, and they had five children.[119] Here I was quite happy, and their kindness made me feel at home and more at my ease than I usually did with strangers, and when they had company, I had no wish to escape from them, as I often have done both before and since that time. Of Betsey, a child of five years old, and Sam, who was younger, I was very fond, and they were much attached to me.[120] The week before we sailed for England, Sam, who did not approve of our intended departure, on hearing a cry of fire and seeing the people running out of meeting, called out, "Oh never mind, 'tis only Mrs. Hazlitt's ship on fire, and now they cannot go to England." How much I should like to know the fate of that dear boy and girl and the rest of that most worthy family. Mrs. Lathrop I know has long since been numbered with the dead. But her look, her manner, her voice is [are] still present with me as if I had seen her but yesterday! How kindly she told me what I ought to do and encouraged me to speak my thoughts of what I saw; and how sweetly she used to sing that soft Moorish ditty, so simple and true to nature.

For some time after our return my father had many correspondents in Boston, and Dr. Lathrop was one of them. And he sometimes heard from Dr. Ewing and Mr. Davidson of Philadelphia, but it is now a long time since we heard from any of our American friends. Many are dead, and but few are left that can remember us. So quickly does this world and the things of it pass away.

I spent much of the last winter at Mrs. Boot's. Mr. Boot was an English merchant who had settled at Boston. Here the society were mostly English. His partner Mr. Pratt, Mr. Gregory, and Sharpe[121] usually spent their evenings at Mr. Boot's house,[122] as he was the only married man among them, yet at times we had other company. But as no one ever thought of asking Mr. Boot's family without inviting the other three, we were always together and spent the Christmas in the old English fashion. At times they spoke of Old England; and Sharpe, who had left his lady love at home, vowed he would go home again, even if he sailed in a *washing tub;* and back he did go, but in some safer vessel, I ween, and married his lady and settled in the Isle of Wight. Mr. Boot had one little girl;[123] she was their first child; afterwards they had several others, who are all settled in Boston. Mr. Boot was all his life a firm friend to my father, and some few years after our return he and Mrs. Boot took a journey from Derby to Wem [in Shropshire] on purpose to see us, although they could stay but one night. He wished to have my brother William and bring him up as a merchant,[124] and they offered to take me back with them as a visitor for a year or two. But William was not destined to be a merchant, and I could not leave home. Yet we felt not the less grateful for their kindness, which has been uniform from first to last. I saw Mr. Boot once afterwards, and John saw him several times, as he often came over on business and to see his father, who lived in Derby. Boot was an uncommonly strong man, but he did not live to be much above fifty.

The last summer my father passed in frequent visits to Boston, to Hingham, and to Salem. At length he made up his mind to return to England in the autumn and try to get settled before we arrived, as we were to follow him in the spring. A most unfortunate resolve! Had he but staid over that winter, it is probable that we should never have left that dear country. For but a few months after he had sailed, old Mr. Gay died and Dr. Gordon came over to London to publish his book. And

at either of these places my father would have been
chosen. But he would have preferred Hingham, where
he had many sincere friends to whom he was warmly attached. Instead of this happy end of our many wander-
ings in this changing world, it was our evil destiny to pass
the best of our days in a little, disagreeable market town
[Wem], where we could not see the green fields and
scarcely the blue vault of heaven. What a contrast to
our transatlantic and sylvan abodes.

This last summer passed quickly away and October
came, and the time of my father's departure drew near.
I recollect his coming to fetch me home from Boston a
few days before he sailed. He talked to me of our sepa-
ration, and the hope of meeting again, and charged me,
above all things, to be careful of and attentive to my
mother, and endeavour by every means in my power to
keep up her spirits and soften every care. I promised to
do all she wished, and never wholly forgot my promise,
though in some instances I might, perhaps, have performed it better!

From my father's journal[125] it appears that he sailed
from the Long Wharf, Boston, on the 23d of October, on
board the *Rebecca,* Captain Folger,[126] went a mile down
the bay, returned to town, and passed the evening at Mr.
Boot's; sailed again on the 24th, and in the afternoon
cast anchor in Nantucket Road,[127] and sent a letter home
by the pilot. "25. A quarter before three P. M. From
the time we sailed yesterday until eleven this morning,
we had a dead calm and hazy weather, but a breeze
springing up, we weighed anchor, and at 20 minutes
before one passed the light house, and are now sailing
pleasantly at 5 knots an hour. I often looked this morning for the habitation of my dear family, or the place on

the hill where we often viewed the light house together, but alas I could see neither the one [n]or the other. May the great God keep them under his holy protection. I feel a continual melancholy in their absence. 26. 11 A.M. We passed the last night very disagreeably. The ship leaked so much as to alarm us, though the wind is fair and not fierce. We have been lying to since 4 this morning, not being able to make for any harbour. I wish myself at Dorchester again, and that I had not been persuaded to leave it before the next spring. My dear family know nothing of my situation. I tremble for them and myself. May they be happy, however Providence disposes of me. Alas, what can I say; God is still able to deliver me. May he give us all consolation.

"This day at noon we sailed with a fair wind. We hope the leakage is diminished. Lon. 67 Lat. 42.25. 27. After sailing yesterday the leakage increased, contrary to the Captain's expectation, which made me lament, in very bitterness, that I should never see my family again. The sea rolled very much until five o'clock, when the wind headed us, which, together with his own alarming apprehensions, determined the Captain to return to Boston. We accordingly tacked about, at six, the wind being S. W. We spoke a fishing schooner at 7. At nine the wind begins not to favour us; so it continues. The wind blew very fresh all night, and the pumps are continually going. This is our situation at nine this morning. But we hope through the divine goodness that we shall be enabled to reach some port in Cape Cod before night. 28. Ten o'clock A. M. The sun shines, the weather is fair, and the wind moderate, but this is a very gloomy morning. The Captain seems determined to keep on his way to England though the leakage seem[s] rather to increase. God be merciful to me and my dear family. He can save the vessel, though men are madly running it into danger. This is my only hope. The wind was very high all night. During that time we were beating up for Cape Cod, excepting two hours when we kept to the eastward to make, I think, a rash and capricious experiment on the vessel. I had a most restless night; the ship rolled disagreeably. Yet I bore this tolerably, in expectation that we were seriously returning to Boston and that we should be safe in harbour before night. How great the reverse this morning. A little after twelve the pump went 210 strokes in a quarter of an hour. This made the Captain irresolute and produced another gleam of hope that he would again endeavour to return to Boston. 29. Yesterday evening when we hoped to continue slanting our way towards Boston, a violent gale of wind sprung up, which placed us [in] a tremendous situation. The pump was kept going so constantly that I sometimes feared the ship could not be kept above water until the morning. The wind still blows very hard. May the great God graciously deliver us."

Several of the next sheets are mislaid, but I recollect his coming back and, after the ship had been repaired, sailing again on the seventh of November. (Oh that he had staid with us that winter.) Sad was our second parting. But we knew not how dreadfully tempestuous a voyage awaited him. But from the remainder of his journal, it appears that nothing ever could exceed the rough and dangerous tempests that attended them from first to last of their most appalling passage. In one place he says: "21 Novbr. This is the first hour since the 17th that I could hold a pen. I then thought the storm had ceased and that the last had been as terrible as could have been expected. But I was mistaken. At four the next morning a gale came on which might be called a perfect hurricane, and continued to blow with increased violence for forty hours. Ever since we have had too much wind, but we now sail pleasantly under two reefed sails, with a fair wind, in Lat. 48 and Lon. 43. When we were passing the banks of Newfoundland, we saw vast multitudes of birds which are called noddies[128] and always cover the banks in winter and by which the sailors can exactly determine their boundaries without an observation. Yesterday our poor owl died." (This bird is mentioned before as the most beautiful that my father had ever seen. It had taken refuge on board, some time before, from the storm that had driven it out of its course.) "23. I hope now, thank God, I shall be able to minute down some of the occurrences of this tempestuous voyage. At four P. M. the 21st the wind blew from the N. E., according to the testimony of the sailors, with the violence of an West Indian hurricane, 46 hours, during which time we ran before the wind, with a close-reefed top sail, at the rate of seven knots an hour, in a most tremendous situation. It then abated a little, but still continued to blow with great fury from the S. W. twenty hours longer. We lay to all this while, tossed about by the dreadful billows and sick at heart that we could not set our feet on any land.

"25. Another chasm has taken place in my journal in consequence of the roughness of the weather. On the 23rd another storm sprung up, from the N. W., and went on increasing with more violence than ever. It was with difficulty that the only sail standing could be pulled down. We some times seemed in danger of oversetting,

the weather being very boisterous until twelve last night
when the wind abated and a calm ensued, followed by a
shifting of the wind to the S. E., where it now stands and
threatens us with another storm. We are now at the half
way house. I can hardly sit to write. The tempest I fear
approaches. I saw no gulls nor Mother Keary's chickens[129] today, but a sea pigeon [130] came on board, which,
after tarrying with us an hour or two, again fled to his
watery habitation. 26. A little before one this morning
a tremendous gale came on, like loud thunder, which
made me apprehensive of the most disastrous consequences. The gale was such as the Captain and Mate
said they had never seen on the ocean. It is now what
is termed moderate for the winter. I am much fatigued.
27. In the morning yesterday we saw a large ship but
could not speak to her, the weather being so boisterous.
Decbr. 1st. Until this morning we have had no quiet
since I last had the pen in hand. Squalls, tempests, and
hurricanes in succession for three days, with heavy rain,
hail, and lightning, etc. are sufficiently terrifying. We
sometimes shipped horrible seas. One broke the chain
which confined the boats and had almost carried them
away. I can write no more. 6. Just after I had laid aside
my pen yesterday, with a thunderstorm came on the
most dreadful gust of wind I ever heard. I thought it
must have shaken the vessel to pieces. But it was soon
over, and we are now supposed to be within an hundred
leagues of the Channel. Four weeks yesterday I left Boston and parted with John. 7. We have passed a fine
moonlight night with a fair wind. We hope to find
soundings this day and our hope is much increased by
the discovery of a noddy, which is one of those birds
that usually enjoy themselves in an 100 fathom water,

within the smell and reach of the cod fish. I had almost forgotten to mention that we were obliged to lie by again the day before yesterday and that one of our gallant yards were [was] broken by a heavy sea. Through what terrors we have passed. I now have better hopes than I have yet had of seeing land again and living to embrace my dear family once more. I bless God for the present favourable weather. May his goodness be still extended towards me and mine. To him be praise. We sounded this morning and found no bottom. It will be five weeks this evening since I returned to Dorchester from my first trip to sea. Decbr. 8. We found soundings this morning at 80 fathoms deep. The weather was hazy, rainy, and very tempestuous from 10 last night till this day at noon. It has been very fine, thank God, ever since. Gulls, hoggletts,[131] a sea hen,[132] etc. were seen, Lat. 49.18, Lon. 9. About 11 last night we had a violent squall which was soon over. After sounding three times this day, we found at six this evening 60 fathom water. We suppose ourselves past the Scilly Islands.[133] Almost twelve at night, something after 7, at Dorchester. Good night to those I left there with a heavy heart.

"9. I thank my good God that I have seen the light of this day and that it has discovered to me the shore of old England. At 9 this morning we were opposite to Ram Island, and could see the Eddistone Lighthouse and the shore, fore and aft, Plymouth. At two yesterday morning a violent gale came on from the south, which blew with unabating fury until 10 last night, whilst heavy rains poured down upon us, and the weather was so foggy that we could not see a mile from us. This gale, though not so violent as some we had passed through, was the most alarming of any we had experienced in the passage, as we only knew that we were in the English Channel, but could not ascertain our latitude, nor know but any moment we might dash to pieces on the French or English coast. The good Lord delivered us; Blessed be his name. We lay by from 10 till 6 this morning. The wind then blew, and still blows fresh. 11. Yesterday was my dear Peggy's birthday. I did not forget it, notwithstanding my perilous situation. I did not forget any of the family but embraced them all with the most tender affection. May Peggy have reason to rejoice forever that she was born yesterday. I ate a bit of Mrs. Boot's cake, and drank many such happy days to my Peggy. Heaven guard the whole of the little family I left at Dorchester.

"13. Yesterday morning began with a heavy gale from the south, accompanied with floods of rain, which prevented our making, or seeing any land. We lay by 18 hours, surrounded by mountainous waves which often struck the ship with such violence as to threaten to shake her to pieces. This was such a storm as we had on the 10th. This morning is pleasant. We see the land and espy a sail, but find ourselves past the Isle of Wight, and are apprehensive that we cannot make Cowes[134] but shall be obliged to run for the Downs[135] and be exposed to the horrors of another night or two in a narrow, horrid channel. 14. Yesterday we were obliged to bear away for Dover. The wind blew all night and this morning, to use the sailor's phrase, *like guns*. The night was dreadful, as we lay by in a narrow sea and heavy waves were continually breaking upon us, and we knew not but we might drift upon the coast on one side or [the] other. We are now in sight of Dover. Twelve o'clock."

This is the last page of the journal, [and] many are missing. Yet what I have transcribed is more than

enough to shew what scenes of terror he must have
passed through. And this winter's voyage was one of the
most stormy and appalling ever performed in safety by
man. But of these sad and overwhelming tempests I
have noticed but a few. Only to think of them is dreadful. How much, then, must our dear father have suffered! But the same pious trust in God that attended
him to the last supported him under them. On what day
he landed at Dover I cannot say.[136] But I know that he
spent nine months in London,[137] and at the house of his
good friend David Lewis, where we also, on our arrival,
found a kind and hospitable welcome.

In the meantime, those he left behind, although they
had many anxious thoughts, looked forward to a meeting with him in the summer and did not suspect his sad
situation on the stormy ocean! The weather was cold,
and except when the snow fell, the sky was bright and
clear. Nor do I recollect any very violent storms of wind
that winter, part of which I spent in Boston at Dr.
Lathrop's and at Mr. Boot's. John was busy improving
himself in painting. For Mr. Sam Vaughan he painted
a picture of two wild turkeys. This picture was sent to
Germany. These birds are very large and beautiful.
About this time he began to teach William the Latin
grammar, to which at that time he gave but little heed.[138]
Yet an year or two afterwards he set himself to work in
earnest and with such intense application as had nearly
cost him his life!

Dorchester was a very pleasant place to live in. It
stood high and commanded a fine prospect on all sides.
We had some good neighbours, and were so near to Boston as to be able to go there at any time. How much
pleasanter those townships are, with a field or two be-

tween every house, than a little country town with its
crooked, narrow, ill-paved streets. We staid there until
the summer, preparing for our departure. At last the
time came when we were to take leave of Dorchester,
and there were some we regretted to leave. But from
none was I so sorry to part as from Susan Butt. She was a
good and kind-hearted girl and much attached to me.
She persuaded my brother to give her a picture he had
done of me in crayons. I have no picture of her, but I
do not forget her fair and open countenance, her light
brown hair, and even the dress she usually wore, a joseph,[139] with buttons of mother of pearl, and a straw hat,
and her cousin Patty Davies, and the rest of our kind
young friends. How much I should like to know how it
was with them in after life. Do they still live and sometimes think of their English friends? How often we have
looked back with regret on the pleasant evenings John
and I used to spend with them, our games and songs, and
the tumbles we got in the snow, returning home by
moonlight, when the rain, freezing on the ice, made the
road slippery as glass. 'Twas then who best could keep
their feet. How delightful a ride in a sleigh was then;
how swift we cut through the air, going over hedge and
ditch, for the snow made all level!

This last Christmas I spent at Mr. Boot's. Here we
had a constant round of visits, and I was more expert at
cards than I have been since. For I was pleased to do as
grown-up people did, though often tired and weary of
cards and sitting up so late. Whist and palm loo were the
games most in fashion, but chess was a favorite with all.
Mrs. Boot took a fancy at this time to dress me like a
woman and had my hair turned up and dressed by an
hairdresser, an operation I did not like; and a queer

figure I must have cut, for Mr. Pratt did not know me, and when he had been sometime in the room cried out, "Is this our Peggy?"

Some days I spent with Mrs. Lathrop, the most amiable of women. At the end of three weeks my brother came to take me home, and I did not see Boston again till the summer. Mrs. Boot was a tall, handsome woman just one and twenty. She was very kind to me, and I shall always remember her and Mr. Boot with gratitude and affection. A curious circumstance took place at Mr. Boot's this winter which was a great annoyance and gave rise to various conjectures. This was the throwing of stones by some persons unseen, which were sure to enter the moment any door or windows were left open, and with so true an aim as always to hit the object intended. Once they struck a turkey the boy was bringing in for dinner, and Mrs. Boot partly closed the shutters before putting out the china when we expected company, a very necessary precaution. For some months nothing could be known but that they were thrown from a sling. At last one of the servants confessed that it was a contrivance of their own, but for what purpose, or how managed, I forget. This avowal put to flight whole armies of ghosts and fairies which the imagination of some neighbours had conjured up. On the whole, the excitement was not unpleasant. It was like living in an enchanted castle, and the frequent question from the servants, "Miss, are you not afraid to stay here?" and the mysterious whisperings of gossips and school boys were not a little amusing.

On the 18th of April this year [1787] a most tremendous fire broke out in Boston. It made a very grand appearance as we viewed it from the orchard, and, though at five miles' distance, the light was so great that the least thing was visible. The column of fire and smoke that rose to the clouds resembled a volcano. John got an horse and attempted to go in to assist our friends and bring away anything for them. He soon returned, saying it was impossible to get into the town as South Street, the only entrance, was burning on both sides. About an 100 houses were burnt and a church. But the damage was not so great as we supposed. Some rum stills had served to increase the splendour of the blaze.[140]

Boston is built on a peninsula, and joins the mainland by a narrow neck of land, four, or perhaps five, furlongs in length. I know not if it is a natural isthmus, or the work of man, but from the swampy meadows on either side, I should think it to be natural. South Street is part of it. The bay in which it stands surrounds it on every other side. The entrance into the bay is defended by Fort William,[141] and no ship can come into the port without passing under its guns. The government keeps a small garrison here and a chaplain. Mr. Isaac Smyth was the chaplain when we were there. He was in England during the war, and settled in Sidmouth in Devonshire.[142] Fort William is nine miles from Boston. The bay is very extensive and contains many beautiful islands, most of them small and wooded to the top. Those we saw from Weymouth and Dorchester had two or three hills of a sugar-loaf form, adding to the beauty of the scene, by the deep indigo of their firs, mixed with the bright and ever-varying green of the other trees. Perhaps when the country is more filled, these untenanted islets will be studded with neat cottages and farms.

At Cambridge, two mile[s] from Boston, there is a very flourishing college, and I believe it is the oldest in

the United States.[143] For as New England was at first settled by those who had fled thither to enjoy liberty of conscience, their first care was to provide means to train up
a race of young ministers worthy to supply the place of
the old, that the religious instruction of the rising generation might not be neglected. Such were these men,
driven out from their native land to seek in a distant and
howling wilderness that peace and security denied to
them at home. But blessed were the fruit of their labours and glorious the result. Little did the bigots who
persecuted these holy men dream that they were laying
the foundation of the happy and widely extended Em-
pire of Liberty in the West! Thus has the "Providence
of God made the wrath of man to praise him."

A ferry divides Cambridge from Boston. Hartford
College in Connecticut is another of their oldest establishments,[144] I believe the second. Boston is more like
an English town in the irregularity of its streets and
houses than any other that I saw on that continent. It
had its government, or State House, and other public
building[s], and churches of every denomination, more
than I can recollect. The people were then in everything
English; their habits, their manners, their dress, their
very names spoke their origin, and the names given to
their towns prove that they still regard the land of their
fathers. Beacon Hill, just at the edge of the Common,
was a pretty object at a distance, and the house of Governor Hancock stood close to it. He was an old man
then.[145] His lady was of the Quincy family, but we did
not know it then, though my father often visited at the
house.

The spring brought letters from my father, full of
hope and anxiety to see us again. And with mingled feel-

ings of expectation and regret we prepared to follow
him, and bid [bade] a last adieu to all that had been
pleasing in that country endeared to us by so many true
and valued friends.

Had I the power of travelling over the world, I
should prefer seeing every place that we have formerly
visited to any new scenes whatever. But how few should
I meet with that would recollect me, and how altered
and changed for the worse would all appear! It is best as
it is. The former time still remains engraven on the
mind, as with a pen of gold, and its glories undimmed
by the sad realities of the present scene are still fair and
beautiful visions.

In June all our preparations were completed, and we
agreed to take our passage to England with Captain
Cushing. It had been proposed that we should sail with
Captain Barnard, and it was desirable as his lady was to
go with him. How it happened, I forget, but I believe
he sailed too early in the spring for us. However, we
were fortunate in our captain, a generous, kindhearted
man, always attentive to everything that could make his
passengers comfortable. In June we left Dorchester, and
spent a fortnight in Boston, paying farewell visits to our
friends there. And now that we were taking a last farewell of them, we felt their value more than ever. Surely
no man ever had so many sincere and steady friends as
my father had in that country, where he went as a
stranger. More than one friend enquired of my brother
if anything was wanted by my mother for our voyage,
offering to supply her with money or any other needful
assistance! These offers were declined with grateful
thanks as we had money enough to take us home, and
we trusted the future to that kind Providence which had

guided and supported us hitherto. After passing these last days with our friends in Boston as pleasantly as the prospect of so soon parting with them would allow, we went on board the *Nonpareil*[146] ready to sail the next morning, the Fourth of July, the grand anniversary of American Independence. Mr. Boot and Gregory went on board with us, and staid some time. Except Mr. and Mrs. Boot, not one of all that we left behind have we ever seen since. But we hope to meet hereafter with all that we have lost and loved. How great will be the blessedness of that happy state when purified from the sins and follies of this life we shall rejoice together forever.

Our passage home was prosperous, and the weather, on the whole, fine. Yet we had some rough days as we went too far north in order to avoid the Algerines who at [that] time captured all American vessels that had not a passport from them, and our captain had not one. With our captain we had reason to be pleased. Mr. Wyatt, the mate, was a worthy man, and the sailors were a quiet, sober set. So far we were happy in our shipmates. Our fellow passengers were four: Mr. Millar, the son of a farmer in Hampshire, who at the age of fourteen had run away from home and [en]listed for a soldier, and being sent off with the first troops to America, had settled (after the war was over) in Nova Scotia, where he had left his wife and children, and was to return there as soon as the object of his present voyage was completed. His chief business in England was to implore the blessing and forgiveness of his father, whom he had not seen since the day that his boyish folly had so unhappily estranged him from the paternal roof. We heard afterwards that his [father] had died two days before he reached home. Poor man, how bitter his disappointment must have been! He appeared to be a very worthy and respectable, plain man. Of our other shipmates, one called Powis was the most amusing. He was an Irishman, a clever, shrewd fellow, with a superabundance of humour. He was an hair dresser, and valued himself on being at the head of his profession, and boasted of having been sent for an hundred miles or more to dress the hair of noble dames on some grand gala days. Happy man! But he should have been a Frenchman to enjoy this high distinction in perfection!

These and the two ladies were all our cabin passengers. Mrs. Cuzeeno entertained us with singing. She had a fine voice and had been a singer on the stage. She also was clever in making plum puddings, cakes, and other dainties for the public good.

One of the sailors had a venture on board of which he hoped to make some profit. This was a young rattlesnake confined on deck in a sort of coop. Twice he got out, but was too feeble to hurt anyone, and the sailor took him up in his hands and replaced him in his cage. I suppose the poor thing was seasick, as he had scarcely tasted food all the voyage. On arriving in London, he was sold for eleven guineas to a showman, but he died eleven weeks afterwards.

We had also on board a number of mocking and other birds, but none of them survived the voyage except one pretty little red bird, a present from our friend Gregory to a young lady, which she received from the hands of my brother. We had also half a dozen American foxes, who looked with longing eyes at some domestic fowls, their near neighbours, whom they could not reach. These foxes were to be sent to some rural Nimrod who may perhaps still boast [of] his Yankee breed and give many a festive hunt to shew the wily strangers off!

On the Fourth of July, a day never to be forgotten by America, we sailed, and directing our course Nor East, in a day or two lost sight of land. Seasickness for a while kept us below, but we soon got on deck and for the most part lived there, only going down to eat or sleep, except when rain or stormy weather drove us below. Yet even here, on the boundless ocean, so often terrific and in most things so very [u]ncongenial to a female mind, we found pleasures of the highest kind: to watch the changing sky, the bright tints of evening, or the dark, heavy mists retiring before the dawn, the moon's pale lustre, the majestic rolling waves, and the whales spouting the water into the air and making a rainbow as they [it] fell. And the most glorious sight of all, the sun rising from, or setting in, the ocean. All this and much more we have seen. It was a beautiful, though not a very pleasant, sight to see the porpoises springing up and playing, some hundreds together, around the ship. They might be seen to a great depth in the sea. But as the sailors looked on their appearance as the forerunner of a storm, they are always unwelcome guests. Sometimes we saw the pretty dolphins sporting over the waves, and the voracious shark often passed, with his large triangular fin erect above the water like a sail.

Once we caught a shark attended by his two little pilot fish, who suffered themselves to be taken rather than desert him. The sailors affirm that these fish always direct his course, and thence they have the name of pilots. It is strange the shark, greedy as he is, never hurts them. They are a little larger than a mackerel and of various beautiful colours.[147]

For a few weeks our voyage was prosperous, but an unhappy accident fell out that cast a gloom on all [a]board. One rainy day when the yards were wet and slippery a lad who had been sent up aloft fell from the top mast, and every exertion to save him was in vain. The boat got near him just as he sunk, and the sailors returned to the ship with a silence that spoke more feelingly than words could their grief and disappointment. He was a fine youth of seventeen and had parted with an only sister when we sailed, hoping to meet again in joy! Poor Hannah! How sad was her loss, for they were orphans. And sadly the sailors lamented poor George, and often in the fine moonlight nights they would fancy they heard soft music and said it was poor George in a little boat astern.

Some time after we passed the banks of Newfoundland, but we staid only three hours to fish there (and caught but three cod), for the weather was unfavourable and it was the captain's wish to get on. One day the cry of an Algerine on board was raised by a wag who wished to amuse himself by alarming the cabin. But we did not believe him, for his voice was firm and we knew the stoutest heart would falter at the sight of so cruel a foe.

The rest of our voyage passed without any incident except the casual sight of a sail, or the bustle occasioned by the shifting wind or sudden squalls. The usual farce of the half way house was acted, which gives an holiday to the merry tars and procures them the ordinary fine of a bottle of rum from the passengers. The boatswain fantastically dressed to personate Neptune appears at the cabin window and pretends to arise from the sea, and having paid his compliments, returns to the deck, where a tub, with a board across, is placed ready to shave with tar the unlucky wight who refuses to give them their usual fees. On entering the English Channel, we saw a great number of ships; many of them were East Indiamen. Our captain told us that it was a very common practice with them to loiter about the Channel for weeks in order to sell to smugglers as much of their goods as they can before they enter them at the custom house.

# III

# The Hazlitts after Their Return to England

On the twelfth of August, 1787, we landed at Portsmouth.[1] It was on a Sunday, the sun shone bright, the bells were ringing, the streets were full of well drest people returning from their different churches, and all things looked gay, while we, not in our best, unsteadily walked to the inn. After dinner my mother lay down, John walk[ed] out to view the town, and I seated myself with William at the window to gaze at the passing crowd. The Isle of Wight, as we passed it, looked very beautiful.

The morning after we landed, we sat [set] off in the stage for London. Mr. Millar, who went with us and was well acquainted with that part of the country, pointed out to us the different seats on the road and among many others that of the unfortunate Captain Peirce who not long before had perished with his two daughters in his arms, in the Halsewell East Indiaman, which was wrecked before getting out of the Channel, and only sixty persons were saved out of the many hundreds on board. The shops at that time were full of prints representing the scene, and china and tea boards were made to exhibit the same sad object.[2] On [our] arriving in London, my father met us at the inn, and before I had time to see him, took me in his arms, out of the coach, and led us to our very good friend David Lewis, and from him and Mrs. Lewis we received the greatest attention and kindness. With them we staid some weeks, but my mother's health being very indifferent, we took a lodging at Walworth, and she was in some measure revived by the fresh air. This is near Ca[m]berwell, where your father saw the garden he speaks of in his works[3] and which had made so strong an impression on his young mind. And being the first gardens he had seen after our long voyage were of course doubly valued.

After staying there a fortnight, David Williams[4] proposed our taking part of an house in Percy Street, which was to be had cheap, and it would be more convenient for my father to attend to anything that might occur. Here we staid eleven weeks, and my grandmother came up from Wisbeach to see us. She staid with us a month; she could walk above two miles, yet she must have been 84 at that time, and she lived above 14 years after. This was a meeting she at one time did not hope for as she was very old when we went to America, and our return to England was not intended. I never saw her after this time, but my mother paid her a visit of nine weeks in 1792. She died at my Uncle Loftus's house at Peterborough in 1831 [1801].

While we were in Percy Street, many plans were proposed to my father by his friends for keeping him in London. One was a school, another to give lectures to

young men, or to teach rhetoric, etc. But my mother's
health was an obstacle to the first, and a little with quiet-
ness was preferred to the uncertain though probable
chance of gaining much. In these plans the Lewises and
David Williams were the most active and when a small
congregation in a distant part of the country was accepted, they said we should not remain there if we did
not find it comfortable, and did everything in their
power to serve my father and would have done much
more if their own misfortunes (which happened six
months after)[5] had not prevented the kindness intended
from being realized.

Mr. Lewis was the son of Mrs. Lewis at Maidstone.
There were six brothers, and all of them warm friends
to my father. The youngest, James, died at New York,
and they had one sister, Mrs. Cooper.[6]

While we remained in London, my chief business
was to attend to William and see that he did not escape
out of the front door and ramble about the streets by
himself, which he was fond of doing. Yet he never lost
his way.

Once my father took us to see a panorama. It was
one of the Isle of Wight, the view we had so lately seen.
Boydell['s] shop[7] had great attractions for me, and I was
quite delighted when my father took me there to buy a
print. It was the *Fish Stealers by Moonlight*.

This autumn was dry and pleasant, and we used to
walk out every afternoon in the neighbourhood of Percy
Street. At Walworth there was a great common, and
Camberwell Green was near. If ever I go to London
again, I will visit these places for "Auld Lang Syne."

I never feel the morning air of an October day with-

out thinking of that autumn and the difference we found
between our English fogs and the American fall.

In November we sat [set] off for Wem in Shropshire,
where it was my father's ill fate to settle and bury his
talents until old age prevented his further usefulness.
John was left in London, under the eye of David Lewis,
to begin his career as a miniature painter, and he went
on prosperously for some years.[8] William went with us
to Wem. We left London on a Thursday and on Saturday reached Shrewsbury. Mr. Wicksteed[9] came to us at
the inn and kindly insisted on our going to his house,
where we staid till the next week. My father went in a
gig to Wem the same evening and took William with
him, and they came back on Sunday evening. The next
day we spent at Mr. Beck's,[10] and were introduced to Mr.
Fownes, the old minister of the High Street meeting.[11]
And we met for the first time Mr. John Rowe,[12] who had
just settled at Shrewsbury as co-pastor with Mr. Fownes.
Our evening passed pleasantly, and I thought if the people of Wem resembled our present company, it would be
well. But this was not exactly the case. Yet there we
found some pleasant companions, and over the faults of
others Time (like the blue mist on the distant mountains) has drawn a beautiful veil!

On our road from London we slept one night at
a lone inn close to the Wreakin (the highest hill in
Shropshire), sixteen miles from Salop [i.e., Shrewsbury].
On Tuesday we proceeded to Wem, and were received at
Mr. Swanwick's,[13] where we remained until Saturday
evening, while the old house was put in order which belonged to the meeting. It was indeed old and ugly, but
there was plenty of room in it. And although it had the
appearance of a place ready to fall, it lasted our time.

William always liked this old house better than many superior ones that we have lived in since, but he liked Wem better than any of us, for it was the scene of his childhood and where he first began to shew those talents which have since shone so brightly.

The road from Salop to Wem is pleasant, and the entrance to the town seemed to promise a better looking place than we found. It was a very small town, but it had a town hall and market and a free school. The rectory is worth 1800, or 3000, an year. It [the town] was once larger and had walls. And they have a story of Cromwell's looking down upon it from the Trench farms and turning back, thinking it not worth taking. It was, indeed, a dismal place to sit down in after all that we had seen.

Here in an obscure inland town and far from all that were dear to us, it was our lot to live for many years, the best years of our lives; but perhaps it was best for us, and we resolved to think it so and to shut our eyes as far as it was possible to all that was disagreeable in our new situation. If my father had but little society, his books made ample amends and the rise and progress of the French Revolution, which happened soon after, gave full scope to his thoughts and diverted them from dwelling too anxiously on his own privations. The dull monotony of our lives was sometimes broken by the visits to and from Mr. Rowe of Shrewsbury and Mr. Jenkins of Whitchurch,[14] which like "a sun beam in a wintry day" cheered at bright intervals our cloudy existence. These two gentlemen were, all their lives, our unchan[g]ing friends. Of Mr. Rowe and his family I shall have often occasion to speak. And to them I shall always feel the warmest gratitude for very many acts of kindness.

Mr. Jenkins was the minister of a still smaller congregation than that of Wem, but he had a sort of free school attached to the chapel, with a few acres of land belonging to it, that served to keep famine from the door. Mr. Jenkins was a joyous, pleasant man, full of wit and glee, abounding with good stories which he dealt out to his younger friends with a marvelous grace. He was besides a pious, judicious, and excellent preacher, firm and unbending in principle. Yet with all this, he could get no better situation than Whitchurch. In the church,[15] perhaps, he might have risen high, but the dissenters would none of him. And why? He was a little man, of no very handsome outward appearance, and worse than all, he was a Welshman and had a strong national accent. Mrs. Jenkins was a lady of good sense and talents that if cultivated might have adorned the highest station. They were both very fat, and not much given to locomotion. But once coming to spend the Christmas week with us, as they often did, they undertook to walk to Wem (a distance of nine miles) and sat [set] out at ten in the morning. It was an hard frost, and after dinner my mother and I walked up the road two miles to meet them, and just after we got home and had put all things in order for tea, they came in, about four o'clock. How pleasant those evenings were, and how refreshing that tea and bright fire after the cold air and hard ground frozen into ruts that almost cut our shoes. These evenings will return no more, but the memory of them still lives, and that is something.

## OCTOBER 27, 1838.

It is now two years since the last page of these notes was written; I wrote them with a pleasure I shall never feel again, for my dear mother was sitting by my side, and she was amused with what I wrote! But the spirit for the work is gone with her,[16] and the brightness of my heaven is become dim.

Soon after we settled at Wem, my father took charge of a small school that had been under the care of Mr. Houghton,[17] the former minister of that place, the father of Pendlebury, a famous orator in his day.[18] In a situation so very different from his former life, more particularly when compared with his active labours in America, where the best and wisest of his brethren cheered and supported him in his arduous task, shut out from the society of men of learning and talents, and relying on the resources of his own mind, my father did not repine but applied himself to the duties of his ministry and to the education of his youngest son, William, now about nine years of age (and whom it was his fervent wish to train up in the way he should go), teaching him "that wisdom's ways are ways of pleasantness, and all her paths are paths of peace." And in these duties he found his great consolation and reward. And the talents of this dear boy (in his affectionate father) met with an able preceptor. There was but one boy in the school who had more than common abilities or could give a spur to his exertions.[19] But he needed it not, for his mind was bent on attaining that excellence to which it was his father's earnest wish to lead him. And he attended so closely to his studies, and [i.e., that] his overexertion (when about fifteen) brought on a fit. And although he had no return of it, it was long before he recovered [from] the effects of it. An accident once befell him; he was seized with the cramp while bathing and but for the timely aid of Wil-

liam Cottam, a lad much older than himself, a sad and
fatal end would have been put to all our hopes.

The first six years after our settlement at Wem he
devoted to study, and under his father's guidance he
made a rapid progress. He was at this time the most active, lively, and happiest of boys; his time, divided between his studies and his childish sports, passed smoothly
on. Beloved by all for his amiable temper and manners,
pleasing above his years, the delight and pride of his own
family, he felt not, like the rest, the sad change from the
society of the most agreeable and worthy friends to the
dullness, petty jealousies, and cabals of a little country
town.

Of the time passed here he always spoke with pleasure. The scenes of childhood are dear to all, and while
safe under the parents' care, their years glide on, in inno-
cence, without one anxious thought or fear of the storms
that await them in after life. So it was with this dear boy.
When he was about 12 years old, he and George Dicken
(the son of a clergyman who lived near us)[20] were invited to spend the summer vacation at Mrs. Tracey's at
Liverpool. Mrs. Tracey was a West Indian, a widow
lady who having [i.e., had] taken up her abode for some
years at Wem to be near her daughters, whom she had
placed at school there, and was now passing a year with
them in Liverpool before returning to Jamaica.[21] William made the best use of his time while here in learning
French, which he had not an opportunity to learn at
home. He and Miss Tracey studied together, and Miss
Tracey was his pupil, he having begun to teach her Latin
before they left Wem. After six weeks my father went to
Liverpool and brought home the two boys. After his return William began to teach me what he had been learn-

ing himself. *Telemachus*[22] was the book we read, and to
read it with him was a double pleasure. The book is still
a favorite with me, and perhaps for that reason.

Mrs. Tracey, after losing her second husband, Mr.
Hodgson, finally settled at Wem. She spent much of her
time at our house, always coming on Sunday to attend
our evening service. I hear she died at Wem, a few years
since, as did also her second daughter. It is not often
that I can trace out the fortunes of our old friends to the
present time. There were some others at Wem for whom
I cared but little then; yet chancing to hear of them
lately, that I knew them so long ago gave an interest to
their history which it would not else have had. But time
and distance blot out a multitude of sins!

But to return to William, he was admitted as a student at Hackney College[23] before the usual age of sixteen. He was intended for the ministry, but his mind
taking another direction he could not, of course, any
longer avail himself of the advantages of that institution.
It was a grievous disappointment to his father to see his
dearest hopes frustrated, but no reproaches or unkind-
ness embittered his return home. And now he spent
years between his father's and his brother's house, unde-
termined what profession to chuse for his advancement
in life. Painting was his favorite study, but his idea of
what a picture ought to be was so far above what he
could attain that he was always discontented with his
best endeavors. From his brother he always received
every proof of fraternal affection, who never thought any
expence or trouble too much that could be of service to
one he loved so well. And in after life when William
was more prosperous, he returned to his brother the
kindness he had received from him. And while they

lived, their bond of brotherly love was never broken. May your sons, my dearest William, in this point tread in the steps of your father and uncle.

Soon after leaving Hackney, William began to write his book *On the Principles of Human Action.* This was his first and favorite work, for it cost him more labour than all he wrote beside, nor [i.e., not] for want of ideas, but of words. This deficiency, the consequence of over-study, I need not say soon wore off. For a year or two he practiced as a portrait painter in Liverpool and Manchester. A friend of his,[24] in the latter place (on the conclusion of the short peace of Amiens, in 1807 [1802]) made him an offer of an hundred guineas to go to Paris and copy for him ten pictures in the Louvre. This he gladly accepted, and rejoiced in the opportunity of seeing those monuments of ancient art of which he was an enthusiastic admirer. He spent the winter in Paris, working in the Louvre, from ten in the morning until four in the afternoon, suffering much from cold and many other deprivations. But he cared little for these things while he had those noble specimens of genius before his eyes.

He brought home some beautiful copies. *The Death of Clorinda,* the *Transfiguration,* and the portrait of Hyppolito de Medici are all that I have seen. The *Transfiguration* he gave to Mr. Northcote;[25] where the others are now I do not know. He returned home just before the detention which took place in the spring. As an artist it is said he would have been exempted from that law.[26] I believe he painted very few portraits after his return home; what he had seen, so far above all that he could hope to attain to, made him despise his own efforts. What he was most deficient in was the mechanical part. Shall I say that if he had had less talent and his perception of what was beautiful in art had been more dim, he would have been more successful. But so it was, and many promising beginnings have been blotted that would satisfy many others who did not aim at perfection.

He now devoted his time to study, and first having by the kind assistance of Mr. J. Johnson[27] published his first metaphysical work, he was employed by him to abridge two or three books, after which he brought [out] his answer to Malthus.[28] In 1809[29] he married Miss Stoddart, and her brother[30] offering them a cottage and garden at Winterslow, a village in Wiltshire, they went to reside there for some years. The next year his first child was born, and died soon after.[31] The loss of this child was a severe stroke to him. I arrived there a day or two after, and never can I forget the look of anguish . . .[32] which at the first moment passed over his countenance, but his grief, though deep, was silent, and he applied [himself] to his literary pursuits with the greatest diligence. The English grammar and the life of Holcroft were written at this time.[33] Yet painting was his great delight, and while at Winterslow it was his custom to go forth into the woods to sketch views from nature, taking with him his canvas, paints, etc., an hammer, and a nail, which he used to drive into a tree which served him as an easel to hang his picture on. A couple of eggs, boiled hard, and some bread and cheese for his dinner, but never any liquor of any kind. Usually coming home at four (except when we went to meet him in that beautiful wood), bringing with him some promising beginning of the beautiful views around, but fated, alas, never to be finished. Several of these I remember, one in particular, the view of Norman Court, the seat of ———

Wall Esqr.[34] I wish I had these rejected landscapes. I should prefer them to many highly finished pictures where the leaves look like silver pennies and country girls are dressed in robes of white satin.

The country around Winterslow was very fine and furnished rich subjects for landscape. Besides the woods round Norman Court (which William was used to call his study), there was thorny down, a wood of the oldest looking trees that seemed as if they had stood there for centuries, so entangled were their branches. It was situated on the top of an hill, from whence Salisbury could be seen, and its flattened top and smooth green walks led us to conjecture that a castle had once stood there, and to fancy many a bevy of fair ladies and gallant knights had had those green walks in ages long gone by that none but ourselves now visited. Lamb and his sister[35] were with us in our rambles about this place, which looked like a grove haunted by druids. After two years passed at Winterslow, it was necessary for my brother to remove with his family to London, where he was engaged to give lectures at the Surrey Institution.[36] But here I must go back a little, for I have passed over many events prior to this time. In 1809 [1808] he married Miss Stoddart, and as he was known by his writing and had a fair prospect of being useful to the world, he devoted his time to literature, and gave up his beloved painting, except at intervals of leisure.[87]

# Appendices

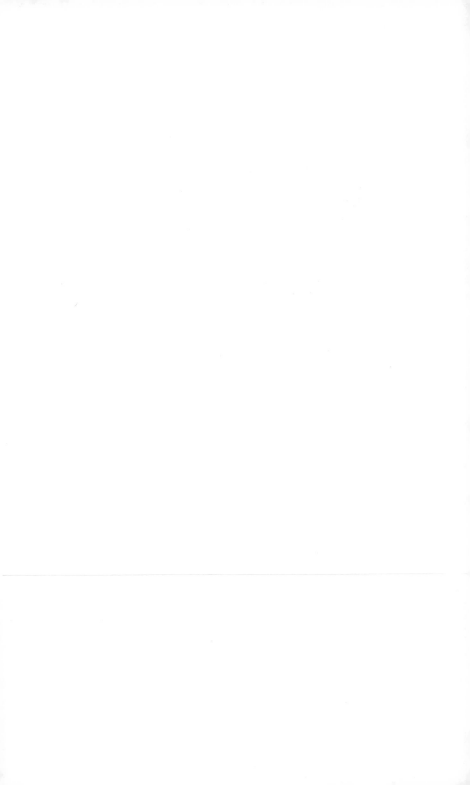

# Appendix I

# "An Account of the State of Rational Religion in America"

In the June, 1808, issue of the *Monthly Repository of Theology and General Literature,* volume III, pages 302-307, the Rev. William Hazlitt, under the pseudonym of "An Old Unitarian," published "An Account of the State of Rational Religion in America; by an Unitarian Minister, Who Travelled in That Country." Addressing his communication to the Editor of the *Monthly Repository,* Hazlitt wrote as follows:

"Upon the authority of Mr. Christie, in your account of Unitarianism in America, you make Mr. Freeman's ordination at Boston to have happened *about fifty years ago.* This is an egregious mistake. For we have not yet seen quite twenty years since that event took place. But, before I proceed farther, you will suffer me to relate some previous circumstances. Mr. Freeman was a young man, when he was chosen by his church to be what they then called *their reader.* As he cherished a generous love

of truth, and was courteous, sociable, and friendly, and
always open to conviction, he became a member of the
Bostonian Association of Ministers, who regularly assembled every Monday and freely conversed upon all subjects, every one declaring his sentiments without offend-
ing or being offended. Doctors Chauncey, Mather and
Lathrop, and Messrs. Clarke, Everit, Eliot, and Smith,
formed the principal part of that venerable band of
brothers, who were true whigs of the old stamp, and
who, whilst they displayed the most amiable manners in
their mutual intercourse, were firmly united in Christian fellowship. They individually agreed to differ, and
maintained this moral and truly religious principle, that
*every man should be fully persuaded in his own mind.*
Some of them, therefore, studied the writings of Priestley, whilst others of them to whom these writings were
not so familiar, expressed no sort of enmity when they
incidentally heard what were the leading doctrines
which he taught. Such was the state of things at Boston,
in the year 1783. In that year, Mr. Freeman's congregation, who had been trained up in all the tenets of high-
churchism, were solicitous to have him receive episcopal
ordination. But, he would not subscribe the 39 Articles,
nor could he submit his conscience to the domination
and capricious dictates of a bishop. The bishop therefore refused to engage in the service, to which Mr. Freeman, upon his own terms, would have gladly acceded.
This conduct of the overseer led Mr. Freeman to think
more deeply upon the subject than he had usually done.
The affair became the topic of general conversation.
Most of the Bostonians were advocates for Mr. Freeman.
But, Mr. Parker, a high priest belonging to the first episcopal Church, exerted himself to the utmost against him,

though with little success, as there was no establishment there, nor any Doctors' Commons, to punish him according to their arbitrary decisions, from a merciful regard to his soul, and a pious discharge of that supreme homage which is ever, *per fas et nefas,* due to the friends of the Church.

"About this particular crisis, a gentleman from this country, who had suffered much for his attachment to the American cause, and who had his share of that evil report, which the orthodox usually circulate amongst their brethren against Unitarians, embarked for America with his family, which his friends humorously told him was his land of promise. After spending some months in the southern States, he arrived at Boston the 15th of May, 1784: and having a letter to Mr. Eliot, who received him with great kindness, he was introduced on that very day to the Association. The venerable Chauncey, at whose house it happened to be held, entered into a familiar conversation with him, and shewed him every possible respect, as he learned that he had been acquainted with Dr. Price. Without knowing at the time any thing of the occasion which led to it, ordination happened to be the general subject of discourse. After the different gentlemen had severally delivered their opinions, the stranger was requested to declare his sentiments; who unhesitatingly replied, that the people, or the congregation, who chose any man to be their minister, were his proper ordainers. Mr. Freeman, upon hearing this, jumped from his seat in a kind of transport, saying, 'I wish you could prove that, Sir.' The gentleman, whom I shall in future call Bereanus, answered that few things could admit of an easier proof: and from that moment a thorough intimacy commenced between him and

Mr. Freeman. Soon after, the Boston prints being under
no *imprimatur,* he published several letters in supporting the cause of Mr. Freeman. At the solicitation of Mr.
Freeman, he also published a scriptural confutation of
the 39 Articles. Notice being circulated that this publication would appear on a particular day, the printer,
apprized of this circumstance, threw off above a hundred
papers beyond his usual number, and had not one paper
remaining upon his hands at noon. This publication, in
its consequences, converted Mr. Freeman's congregation
into an Unitarian Church, which, as Mr. Freeman repeatedly acknowledged, could never have been done
without the labours of Bereanus. A committee was appointed to reform the book of Common Prayer, and to
strike out all those passages which savoured of Trinitarian worship. This object being pursued with great de-
liberation, the ordination of Mr. Freeman by his congregation, did not take place before the end of the year
1788 [1787], and this congregation is now as flourishing
since it has learned to say sumpsimus, as it had formerly
been under its old mumpsimus. Thus, then, 700 or 800
people, who had been accustomed to worship three gods,
and to believe one of these, as consisting of two persons,
to be in reality two gods, are now become so enlightened
as to worship only the One God and Father of our Lord
Jesus Christ.

"But, to say something more of B., he passed the pre-
ceding year in Pennsylvania, and Maryland. In his way
from New York, he preached, at their request, to the
House of Commons belonging to New Jersey. He next
preached Unitarianism with acceptance, at Philadelphia,
to some orthodox churches, and might have done so to
this day, had not some cunning ones and busy bodies

circulated the report that the worship of the great god-
dess Diana was in danger. He afterwards repeatedly
preached to a numerous congregation at New London,
where no exceptions were made to his doctrines, but
handsome compliments paid to him by his principal au-
ditors. At the particular recommendation of his truly
catholic and hospitable friend Dr. Ewing, he preached
also at Carlisle, where there was then a vacancy, and an
expectancy of 400 guineas a-year to the preacher who
should be chosen to fill it up. But, the zealous Dr. Duffield of Philadelphia, had taken care to send off his
character before him as an heretic, with such additional
suggestions of his own as orthodoxy usually supplies. He
therefore appeared before a prejudging audience. But,
after he had preached twice, the endeavours of Dr. Duffield not being deemed sufficiently efficacious, General
Armstrong applied to a Mr. Lynn [Rev. William Linn]
in the neighbourhood, to appear there the following
Sunday, and to take a part of the services of the day.
Lynn was punctually obedient to the commands of his
master. He ascended the pulpit with rancour in his
countenance. He bitterly declaimed against all heresy,
and warned a thousand people who stood before him to
be armed against the greatest danger which then threatened them, a greater danger than all the evils of the late
war, the introduction of heresy by foreigners. Such was
his modesty, forbearance, and charity, and such his rude
treatment of a stranger, who, to his own hurt, had re-
leased some hundreds of his countrymen from a loath-
some prison, and from famine. But, notwithstanding
the indefatigable exertions of Lynn, B. might have remained at Carlisle, if he would have subscribed the confession of faith, *as far as it was agreeable to the word of*

*God.* To this suggestion he replied, that he came there a free man, that he would continue such as long as he lived, that he would give way to nothing which had the most distant resemblance to trimming, and that he would not even subscribe those things which he most firmly believed, lest he might throw a stumbling block in his brother's way. He therefore took his leave of his friends at Carlisle, rather too hastily, it was afterwards said, as Dr. Ewing was informed, that, if he had remained there a fortnight longer, he would have been accepted upon his own terms, and been appointed a Principal of the College. Such is frequently the course of human affairs.

"B. afterwards travelled into Maryland, where he preached in a *quondam* Episcopalian Church, using his own prayers, and declaring to a numerous audience what he believed to be the doctrines of the New Testament. He might probably have settled there, had not some difficulties arisen concerning an Unitarian liturgy, and had he not been seized with a violent fever, which brought him to the brink of the grave. During his illness, he received the most Christian treatment, and the most generous and affectionate hospitality at the house of a Mr. Earl, for whom and his son-in-law, an excellent physician, he has ever since retained the most grateful and heart-felt remembrance.

"In the succeeding winter, he preached a series of sermons on the evidences for the truth of Christianity, at the Common Hall of the University of Philadelphia, which, to the honour of America, is open to all preachers, to whatever sect they belong. At first the place was well filled. But afterwards, through the artifices of those who never attended, the audience was greatly diminished, though Dr. Ewing from his pulpit had strenuously recommended the lecture to his hearers. Dr. Carson, a medical gentleman, was anxious to have the sermons published, and offered to this purpose to procure 500 subscribers. But B. with grateful acknowledgments declined the proposal, as his compliance would have detained him longer at Philadelphia than he then wished to continue there. Before he left the place, however, he published Dr. Priestley's Appeal, &c. to which he prefixed three short addresses of his own. It was purposely contrived that this piece should be ready for sale on the first day of the meeting of the Synod. Some alarmists accordingly, having heard the awful tidings, introduced the subject into their venerable body, which was considered of such high importance, that it occupied their whole attention during two days of their sitting. At last, Dr. Sprout [James Sproat] made a motion, to address a printed circular letter to their respective flocks, to introduce into the letter extracts of all the heresies contained in the book, and solemnly to guard their hearers against the reading of it. The Dr. was seconded by a learned auctioneer belonging to his Church. But Mr. Lynn, already noticed, and the father probably of Dr. Lynn [John Blair Linn], Dr. Priestley's feeble antagonist, seeing farther into the consequences of such a measure than Dr. Sprout, opposed the motion, shrewdly observing, that such a letter would awaken a general curiosity, and instead of suppressing the heresy would spread it far and near, and be the occasion of driving those very persons into heresy whom they intended to guard against it. But, though Mr. Lynn carried his point, his arguments did not seem conclusive to all his brethren. For, one clergyman, who lived 150 miles from Philadelphia, returned home so full of the subject, that he preached the whole of the following Sunday against the heresy, and earnestly cautioned his hearers never to look into so poisonous a book. This proceeding so whetted their curiosity, that the very week after they had 57 copies of it imported into their township. So well founded was the remark of Mr. Lynn. In short, the labours of B. laid the foundation of Unitarianism in that country, he having left behind him some warm friends to the cause wherever he went. At Philadelphia, he was much attached to the Vaughan family, to Dr. Ewing, professor Mr. James Davidson, Dr. Carson, Mr. Justice Bush [Jacob Rush?], Mr. Tenche Coxe, General Irvine, Mr. Porter, &c. who treated him with brotherly affection. There was only one man there of whom he complained, who, upon his first introduction to him, paid him some fulsome flattery, and expressed his anxious wish that they could have many such men in that country. This was the celebrated Dr. Rush, who afterwards told him that he was satisfied with the religion of his ancestors, and abused Dr. Ewing for the friendly regards he had shewn him.

"Bereanus afterwards proceeded to Boston, as we have already seen. He preached repeatedly there the Thursday's Lecture, and to many congregations in that city. He also preached at Dorchester, Jamaica Plain, Weymouth, Marshfield, Scituate, Providence, Salem, Halawell [Hallowell], &c. At Old Hingham, where the venerable Mr. Gay was the pastor, he preached above forty times, and the noble-minded General Lincoln was one of his 1200 hearers. This congregation was founded 1635. They, with their minister, fled from the persecution of the detestable house of Stuart, and settled in this place which was then a wilderness. What is very remarkable is, that from that period until the year 1786, the space of 151 years, this congregation had only three ministers, the last of them, Mr. Gay, having been their pastor above 70 years. The friendly and enlightened Mr. Shute was the minister of New Hingham, and Dr. Barnes the minister of one of the Marshfield Churches, who was also a liberal man. Many other Churches might be mentioned, from which the Calvinistic gloom is gradually dispersing. But, I must particularly notice Salem. There was there one thoroughdox congregation, which was not in a very flourishing state. There were also three large congregations, where Unitarian ministers were generally heard with acceptance. One of these, indeed, became wholly Unitarian in a little time, through the fearless and indefatigable labours of Mr. Bentley, a very learned man, and an unbiassed and strenuous advocate for what appeared to him to be the good word of truth according to the gospel. The two others were mostly Arians. Mr. Barnard, an hospitable, open-hearted man, who readily entered into the circumstances of a stranger, was the minister of the second of these churches, and had so well instructed his flock, that nothing was offensive to them which appeared to flow from an honest mind. Mr. Darby [Derby], a rich merchant, rendered the third respectable by his courteous and bountiful disposition. B. often preached to these congregations, and was treated with civility by them all. Besides Unitarianism becoming now the subject of much conversation far and near, he found many friends in almost all places, though the majority were not in his favour. Near Portland, in his way to Kennebec, he was sought out by Mr. Thatcher, an enlightened member of Congress, who preferred truth to all the world. Being requested by him to lend him a sermon of which he had heard, and to give him leave to publish it, he readily acquiesced. The sermon, which was on the Mystery of Godliness, was immediately printed, and 400 copies of it sold in one week. People in this country cannot well conceive, what a rapid progress truth may make where there are no establishments, nor any temporal emoluments to fetter the mind against it. A little seed sown may be so productive in three or four years, as to furnish a supply to the greatest part of a whole country. The appeal published at Philadelphia was found at Kennebec the year following, and, there is every reason to expect, that in thirty or forty years more the whole of Massachuset[t]s will be Unitarian.

"Such were the labours of B. in America, during a residence of four years. He saw the doctrines of the Bible taking root, and acquiring every day a more extensive spread. He therefore would have gladly remained in that country, to carry on the cause in which he had long laboured. But after laying a foundation on which a spacious superstructure has ever since been growing up, he finding his finances exhausted, was compelled to return to this country, where some, even of his *quondam* Unitarian friends, whilst they congratulated him upon his successful transatlantic services, gave him but a cool reception.

"Our fashion is to expend large sums of money in training up young men for the ministry, and to desert those who have spent their best days in our service, or to suffer them to sink unpitied under the burden of age and infirmities, whilst we follow our pleasures, or act only upon the spur of caprice. I devoutly wish for the spread of Unitarianism. But I wish also to see Unitarians maintain a consistent character as the followers of their blessed Master, and to make their light to shine. I am sorry, when any of them disgrace their profession, by generally absenting themselves from the public worship, or by turning their backs upon a little flock, and attending the idol temple in those places where all the rich and the fashionable resort to it.

"AN OLD UNITARIAN."

# Appendix II

# The Shronell Hazlitts

On her father's side of the family, Margaret Hazlitt's grandfather was John Hazlitt (the name is spelled in a variety of ways), who was born about 1710. With his wife, Margaret, he left Coleraine, Derry, and about 1735 was living in more or less humble circumstances at Shrone Hill, or Shronell, near Tipperary, Ireland. In published documents of 1756 and 1762, cited by W. Carew Hazlitt in his *Memoirs of William Hazlitt, with Portions of His Correspondence* (London, 1867), I, 3, John Hazlitt was described as *mercator,* i. e., a merchant. John and Margaret Hazlitt lie buried in Shronell churchyard.

The following chart lists the members of the Hazlitt family with whom we are directly concerned:

John and Margaret Hazlitt
of Shronell

Elizabeth
m.
Robert McClelland
Jane; other
children in
America

William
(1737-1820)
m.
Grace Loftus
(1746-1837)

James
(1748-1808)
m.
3 times

John
Supposedly
a colonel
in America

Sara     Jane     Maria

John
Kilner

John
(1767-1837)
m.
Mary Pierce

Loftus, died
in infancy

Margaret
(1770-1841)

William (1778-1830)
m.
(1) Sarah Stoddart
(1774-1840)
(2) Isabella Bridgewater
(     -1869)

Thomas
died in
infancy

Harriet
died in
infancy

Esther
died in
infancy

Harriet     Mary     William

A son
died in
infancy

William
(1811-1893)
m.
Catherine Reynell
(1804-1860)
William Carew
(1834-1913)

John, died
in infancy

On her mother's side of the family, Margaret's grandfather was Thomas Loftus, who married Grace Pentlow in 1725.

The following chart lists the members of the Loftus family with whom we are directly concerned:

Father came from Hull                 Father came from Oxfordshire

Thomas Loftus    m.    Grace Pentlow (1708-1801)

Thomas        Grace (1746-1837)      2 children who died young
m.             m.
Miss Coulson   William Hazlitt (1737-1820)

# Notes

## INTRODUCTION

1. For further information about the Rev. Mr. Hazlitt and the American prisoners at Kinsale, see E. J. Moyne, "The Reverend William Hazlitt: A Friend of Liberty in Ireland During the American Revolution," *William and Mary Quarterly*, Third Series, XXI (April, 1964), 288-297.

2. For the full story concerning Dr. Ewing's recommendation of Mr. Hazlitt and Dr. Rush's opposition to him, see E. J. Moyne, "The Reverend William Hazlitt and Dickinson College," *Pennsylvania Magazine of History and Biography*, LXXXV (July, 1961), 289-302.

3. See Henry Wilder Foote, *James Freeman and King's Chapel* (Boston, 1873), pp. 6, 7; this pamphlet is reprinted from the *Religious Magazine and Monthly Review*, XLIX (June, 1873), 505-531. See also Foote, *Annals of King's Chapel* (Boston, 1882-96), II, Chapter XXI; and Conrad Wright, *The Beginnings of Unitarianism in America* (Boston, 1955), pp. 210-211.

4. An Old Unitarian [William Hazlitt, Sr.], "An Account of the State of Rational Religion in America," *Monthly Repository*, III (June, 1808), 303. Since the Rev. William Hazlitt's article contains further information about his relationship with the Rev. James Freeman and otherwise supplements many of the points that Margaret Hazlitt makes in her journal, "An Account of the State of Rational Religion in America" has been reprinted in its entirety as Appendix I.

5. See Appendix I.

6. Foote, *Annals of King's Chapel*, II, 381.

7. *Ibid.*, pp. 383-394.

8. Thomas Belsham, *Memoirs of the Late Reverend Theophilus Lindsey, M. A.* (The Centenary Volume; London, 1873), p. 154 n.

9. *Ibid.*

10. Joseph G. Waters, "A Biographical Sketch of Rev. William Bentley," in *The Diary of William Bentley, D. D.: Pastor of the East Church, Salem, Massachusetts* (Salem, Mass., 1905-14), I, xv.

The Rev. Mr. Hazlitt also preached for other ministers in Salem, and "in one of his sermons, before the North parish, he openly disavowed his belief in the doctrine of the Trinity, much to the surprise of his hearers" (Joseph B. Felt, *Annals of Salem* [2nd ed.; Salem, 1845-49], II, 605).

11. See a letter from the Rev. James Freeman to the Rev. Mr. Hazlitt, November 20, 1787, in "The Hazlitt Papers," *Christian Reformer*, VI (January, 1839), 16.

12. W. Carew Hazlitt, *Memoirs of William Hazlitt, with Portions of His Correspondence* (London, 1867), I, 270.

13. Bereanus Theosebes [William Hazlitt, Sr.], *A Discourse on the Apostle Paul's Mystery of Godliness Being Made Manifest in the Flesh* (Falmouth, 1786), p. 3.

14. See a letter from the Rev. Jeremy Belknap to Ebenezer Hazard, August 16, 1784, in "The Belknap Papers," *Collections* of the Massachusetts Historical Society, Fifth Series, III (1877), 168-169.

15. W. Carew Hazlitt, *Four Generations of a Literary Family: The Hazlitts in England, Ireland, and America* (London, 1897), I, 19.

16. [W. Carew Hazlitt], *The Hazlitts: An Account of Their Origin and Descent* (Edinburgh, 1911), p. 212.

17. *The Diary of William Bentley, D. D.* (Salem, 1905-14), IV, 561. At a later date the Rev. Mr. Bentley received from Mr. Winthrop a miniature of the first Governor Winthrop done by John Hazlitt (*The Diary of William Bentley, D. D.* [Salem, 1905-14], I, 187; and III, 96).

18. See Henry T. Tuckerman, *Book of the Artists: American Artist Life* (New York, 1867), p. 54.

19. See Francis H. Lincoln, "The Thaxter, Now the Wompatuck Club, House," in *Hingham: A Story of Its Early Settlement and Life, Its Ancient Landmarks, Its Historic Sites and Buildings* (n. p., 1911), pp. 112-114.

20. See, for instance, Benjamin F. Stevens, "A Reminiscence of the Past," *Hingham Magazine* (1898), pp. 43-44, and Edward B. Allen, *Early American Wall Paintings, 1710-1850* (New Haven, 1926), p. 18.

21. *American Decorative Wall Painting, 1700-1850* (Sturbridge, Mass., 1952), p. 37. See also pp. 39, 133-134.

22. "Joseph Hunter on the Hazlitts," *Notes and Queries,* CCII (June, 1957), 266.

23. *Heralds of a Liberal Faith,* ed. Samuel A. Eliot, II, *The Pioneers* (Boston, 1910), 4.

24. [W. Carew Hazlitt], *The Hazlitts,* p. 377.

25. *Ibid.,* pp. 381-382. Although dated March, 1790, by W. Carew Hazlitt, William's letter must have been written in July of that year.

In a letter of June 3, 1789, to the Rev. Mr. Hazlitt, the Rev. James Freeman wrote from Boston: "Your son Billy must not like America better than England, because this is certainly not so fine a country as yours. Bid him remember that we have here many such places as Cape Cod, where we are obliged to walk up to our knees in sand, and have little else except fish to eat" ("The Hazlitt Papers," *Christian Reformer,* VI [January, 1839], 19). Apparently young William longed to be back in America until he got accustomed to life in England.

26. *The Hazlitts,* p. xiv. In his letter of June 3, 1789, to the Rev. Mr. Hazlitt, Freeman wrote: "I remember that Miss Peggy gave some

specimens of her talents in drawing before she left Boston. I should be happy to see one of her landscapes" ("The Hazlitt Papers," *Christian Reformer*, VI [January, 1839], 19).

27. [W. Carew Hazlitt], *The Hazlitts*, p. 338.

28. Thomas Addis Emmet, *Memoir of Thomas Addis and Robert Emmet with Their Ancestors and Immediate Family* (New York, 1915), I, 193.

29. Anne Holt, *A Ministry to the Poor, Being the History of the Liverpool Domestic Mission Society, 1836-1936* (Liverpool, 1936), pp. 20-21.

30. Margaret's brother William had died on September 18, 1830, and was buried in the churchyard of St. Anne's, Soho, in London.

31. *Christian Reformer*, VIII (October, 1841), 664. Both in his *Memoirs of William Hazlitt*, 1867, and in *The Hazlitts*, 1911, W. Carew Hazlitt incorrectly gives 1844, instead of 1841, as the year in which Margaret Hazlitt died.

32. *Ibid.* The warmth of Margaret's heart is further illustrated by her friendship with Mary Lamb and her close relationship with her sister-in-law Sarah Stoddart Hazlitt.

33. Holt, *A Ministry to the Poor*, pp. 48-49.


## DEDICATION

1. John Johns, the son of Ambrose Bowden Johns of Northill, Plymouth, an artist who painted in the style of Turner, was born in Plymouth on March 17, 1801. He was educated at the Plymouth Grammar School and attended the University of Edinburgh. Appointed minister to the congregation of English Presbyterians at Crediton, Devon, on January 21, 1821, he served there until 1836, when he went to Liverpool. He died on June 23, 1847.

In 1833 the Rev. Mr. Johns married Caroline, daughter of Henry Reynell, of Newton Abbot. Before his marriage he apparently boarded in Crediton with Margaret Hazlitt and her mother, and it may well be that after their marriage he and his wife lived with the Hazlitts.

During November, 1836, the poetically gifted Mr. Johns preached in Liverpool, and accepting the appointment offered to him, he became the first minister to the poor of the Liverpool Domestic Mission Society on December 16, 1836. Margaret's dedication of her recollections to her good friends on December 10, 1836, her sixty-sixth birthday, probably occurred on the departure of Mr. and Mrs. Johns from Crediton for Liverpool.

# I

## THE ORIGIN OF THE HAZLITTS AND THEIR EXPERIENCES IN ENGLAND AND IRELAND

1. William Hazlitt (1811-1893), Margaret's nephew, was the son of William and Sarah Stoddart Hazlitt.

2. Margaret's father, William Hazlitt, was born at Shrone Hill, or Shronell, in Tipperary. He died on July 16, 1820.

3. The Civil Wars of 1642-1646 and 1648-1651.

4. The Rock of Cashel in Tipperary is a mass of limestone which rises abruptly to a height of about 300 feet above the plain, and can be seen for many miles around.

5. For certificates testifying to his attendance at lectures on the Greek language by Professor James Moor at the University of Glasgow, see [W. Carew Hazlitt], *The Hazlitts: An Account of Their Origin and Descent* (Edinburgh, 1911), pp. 6-7.

6. For a genealogical account of the Shronell branch of the Hazlitt family, see Appendix II.

7. According to the Index to Cashel Marriage Licence Bonds at the Public Record Office in Dublin, Elizabeth Hazelitt [Hazlitt] married Robert McClelland in 1761.

8. This cousin was John Haslett (or Haslet), the oldest of the four sons of Joseph Haslett of Straw, County Derry. According to the *Fasti of the Irish Presbyterian Church*, Part VII, arranged and edited by the Rev. David Stewart (n. p., n. d.), p. 146, John Haslett was educated at the University of Glasgow, where he took his master's degree in 1749. He was licensed for Derry in 1750, and was ordained at Ballykelly on April 21, 1752. He resigned in 1757, and emigrated to America, where he became a medical doctor, and fell at the Battle of Princeton.

In America, John Haslet (as he spelled his surname) practiced medicine in Kent County, Delaware, where he was also active in public affairs before the Revolution. In 1776 he was made a Colonel by the Continental Congress and served with distinction as a leader of Delaware troops until his death at Princeton on January 3, 1777.

At least two of John Haslet's brothers also emigrated to America. Joseph Haslett, who settled in Queen Anne's County, Maryland, practiced medicine there, and was active in St. Paul's Church in Centreville, Maryland. William Haslett, who settled in Greensboro, Caroline County, Maryland, was at various times a farmer, merchant, and innkeeper, and served as a Colonel during the Revolution.

9. If Margaret is right, then our records must be at fault. Her

father's cousin, Colonel John Haslet, of Delaware, was killed at the Battle of Princeton, but none of the histories of the American Revolution consulted by the editor mention two Colonel Hazlitts as serving under General Washington.

10. James Hazlitt matriculated at the University of Glasgow in 1762 and received his M. A. in 1767 (W. Innes Addison, *A Roll of the Graduates of the University of Glasgow from 31st December, 1727 to 31st December, 1897* [Glasgow, 1898], p. 258; and *The Matriculation Albums of the University of Glasgow from 1728 to 1858,* transcribed and annotated by W. Innes Addison [Glasgow, 1913], p. 67). On June 15, 1773, when he signed the dedication of his *Eight Sermons upon Different Subjects,* published in Dublin in 1773, he was curate of Rosenallis, Mountmellick, Ireland.

11. According to *Wilson's Dublin Directory, for the Year 1780* (Dublin, 1780), p. 90, the Rev. James Hazlitt, A. M., was curate of St. Paul's Church, not St. Mary's, in 1780, the year in which the Hazlitts visited Dublin. Apparently Margaret's memory failed her slightly in this instance.

12. W. Carew Hazlitt writes of James Hazlitt: ". . . the tradition in the family itself is that he [James] married a Miss Anne Brazier of Limerick County, with whom the story used to go that he eloped, taking her on a pannier behind his saddle, and swimming across the Shannon. One of his sisters, Jane or Jennie, having married James Sayers of Fethard, he was perhaps induced to migrate thither, where he purchased the lease of a property in the town on July 15, 1797, and acquired in 1800 the fee for £4000. He had established a tan-yard in Fethard and flour mills in Maryville, outside the town, and accumulated a considerable fortune in land and money. He was evidently a man of signal commercial ability, and was held in the highest respect. He died on the 17th April, 1808, aged sixty, and the freemen, burgesses, and general inhabitants of Fethard erected to his memory in the churchyard a marble monument commemorative of his excellent qualities in all the relations of life. The estate was assessed for duty at £17,000, which would represent upward of £20,000 of current money, especially in Ireland, and may not have included all his possessions" (*The Hazlitts,* pp. 9-10).

13. The Index to Dublin Marriage Licence Bonds shows that the Rev. James Hazlitt, clerk, married Margaret Moffet, Dublin, spinster, on November 26, 1778, and that three years later, on January 5, 1782, he married Margaret Sherlock, Dublin, spinster. Apparently neither of his first two wives lived very long, for the Index to Cashel Marriage Licence Bonds shows that James Hazlitt married Anne Brasier in 1785.

W. Carew Hazlitt does not mention how many times James Hazlitt married, but he does refer to James's marriage to Anne Brazier and tells us that James left three sons, Kilner, James, and Samuel, and two daughters (*The Hazlitts*, p. 10).

14. William Hazlitt matriculated at the University of Glasgow in 1756, instead of 1758 as Margaret says, and he received his M. A. in 1760 (*The Matriculation Albums of the University of Glasgow*, p. 54; and W. Innes Addison, *A Roll of the Graduates of the University of Glasgow*, p. 258). In *A History of the University of Glasgow, from Its Foundation in 1451 to 1909* (Glasgow, 1909), p. 213, James Coutts writes: "The last [the elder William Hazlitt] having come over from Ireland in expectation of a bursary which he did not obtain, was more than once helped by small grants of money voted to him by the administrators of the College."

15. For some of these certificates, see [W. Carew Hazlitt], *The Hazlitts*, pp. 6-7.

16. Margaret must have meant Sir Conyers Jocelyn, 4th Bart. of Hyde Hall, Hertford, who died unmarried in 1778 (*Burke's Genealogical and Heraldic History of the Peerage, Baronetage, and Knightage*, ed. Peter Townend [103rd ed.; London, 1963], p. 2080).

17. Grace Loftus, who became Mrs. William Hazlitt, was born on July 21, 1746, and died on June 10, 1837. For a genealogical chart of the Loftus family, see Appendix II.

18. W. Carew Hazlitt gives the date as January 19, 1766 (*The Hazlitts*, p. 13). Since there is an obvious discrepancy in Margaret's account here, perhaps the Rev. William Hazlitt settled in Wisbeach in 1763 or remained there for only one year instead of two and then returned to marry Grace Loftus after an absence of a year.

19. Miss Coulson married Thomas Loftus.

20. William Godwin, author of *Political Justice* and *Caleb Williams*, was born in Wisbeach on March 3, 1756. His father, John Godwin, was a dissenting minister at Wisbeach, and his mother was Anna Hull Godwin, the daughter of a shipowner in Wisbeach (Ford K. Brown, *The Life of William Godwin* [London, 1926], pp. 2-3).

21. A Thomas Pentlow is mentioned in Alfred Beesley's *History of Banbury* (London, n. d.), p. 407, as a member of the Northampton Committee in 1645. W. Carew Hazlitt believed that the Pentlows of Oxfordshire might have been connected with Pentlow and Pentlow Hall, a parish and manor in Essex (*The Hazlitts*, p. 14, n. 1).

22. For an account of the "State of Religious Liberty during the Reign of Queen Anne," see David Bogue and James Bennett, *History of Dissenters from the Revolution in 1688, to the Year 1808* (London, 1808-12), I, 228-277.

23. Thomas Loftus, the "old hair-brained uncle," whose taste in pictures was like William Hazlitt's. He is mentioned in Hazlitt's essay "On Personal Character."

24. Mr. Oland probably was William Oland, whose poetic inscription appeared on the foundation stone of the meetinghouse in Marshfield built during the ministry of Mr. Evan Thomas, 1748-1762. Mr. Shapland may have been a son of Angel Shapland, a former minister in Marshfield, who died in 1748 (Jerom Murch, *A History of the Presbyterian and General Baptist Churches in the West of England* [London, 1835], pp. 37-38, 41). Reed, Freeme, and Osburne have not been further identified.

25. Perhaps this was Joseph Smith (1745-1815), iron merchant of Bristol, who was a great supporter of Edmund Burke and a Presbyterian (*The Correspondence of Edmund Burke,* ed. George H. Guttridge, III, *July 1774-June 1778* [Cambridge, Eng., and Chicago, 1958-65], 119, 131; and Stanley Hutton, *Bristol and Its Famous Associations* [Bristol, 1907], pp. 229, 324, and 326).

26. John Hazlitt was born on May 13, 1767; his father baptized him on July 6th of that year.

27. David Evans (1750-1817) was minister at Marshfield from 1770 to 1791 and again from 1796 to 1815. He died on June 14, 1817, and was buried in Marshfield (Murch, *A History of the Presbyterian and General Baptist Churches in the West of England,* p. 41).

28. The Rev. David Evans lived in Bath and went to and from Marshfield every Sunday (Murch, p. 145).

29. Margaret probably visited Maidstone in 1790 ([W. Carew Hazlitt], *The Hazlitts,* p. 393, n. 1).

30. Dr. Joseph Priestley (1733-1804), theologian and man of science; Dr. Richard Price (1723-1791), nonconformist minister and writer on morals, politics, and economics; Dr. Caleb Fleming (1698-1779), dissenting minister; Dr. Andrew Kippis (1725-1795), nonconformist divine and biographer; Theophilus Lindsey (1723-1808), Unitarian divine; and John Palmer (1729?-1790), Unitarian divine, minister at New Broad Street Chapel, London.

31. The Birmingham Riots occurred in July, 1791. On the second anniversary of Bastille Day, July 14, 1791, a mob in Birmingham stormed Dr. Priestley's house and burned it down.

32. John Wiche (1718-1794) was minister of a Baptist congregation in Maidstone from December, 1746, until his death in 1794. Arian in his earlier views, he became a Socinian in 1760.

33. Thomas Viny (1731-1812), a wheel manufacturer of Tenterden, Kent, was a close friend of Benjamin Franklin. See *The Writings of Benjamin Franklin,* ed. Albert H. Smyth (New York, 1905-07), V, 248-

250, and VII, 301-302, for letters from Franklin to Viny. See also VIII, 426, and IX, 143, for Franklin's references to Viny.

34. Samuel Thomas (1739-1786) was educated at Carmarthen Academy and served as minister at Yeovil from 1759 until 1767, when he accepted an invitation to succeed Dr. John Leland, as colleague with Dr. Isaac Weld, in the care of the Presbyterian congregation, Eustace Street, Dublin (Murch, *A History of the Presbyterian and General Baptist Churches in the West of England,* p. 215).

35. Actually at the age of seventy-six.

36. The Rev. Israel Lewis (1717-1770) a Welshman, died at the age of fifty-three, and was buried in All Saints' Churchyard (J. M. Russell, *The History of Maidstone* [Maidstone, 1881], p. 159). The List of Subscribers for the Rev. Mr. Hazlitt's *Discourses for the Use of Families* (London, 1790) includes Mrs. Lewis, Maidstone; Israel Lewis, Esq., Hampstead; Leyson Lewis, Norwich; George Lewis, New York; and James Lewis, Halifax, Nova Scotia.

37. The List of Subscribers for Hazlitt's *Discourses* includes Thomas Milner, M. D., of Maidstone, and James Jacobson, of Maidstone. According to the Clement Taylor Smythe Manuscripts, Volume IV, Folio 314, Maidstone Museum and Art Gallery, Maidstone, England, James Jacobson (died 1807) and Samuel Jacobson (died 1791) were the sons of Ayscough and Susanna Jacobson.

38. James Jacobson, son of James and Ann Bond Jacobson.

39. Margaret Hazlitt was born on December 10, 1770, and baptized on January 30, 1771. William Hazlitt was born on April 10, 1778, and baptized on June 21, 1778.

40. Penmaenmawr was a great obstacle to travelers to Holyhead. In 1774, only six years before the Hazlitts traversed it, Dr. Samuel Johnson traveled the road over Penmaenmawr with some anxiety.

41. St. Stephen's Green and the Basin, or reservoir, were famous landmarks in Dublin. According to *Wilson's Dublin Directory,* the Rev. James Hazlitt lived on Barrack Street in 1780.

42. Kilkenny is sometimes known as the "Marble City" because of the fine limestone quarried in the neighborhood.

43. The Rev. Mr. Clugston, who was ordained in 1745, was the only son of Josias Clugston, of Larne, in the County of Antrim, one of the founders of the Presbytery of Antrim. He was the third minister of the congregation at Bandon, County of Cork (J. C. Ledlie, "Anti-Trinitarianism in the South of Ireland," *Unitarianism Exhibited in Its Actual Condition,* ed. J. R. Beard [London, 1846], p. 187).

44. "The house in which the Reverend Mr. Hazlitt lived was in Gallow-hill Street, near where the mill-stream crosses the roadway, and it adjoined the cross lane leading north to the Castle Road. Every trace

of this house is now completely gone" (George Bennett, *The History of Bandon, and the Principal Towns in the West Riding of County Cork* [enlarged ed.; Cork, 1869], p. 440).

45. The congregation of Bandon was "founded by Puritans, chiefly from Bristol and its neighbourhood, and their first minister, of whom any record can be traced was the Reverend Mr. Harding, who was ordained to the pastoral charge in 1679. The forms of the English Presbyterians are still observed in the Chapel at Bandon, and the Hymn Book long in use is that edited by Kippis and Rees. At what particular time the congregation became avowedly Unitarian, it would be now difficult to trace; the change of opinion, as in other cases, was no doubt gradual, and the natural result of inquiry unfettered by human creeds and confessions of faith" (J. C. Ledlie, p. 187).

It is interesting to note that the Rev. William Hazlitt's cousin, John Haslet, who took his M. A. at the University of Glasgow in 1749, apparently was the minister of this same congregation from 1757 until he departed for America (W. Innes Addison, *The Matriculation Albums of the University of Glasgow*, p. 39).

46. For the letters exposing the mistreatment of American prisoners at Kinsale which the Rev. Mr. Hazlitt published in a Cork newspaper under various pseudonyms, see E. J. Moyne, "The Reverend William Hazlitt: A Friend of Liberty in Ireland During the American Revolution," *William and Mary Quarterly,* Third Series, XXI (April, 1964), 288-297.

47. George Bennett records the following account of the same affair: "This excitement [i.e., the excitement caused by the English officers' throwing sods of turf at Irish women passing by on the street in order to make them drop their earthen jugs or pitchers full of milk], however, lost novelty and interest, and the military sent over to reconcile the Irishry discovered one of higher zest. Bandon did not then enjoy public shedded-in meat-markets; and the meat was exposed for sale in the streets, and on the 'big bridge.' The sport-seeking heroes noticed this facility for fun; and, seeing a poor Papist eyeing the beef on a Friday or a fastday, they compelled him to turn up the knees of his breeches, kneel down on his knees in the street, and eat a bit of raw beef at the point, and from the point of the sword" (*History of Bandon,* pp. 439-440).

48. Cornet John Gamble, Lieutenant John King, and Cornet Joseph Keighley were members of the Fourteenth Regiment of (Light) Dragoons, Ireland, in 1782 (*A List of the General and Field Officers, as They Rank in the Army; of the Officers in the Several Regiments of Horse, Dragoons, and Foot, on the British and Irish Establishments* [Dublin, 1782], p. 50).

49. Apparently Hazlitt was worried about the outcome of this affair and appealed to his friends in England for help. Dr. Richard Price, eminent nonconforming minister, immediately wrote to Lord Shelburne, who interceded in Hazlitt's behalf ([W. Carew Hazlitt], *The Hazlitts,* p. 374).

50. The Fourteenth Regiment of Light Dragoons was stationed in Bandon and Innishannon from 1780 until June 30, 1782, when a change of quarters took place (Henry Blackburne Hamilton, *Historical Record of the 14th (King's) Hussars from A. D. 1715 to A. D. 1900* [London, 1901], p. 33).

51. Perhaps the writer was referring to a great row which happened in 1785. "It seems that one of the 5th Dragoons, passing over the bridge, met a countryman, and taking a fancy to his stick, tried to wrest it from him; and would probably have succeeded, had not the countryman's companion come to his assistance, and knocked the soldier down. A well-known mischief-maker named Joan Cunningham, who happened to be present, immediately ran off, and told some of the troopers, whom she met in Irishtown, what had occurred. These instantly hastened to their comrade's help. The townspeople sided with the countryman, and a regular battle took place. In a short time, all the troops in the barracks turned out, armed with swords, and attacked indiscriminately every civilian; but the country people were the special objects of their vengeance. Of these, forty-two were wounded, several severely injured, and two killed" (Bennett, *History of Bandon,* p. 444). See also *The Journal of the Rev. John Wesley,* ed. Nehemiah Curnock (London, n. d.), VII, 77, for an account of the same incident.

52. Margaret here refers to the "Rebellion of 1798." She was particularly aware of this insurrection because of her close friendship with Catherine Emmet, the niece of Thomas Addis Emmet and Robert Emmet. Seriously involved in the events of 1798, Thomas Addis Emmet had to leave Ireland, going with his family to the United States (Thomas Addis Emmet, *Memoir of Thomas Addis and Robert Emmet with Their Ancestors and Immediate Family* [New York, 1915], I, 192-194).

53. The List of Subscribers for Hazlitt's *Discourses* includes Peter Kingston, Bandon; George Kingston, Bandon; Isaac Kingston, Cork; John Wheeler, Bandon; Jos. Wheeler, Bandon; Jonathan Wheeler, Bandon; John Wheeler, jun., Bandon; Jos. Wheeler, jun., Bandon; and Thomas Wheeler, Bandon. See also Bennett, *History of Bandon,* pp. 407, 529, 545, and 549.

54. The List of Subscribers for Hazlitt's *Discourses* also includes Mrs. Vize, Cork, and John Vize, M. D., Limerick. Dr. Vize took his medical degree at Edinburgh in 1778 (*Nomina Eorum Qui Gradum Medi-*

*cinae, Doctoris in Academia Jacobi Sexti Scotorum Regis, Quae Edin-burgi Est, Adepti Sunt. Ab Anno MDCCV. Ad Annum MDCCCXLV* [Edinburgh, 1846], pp. 14, 270).

55. The List of Subscribers for Hazlitt's *Discourses* includes Thomas Biggs, Esq., Bandon; Ab. Biggs, Bandon; Jacob Biggs, Cork; John Popham, Bandon; William Popham, Bandon; Charles Popham, Bandon; Robert Popham, Bandon; Miss Popham, Bandon; and Bradshaw Popham, Cork. See also Bennett, *History of Bandon,* pp. 447, 448, 500, 531, and 548.

56. Hazlitt's advocacy of American independence brought upon him the reproaches of some of his fellow-townsmen, who, when they saw him in the street, would cry out to beware of the black rebel. "To some of the members of his congregation, too, his advocacy of American notions was not agreeable. One Sunday morning he was more than usually vehement in advocating the right of our Transatlantic cousins to govern themselves, when up started one of his hearers, and hurriedly pulling his plug of tobacco out of his mouth—'I didn't come here to listen to treason!' said he, addressing the preacher; then taking up his hat and cane, he indignantly walked out" (Bennett, *History of Bandon,* p. 440).

57. The Volunteers were organized in 1778. "They were brought into existence ostensibly to protect the Irish from an attack by a foreign foe during England's troubles with America and France, but they soon began to appear as the most eloquent factor in the appeal of Ireland for an independent Parliament" (Arthur Lynch, *Ireland: Vital Hour* [London, 1915], p. 170). See also Bennett, *History of Bandon,* pp. 438-439; and especially William E. H. Lecky, *A History of Ireland in the Eighteenth Century* (new ed.; London, 1909-23), II, 218 ff.

58. Samuel Perrot (died 1796) was educated at Carmarthen Academy, of which his father, the Rev. Thomas Perrot, was president for many years. The Rev. Samuel Perrot officiated successively at Frome, Devizes, and Yeovil before going to Cork, at which place he was minister until his death in 1796 (Murch, *A History of the Presbyterian and General Baptist Churches in the West of England,* p. 215).

59. Perhaps this was the Bradshaw Popham, of Scortnamore, who married Martha Stewart (W. Maziere Brady, *Clerical and Parochial Records of Cork, Cloyne, and Ross* [Dublin, 1864], III, 253).

60. Reuben Harvey (1734-1808) married Elizabeth Wheddon in 1761, and they had twelve children, of whom ten survived their father. Harvey's estate, Pleasant Field, later became the Ursuline Convent, Black Rock, Cork. Harvey was a strong advocate for America during the Revolution, befriending American prisoners in Ireland and writing in their favor in the local newspapers under a fictitious name. It has

been claimed that he made himself serviceable to the American cause by corresponding with General George Washington and transmitting accurate news of what was happening in America to members of the British Parliament friendly to America (Margaret B. Harvey, *A Journal of a Voyage from Philadelphia to Cork in the Year of Our Lord 1809* [Philadelphia, 1915], pp. 40-42, 69-70). Harvey did correspond with Washington, and also with Benjamin Franklin (*The Writings of Benjamin Franklin,* ed. Albert H. Smyth [New York, 1905-07], I, 204).

61. The name of Cove was changed to Queenstown in 1849, after the visit of Queen Victoria, and today the place is known as Cobh.

62. In 1809 Margaret B. Harvey described Passage as a busy town with but one street (Harvey, p. 25).

63. The *Letters from an American Farmer,* by J. Hector St. John de Crèvecoeur, was first published in London in 1782. It may well be that Benjamin Franklin had referred Reuben Harvey to Crèvecoeur's work in replying to Harvey's inquiries about America, for we are told by Smyth (I, 204) that Franklin was accustomed to reply to inquiries for information about America by a reference to the *American Farmer.* If so, Harvey may have recommended the work to the Hazlitts; and we know that Crèvecoeur's *Letters from an American Farmer* was one of the favorite works of William Hazlitt the essayist.

64. Concerning the captain, W. Carew Hazlitt writes: "The story goes that the minister's lady, still in the possession of her original comeliness, was an object of more special attention on the part of the captain of the *Henry* than her husband quite approved. Just a little flirtation to beguile the monotony of the life. She was seven-and-thirty; Mr. Hazlitt was nine years her senior. At the same time, she always entertained the highest respect for him; and in later days, when her sons were married, he was *my* Mr. Hazlitt" (*The Hazlitts,* p. 23).

65. Actually seven weeks.

66. The *Pennsylvania Packet, or the General Advertiser* for June 3, 1783, reported that on Monday, May 26, there arrived in New York "the brig Henry, Captain Jefferson, from Cork, in a passage of seven weeks and four days." The May 28, 1783, issue of the New York *Royal Gazette* carried an advertisement, dated at New York, May 27, 1783, in which Banan (who may have been the person Margaret called Bannon) and Burke, merchants, announced their arrival from Cork, in the *Henry,* of White-Haven, Henry Jefferson, Master. Note that Margaret later refers to the captain as Captain Jeffries. Apparently her memory was not quite accurate in this instance.

67. See Joseph F. W. Des Barres, *The Atlantic Neptune* (London, 1774-81), III, Part 3, no. 12, "A Chart of the Coast of New York, New Jersey, Pensilvania, Maryland . . ." for the "Highlands of Neversink,"

and no. 13, "A Chart of New York Harbour with the Soundings . . ." for the "Highlands of Neversunk." Apparently both terms, *Neversink* and *Neversunk*, were used in the eighteenth century.

68. Every ship that arrived brought news of the impending treaty of peace, but the final treaty between the United States and Great Britain was not signed until September 3, 1783. Perhaps the brig *Henry* brought more news than was known from the first despatches, which reached Philadelphia on March 12, 1783, about the Preliminary Articles signed on November 30, 1782. See *Letters of Members of the Continental Congress,* ed. Edmund C. Burnett (Washington, D. C., 1921-36), VII, vi.

## II

### THE HAZLITTS IN AMERICA

1. Tench Coxe (1755-1824) was a Philadelphia merchant with New York connections. During the Revolution he had British sympathies, but tried to remain neutral. After the war he supported the new Constitution, and was a member of the Constitutional Congress of 1788. A Federalist, he became Assistant Secretary to the Treasury in 1789 and Commissioner of Revenue in 1792. Dismissed by President John Adams in 1797, Coxe became a Democrat. In 1803 President Jefferson made Coxe Purveyor of Public Supplies. Coxe wrote much on economic matters, his best-known work being *A View of the United States of America,* published in 1794.

Interestingly enough, Tench Coxe was closely associated with a branch of the Hazlitt family in America, the Hazletts of New Jersey. In 1783, when the Hazlitts landed in New York, a Hazlett family was living on Coxe property in Mansfield Woodhouse, Sussex County, New Jersey. This property of three hundred acres had passed by a deed dated October 10, 1766, from Rebecca Coxe, aunt of Tench Coxe, to Robert Hazlett of Sussex County, New Jersey. Robert Hazlett left his land to his sons James and Samuel, as shown by his will drawn January 22, 1774, and proved February 26, 1774 (*New Jersey Archives,* First Series, XXXIV, 237). The sons sold the property in 1785.

At this point we may be forgiven for wondering whether the fact that the Rev. William Hazlitt brought to America a letter of introduction to Tench Coxe, whose Aunt Rebecca seventeen years earlier had sold 300 acres of her 1250-acre inheritance, a part of a much larger tract of land known as Indian Purchase, to Robert Hazlett of New Jersey, and which property was next door to Tench Coxe's own portion of the same tract, was merely coincidence. This seems to suggest rather that there was a connection between the Rev. William Hazlitt's family and the New Jersey Hazletts.

2. Honour apparently was the servant brought from Ireland by the Hazlitts.

3. This evidently refers to Bath Springs, for Bath, Pennsylvania, is in Northampton County, not in Bucks County, where Bristol is located. However, the "Bath Springs, known from the earliest settlement of Bucks County, and for years a fashionable watering place, were situated on the edge of the borough of Bristol. The waters are chalybeate and had celebrity as early as 1720, when they were a summer resort" (William W. H. Davis, *History of Bucks County Pennsylvania from the Discovery of the Delaware to the Present Time* [2nd ed.; New York, 1905], I, 99).

4. The published proceedings of the Jersey Assembly meeting in Burlington at this time do not contain any references to the Rev. Mr. Hazlitt's preaching to the Assembly.

5. William Franklin (1729-1813), illegitimate son of Benjamin Franklin, was the last of the Royal Governors, from 1763 until 1774, when he moved from Burlington to Perth Amboy. The Governor's mansion on the Green Bank in Burlington was "an imposing three storied brick building with a colonial portico extending across the front" (George DeCou, *Burlington: A Provincial Capital* [Philadelphia, 1945], pp. 106, 142).

6. Clement Biddle's *Philadelphia Directory* (Philadelphia, 1791), p. iii, describes Philadelphia as follows: "The ground plot of the city is an oblong square, about one mile North and South, and two miles East and West, lying in the narrowest part of the isthmus between the Delaware and Schuylkill rivers, about five miles in a right line above their confluence."

7. Biddle's *Philadelphia Directory* for 1791, p. ix, lists the principal houses for public worship as follows: "Of the church of Rome three, of the Protestant Episcopal church three, of the people called Quakers five, of the Presbyterians of different sects six, of the Baptists one, of the German Lutherans two, of the German Calvinists one, of the Moravians one, of the Methodists two, of the Universalists one, and of the Hebrews one."

8. The State Society of the Cincinnati of Pennsylvania met at the City Tavern in Philadelphia on October 4, 1783, and at other times during the fall of 1783 and the spring of 1784. The first general meeting of the General Society of the Cincinnati was held in Philadelphia from May 4 to May 18, 1784. The Rev. William Hazlitt may have dined with the Society of the Cincinnati on the banks of the Schuylkill on one of these occasions (*Institution of the Society of the Cincinnati: Organiza-*

*tion of the State Society of Pennsylvania* [Philadelphia, 1863], p. 19; and Francis A. Foster, *The Institution of the Society of the Cincinnati Together with Standing Resolutions, Ordinances, Rules, and Precedents of the General Society of the Cincinnati, 1783-1920* [Boston, 1923], p. 22).

9. The first time the Rev. Mr. Hazlitt and his son John could have seen General Washington in Philadelphia was during his visit there from December 8 to December 15, 1783 (William S. Baker, *Itinerary of General Washington from June 15, 1775, to December 23, 1783* [Philadelphia, 1892], pp. 316-317). General Washington also visited Philadelphia from May 1 to May 18, 1784, to attend the first general meeting of the Society of the Cincinnati (William S. Baker, *Washington after the Revolution, MDCCLXXXIV-MDCCXCIX* [Philadelphia, 1898], pp. 7-8). Since the Rev. Mr. Hazlitt left Philadelphia for Boston, where he arrived on May 15, 1784, he must have seen General Washington either in December, 1783, or May, 1784.

Washington was accustomed to worshipping at St. Peter's Church at Third and Pine Streets or at Christ Church when he was in Philadelphia (C. P. B. Jefferys, *George Washington, St. Peter's and the Episcopal Church* [Philadelphia, n. d.]).

10. About five miles north of the New London Presbyterian Church, where the Rev. Mr. Hazlitt preached, is the Fagg's Manor Presbyterian Church. Living near the Fagg's Manor Church and belonging to it were many members of the Hazlitt family. In speaking of her father's meeting in New London "some of his own name and kindred," Margaret was referring to the Fagg's Manor branch of the Hazlitt family in America. The most prominent member of this family was William Haslett, Jr., a large landowner, a justice of the peace, and an elder in the Fagg's Manor Presbyterian Church.

11. On November 13, 1783, Polly Hazlet and Robert McGormot (McGarmot) were married in the First Presbyterian Church in Philadelphia ("Record of Pennsylvania Marriages, Prior to 1810," in *Pennsylvania Archives,* Second Series, IX [1890], 89, 95).

12. For an account of the Rev. Mr. Hazlitt's activities in Carlisle, see E. J. Moyne, "The Reverend William Hazlitt and Dickinson College," *Pennsylvania Magazine of History and Biography,* LXXXV (July, 1961), 289-302.

13. Benjamin Rush (1745-1813)), physician and patriot, studied at the College of New Jersey and at the University of Edinburgh. In 1769 he began practice in Philadelphia and was appointed professor of chemistry at the College of Philadelphia. He became professor of the institutes of medicine and clinical practice at the University of Pennsylvania in 1792, and in 1796 he became professor of theory and practice

as well. A signer of the Declaration of Independence, Rush served as surgeon-general with the Continental Army, 1777-1778, and as Treasurer of the United States Mint, 1799-1813.

14. John Carson (1752-1794) graduated from the University of Pennsylvania in 1771, and received his medical degree from the University of Edinburgh in 1776. He was a physician at the Philadelphia Dispensary, 1786-1787, and was an incorporator and original Fellow of the College of Physicians in Philadelphia in 1787. He was a trustee of the University of Pennsylvania, 1791-1794, and was appointed professor of chemistry at the University in 1794. He became a member of the American Philosophical Society in 1785.

15. Francis Dana (1743-1811) graduated from Harvard in 1762, and was admitted to the bar in 1767. He was a delegate to the first provincial congress of Massachusetts in 1774, a member of the Massachusetts Executive Council, 1776-1780, and a delegate to the Continental Congress, 1776-1778. In 1779 he was secretary of legation in Paris under John Adams, and United States representative to Russia from 1781 to 1783. During the spring of 1784 he was again appointed delegate to the Continental Congress meeting in Philadelphia, and the Rev. Mr. Hazlitt must have become acquainted with him at this time. In 1785 Dana was appointed a justice of the Supreme Court of Massachusetts, and in 1791 he became Chief Justice. His brother, the Rev. Edmund Dana, was settled in Shropshire (Richard H. Dana, Jr., "Francis Dana," *PMHB,* I [1877], 86-95).

16. John Ewing (1732-1802), a graduate of the College of New Jersey in 1754, was pastor of the First Presbyterian Church in Philadelphia from 1759 until 1802. He received an honorary doctorate from Edinburgh in 1773. He became provost and professor of natural philosophy in the University of the State of Pennsylvania in 1779, and continued in these positions after the reorganization of the institution as the University of Pennsylvania in 1791. He became a member of the American Philosophical Society in 1768.

17. James Davidson (1732-1809), Professor of Greek and Latin Languages at the University of Pennsylvania, 1768-1779 and 1782-1802, and Rector of the Academy, 1780-1791, was in charge of the academy in Newark, Delaware, before going to Pennsylvania. He became a member of the American Philosophical Society in 1768. His wife was Margaret Linn Davidson. According to Edward Potts Cheyney, in his *History of the University of Pennsylvania, 1740-1940* (Philadelphia, 1940), p. 134, James Davidson was a brother of Robert Davidson (1750-1812), Professor of Greek and Latin Languages at the University of Pennsylvania, 1780-1782, and Professor of History, 1782-1784.

A Presbyterian clergyman, Robert Davidson taught at the University of Pennsylvania and acted as assistant to Dr. Ewing at the First Presbyterian Church in Philadelphia until 1784, when he was called to Carlisle, Pennsylvania, as Professor of History, Geography, Chronology, Rhetoric, and Belles-Lettres at Dickinson College and pastor of the Presbyterian Church. In 1796 he was chosen moderator of the General Assembly of the Presbyterian Church. He was president of Dickinson College from 1804 to 1809. In 1784 appeared his *Geography Epitomized; or, a Tour Round the World: Being a Short but Comprehensive Description of the Terraqueous Globe Attempted in Verse for the Sake of the Memory: And Principally Designed for the Use of Schools.*

18. Moses Daniel Gomez was born in New York on May 29, 1728, and died in New York on April 12, 1789. During the Revolution he and his family, as well as his father, Daniel Gomez, refused to remain under Tory rule in New York, and moved to Philadelphia. The war, and particularly the occupation of New York by the British, greatly diminished the Gomez fortune accumulated in earlier years by Daniel Gomez.

Moses D. Gomez married his first cousin Esther, daughter of Isaac and Deborah De Leon Gomez, on May 14, 1755, and had several children; all died young except Daniel and Isaac Gomez, Jr. Since Moses' mother died in 1729, it must have been his mother-in-law, Deborah De Leon Gomez, who was living with the Gomez family in Philadelphia. Moses' only brother died young; the two boys and two girls living in the Gomez family were the orphaned children of his brother-in-law Mattathis (Matthias) and Rachel Gomez, who died in 1781 and 1776, respectively. These children were Esther, Deborah, Isaac, and Benjamin. Deborah Gomez died single in Philadelphia on October 5, 1783 ("Genealogy of the Gomez Family in America," *Publications of the American Jewish Historical Society,* XVII [1909], 198-199; and "Items Relating to the Gomez Family, New York," *PAJHS,* XXVII [1920], 284).

19. Captain Atkinson was probably Captain George Atkinson, who paid various taxes in Dock Ward, South Part, in the early 1780's ("Provincial Papers," *Pennsylvania Archives,* Third Series, XV [1897], 212, 218, 758, 759; XVI [1898], 334, 335, 752, and 753).

According to the "Record of Pennsylvania Marriages, Prior to 1810," *Pennsylvania Archives,* Second Series, VIII [1890], 18, 180, George Atkinson married Catharine McGinnis in Christ Church, Philadelphia, on August 9, 1756. The same source, pages 306 and 322, lists the marriage of Margaret Atkinson and Jonathan Brewer in the Swedes' Church (Gloria Dei) on May 26, 1778.

20. Since the name of Captain Lieutenant Jonathan Brewer appeared on the "Muster Roll of Detachment of [Mutilated] Stationed at Fort Island" and he sought leave to resign his commission in 1779, it is

reasonable to assume that he had been so seriously wounded, or his health so badly undermined, that by 1783 Mrs. Brewer was a widow ("Continental Line. Fourth Regiment of Artillery, February 6, 1777—November 3, 1783," *Pennsylvania Archives,* Fifth Series, III [1906], 961, 974, 986, 988, and 1006; see also the *Journals of the Continental Congress, 1774-1789,* ed. Worthington C. Ford [Washington, D. C., 1904-37], XII, 949, 982, 1072-73; and XIII, 159).

21. The "Mitchels" could have been either the Thomas Mitchells or Joshua Mitchells. Thomas Mitchell, carpenter, and Joshua Mitchell, cryer, both paid taxes in Dock Ward, South Part, in 1781, 1782, and 1783 (*Pennsylvania Archives,* Third Series, XV [1897], 759; XVI [1898], 333-334, 751-752). It is very likely, however, that Margaret was referring to the family of Joshua Mitchell. According to Francis White's *Philadelphia Directory* (Philadelphia, 1785), p. 51, Joshua Mitchell, hatter, lived on Union Street, between Third and Fourth Streets. For more about the Mitchells, see "Notes and Queries," *PMHB,* XXXVII (July, 1913), 384.

22. Samuel Vaughan (1720-1802), of London, married Sarah Hallowell (1727-1809), daughter of Benjamin Hallowell of Boston, and they had eleven children, three of whom died in infancy. The two sons in Philadelphia were John Vaughan (1756-1842) and Samuel Vaughan (1762-1802). The daughters in the family were Ann Vaughan (1757-1847), who married John Darby; Sarah Vaughan (1761-1818); and Rebecca Vaughan (1766-1851), who married John Merrick. The other sons were Benjamin Vaughan, M. D., M. P. (1751-1836); William Vaughan (1752-1850); and Charles Vaughan (1759-1839) (*Early Recollections of Robert Hallowell Gardiner, 1782-1864* [Hallowell, Me., 1936], p. 118).

23. Yellow fever ravaged Philadelphia in 1793. However, Germantown remained strangely uninfected (J. H. Powell, *Bring Out Your Dead: The Great Plague of Yellow Fever in Philadelphia in 1793* [Philadelphia, 1949], p. 230).

24. Stephen Kingston carried on a shipping business, at 39 Pine Street, in partnership with James Campbell. This partnership was dissolved in 1789 (W. A. Newman Dorland, "The Second Troops Philadelphia City Cavalry," *PMHB,* XLV [October, 1921], 386). The List of Subscribers for Hazlitt's *Discourses for the Use of Families* includes Peter Kingston and George Kingston, of Bandon.

25. The List of Subscribers for Hazlitt's *Discourses* includes both Joseph Wheeler and Jonathan Wheeler, of Bandon.

26. The place was Centreville, Maryland, and contrary to Margaret's version of her father's failure to settle there, the Rev. Mr. Hazlitt was denied admission into St. Paul's parish in Centreville. According to

vestry records for October 4, 1783, "on application of the Rev. Mr. William Hazlitt to be admitted into St. Paul's parish as a minister and preacher of the gospel, the vestry was unanimously of opinion, he being a dissenter, that they have no authority for admitting him" (Frederic Emory, *Queen Anne's County, Maryland: Its Early History and Development* [Baltimore, 1950], p. 176; see also E. J. Moyne, "The Reverend William Hazlitt in Maryland," *Maryland Historical Magazine,* LI, [March, 1956], 59-61).

The Rev. Mr. Hazlitt may have been invited to preach in Centreville because his cousin Dr. Joseph Haslett, who died in 1770, had been active in St. Paul's Church and the doctor's son, Joseph, was still affiliated with St. Paul's in 1783.

27. Mr. Earl probably was Richard Tilghman Earle, the elder vestryman of St. Paul's Parish in 1783 ("Vestry Proceedings, 1762-1819, of St. Paul's Episcopal Church, Queen Anne's County," II, 139, at the Maryland Historical Society). James Earle also was active in the affairs of St. Paul's Parish at this time.

28. By "Columbia root" Margaret probably meant Columbo (Calumba) root, used as a stimulant.

29. Jacob Hiltzheimer, of Philadelphia, recorded an earthquake in his journal on November 29, 1783: "About twenty minutes after ten o'clock this evening I felt the shock of an earthquake as I was walking through my room upstairs, which lasted half a minute" (*Extracts from the Diary of Jacob Hiltzheimer, of Philadelphia, 1765-1798,* ed. Jacob Cox Parsons [Philadelphia, 1893], p. 59). Margaret's memory may not have been entirely accurate as to the exact date of the earthquake.

30. These lectures were given at the Common Hall of the University of the State of Pennsylvania. For the Rev. Mr. Hazlitt's comments on the lectures, see Appendix I.

31. Dr. Priestley did not come to America until 1794, eight years after the Rev. Mr. Hazlitt had returned to England.

32. An inadvertence for South Carolina. After the Revolution the Presbyterians in South Carolina were in need of ministers. "This church [the Presbyterian] would have none except highly educated men for its ministers. Not enough of them were to be found and some Presbyterians, lacking pastors, turned to other churches. The colleges eagerly sought Presbyterian ministers as professors, because they were educated and able to teach the youth of the land many branches of learning" (William Gilmore Simms, *The History of South Carolina,* ed. Mary C. Simms Oliphant [Columbia, S. C., 1927], p. 152).

33. Pittsburgh is almost 300 miles, rather than 200 miles, from Philadelphia.

The. Rev. William Wilson McKinney, an authority on the early development of the Presbyterian Church in Pittsburgh, wrote in 1919: "Although several men had made missionary tours through the Pittsburgh district, and although there were Presbyterian chaplains at Fort Pitt, yet the first call for supplies from Pittsburgh was on April 13, 1784, three years after the formation of the Redstone Presbytery. Other requests were made at infrequent intervals until the arrival of Reverend Samuel Barr in October of 1785" ("Eighteenth Century Presbyterianism in Western Pennsylvania," *Journal of the Presbyterian Historical Society,* X [September, 1919], 101).

34. John Wilkins, Sr., who arrived in Pittsburgh at the end of 1783, said that "all sorts of wickedness were carried on to excess, and there was no appearance of morality or regular order . . . . it seemed to me that the Presbyterian ministers were afraid to come to the place lest they should be mocked or mistreated." The streets were muddy and filthy; the houses were ramshackle and unpainted log structures with makeshift and ugly furnishings (Leland D. Baldwin, *Pittsburgh: The Story of a City* [Pittsburgh, 1937], p. 104).

35. It is interesting to speculate whether or not these two farmers were sent by Hugh Henry Brackenridge, author of *Modern Chivalry,* who had settled in Pittsburgh in 1781 and was instrumental in the founding of the Presbyterian congregation in Pittsburgh.

36. After the death of Dr. Samuel Cooper on December 12, 1783, the pulpit of Brattle Street Church was supplied by visiting ministers until October, 1784, when the Rev. Peter Thacher, of Malden, was chosen as the regular pastor (Samuel Kirkland Lothrop, *A History of the Church in Brattle Street, Boston* [Boston, 1851], p. 125). In August, 1784, the Rev. Jeremy Belknap, of Dover, New Hampshire, wrote to his friend Ebenezer Hazard, of Philadelphia, that Hazlitt had preached "in one of the politest *vacant* assemblies [Brattle Street Church], and been much admired; but his company is as perfect a contrast to their *late* minister's as can be" (Belknap to Hazard, August 16, 1784, in "The Belknap Papers," *Collections* of the Massachusetts Historical Society, Fifth Series, III [1877], 169).

37. In answer to Jeremy Belknap's inquiry about what had become of Hazlitt, the Rev. John Eliot wrote to his friend on August 26, 1784: "Poor fellow, I am afraid he is in trouble. His wife and family are now come, and put themselves upon him, understanding, as I learn, that he was to be settled at Dr. Cooper's. He was buoyed up with such an idea, and flattered himself that there were no difficulties at all in the way. It was only to hear him, and they would be too much captivated to let him go. In short, he is the most conceited and most imprudent man I ever met with, and yet hath many good qualities both of head and

heart" (Eliot to Belknap, August 26, 1784, in "The Belknap Papers," *Collections* of the MHS, Sixth Series, IV [1891], 274).

38. Daniel Gomez (1759-1784), son of Moses D. Gomez, served in the Revolution as a private in Captain John Corrush's Company in the Fourth Battalion of the Philadelphia Militia. He died on August 27, 1784 (David and Tamar de Sola Pool, *An Old Faith in the New World: Portrait of Shearith Israel, 1654-1954* [New York, 1955], p. 505; see also "Items Relating to the Gomez Family, New York," *PAJHS*, XXVII [1920], 284).

39. For a more detailed account of the havoc and desolation wrought in Newport by the British, see Samuel Greene Arnold, *History of the State of Rhode Island and Providence Plantations* (New York, 1859-60), II, 446-448.

40. Perhaps the tautog, *Tautoga onitis,* or the black sea bass of the northeastern United States, *Centropristes striatus.*

41. Providence is located at the mouth of the Providence River and the head of Narragansett Bay, about 28 miles from the ocean. Here and in the following sentence Margaret means the Narragansett Bay, not the river.

42. The Governor of Rhode Island from May, 1778, to May, 1786, was William Greene, Jr., and the Deputy-Governor from May, 1781, to May, 1786, was Jabez Bowen. In 1784 the State House was in Newport (Samuel Greene Arnold, *History of the State of Rhode Island and Providence Plantations,* II, 510, 566).

43. William Gordon (1728-1807), minister of the Third, or Jamaica Plain, Parish Church in Roxbury, left for England on March 17, 1786, to publish his history of the American Revolution on more favorable terms than were possible in this country. In 1788 his *History of the Rise, Progress, and Establishment of the Independence of the United States of America* was published in four volumes. An American edition in three volumes appeared in New York in 1789.

Dr. Gordon spent the last years of his life in England as minister of a congregation at St. Neots in Huntingdonshire from 1789 to 1802, when he went to Ipswich, where he lived in great poverty until his death in 1807.

44. The first *Boston Directory* in 1789 lists Catherine Gray as keeping a boarding house in State-Street (*Boston Directory* [Boston, 1789], p. 23).

45. Ebenezer Withington and Molly Preston, both of Dorchester, were married on December 9, 1755. Mather Withington, the son of Ebenezer and Molly Withington, was born on July 28, 1757 (*A Report of the Record Commissioners of the City of Boston, Containing Dor-*

*chester Births, Marriages, and Deaths to the End of 1825* [Boston, 1891],
pp. 155, 226).

Cotton Mather (1663-1728) was, of course, the well-known clergyman
and author.

46. Richard Cranch (1726-1811) was married to Mary Smith (1741-
1811), daughter of the Rev. William Smith and his wife, Elizabeth
Quincy Smith, daughter of Colonel John Quincy (1689-1767). He served
as Justice of the Court of Common Pleas for Suffolk County, Massachusetts, and also as a state senator.

47. The house in Weymouth in which the Hazlitt family lived
from November, 1784, to July, 1786, was the home of the Rev. William
and Elizabeth Quincy Smith, whose daughter Mary married Judge
Richard Cranch; Abigail married President John Adams; and Elizabeth
married the Rev. John Shaw, and after his death, the Rev. Stephen
Peabody. The Rev. William Smith died in 1783, leaving the house to
his oldest child, Mrs. Mary Cranch.

In a letter to her sister Abigail, who was in France, Mary Cranch
wrote on November 6, 1784: "I have forgot whether there was a Mr
Hazlett an Irishman preaching at Doctor Coopers meeting before you
went away—He is a very sensible fine preacher but alass is not orthodox,
& takes no pains to secrete it—He wishes to be settled in this State but
unless he will be more prudent (I call it) he says tis cun[n]ing he never
will get a Parish. He has a Family, a wife a very pretty sensible well
Bred woman & three very likely children. He was settled in england
was a high Whig & was as explicit in Politicks there, as he is here in
his sentiments of religion. His Life became so uncomfortable that he
removed to Ireland of which Island he is a native as I said before.
There he secreted prisoners & refused preaching upon a Fast day, etc.
His life was then threatened by the the [*sic*] soldiers but being an acquaintance of Lord Shelburne who arri[ved] there about that time he
was protected & proc[ured] a court martial for the trial of the
sold[i]ers. I should not be so particular about this Family if they did
not live in one part of our House at Weymouth. He has been preaching at Hingham & Situate. The people like him much. The people at
Weymouth I hear wish to hear him but however they might like him
as a preacher, I fear his freedom of speech would prevent there ever
settling him let his Heart & his Head be ever so good—" (*Microfilms
of the Adams Papers*, Part IV, "Letters Received and Other Loose
Papers," Reel 363).

48. John Adams did not become the first minister of the United
States to Great Britain until 1785.

49. Margaret Hazlitt claims a relationship to the Adams family
through the Quincys several times in her journal, but the basis for her

claim is not clear. W. Carew Hazlitt has suggested an answer to this problem, but it does not have much merit. In *Four Generations of a Literary Family* (London and New York, 1897), I, 6-7, he wrote: "When our family visited Boston in or about 1785, there was a lady, whom I take to have been the widow of Colonel John Hazlitt of Coleraine [Colonel John Haslet of the Delaware Continentals], living there. She was still in the possession of her youthful beauty, and the miniature-painter, though much her junior, was smitten by her personal attractions. She subsequently visited England, and John Hazlitt painted her portrait. Mrs. Harriet Hazlitt must have married very early in life, for the miniature, taken somewhere about the end of the century, represents her as a woman not even yet in her prime. It was through the Coleraine branch and this lady that we acquired consanguinity with the two Presidential families of Quincy and Adams." The difficulty with this conjecture is that the wife of Colonel John Haslet died soon after hearing the news of her husband's death in the Battle of Princeton in 1777. In *The Hazlitts,* pp. 4-5, W. Carew Hazlitt says that the Hazlitt family met the widow of Colonel John Hazlitt in Philadelphia in 1785, and that John Hazlitt's miniature of her represents her as a woman hardly beyond her prime. Here he was merely compounding the confusion already existing in his mind about the identity of Mrs. Harriet Hazlitt. The miniature on which he based his conjectures was in his possession in 1911.

50. Lucy Quincy (1729-1785), daughter of Colonel John Quincy, of Mount Wollaston, married Dr. Cotton Tufts in 1755.

51. Dorothy Quincy (1747-1830), daughter of Justice Edmund Quincy, married John Hancock in 1775.

52. Since John Singleton Copley (1738-1815) experimented with classic, Scriptural, and historical subjects in his early paintings, it is possible that the picture in oil of the meeting of Esau and Jacob was one of his early attempts.

53. Benjamin West (1728-1820), historical painter.

54. The Rev. William Smith (1707-1783).

55. In 1776 the Americans fortified Dorchester Heights, which had complete command of Boston and of Boston Harbor. "The American works were now very strong, and in order to render the passage up the hill, should it be attempted, still more difficult, a large number of barrels filled with stones and sand were placed on the brow of the hill. These were to be rolled down the embankment as the columns were advancing. It is said that one of these barrels was sent down the hill in order to see how far it would roll, and in its course it cut off a large elm tree at the root, and made an indenture a foot deep in another tree which was in its path" (Thomas C. Simonds, *History of*

*South Boston; Formerly Dorchester Neck* [Boston, 1857], pp. 51-52). Apparently this incipient battle of the kegs, not the one immortalized by Francis Hopkinson, was still fresh in the minds of people in Massachusetts in 1784.

56. The Battle of Bunker Hill was fought on June 17, 1775, with a great British loss in killed and wounded.

57. Captain Abiah Whitman, the son of Abiah and Sarah Whitman, was born in Weymouth on May 4, 1741, and died on May 7, 1807. On May 15, 1766, he married Abigail Giles (1742-1805) (*Vital Records of Weymouth, Massachusetts to the Year 1850* [Boston, 1910], I, 347; II, 217, 370, 372). In *Massachusetts Soldiers and Sailors of the Revolutionary War* (Boston, 1896-1908), XVII, 185, Captain Whitman is listed as two separate men, Lieutenant Abiah Whitman and Captain Abijah Whitman.

58. For further accounts of the actions of the British regulars near Weymouth, see *Adams Family Correspondence,* ed. L. H. Butterfield *et al.* (Cambridge, Mass., 1963), I, 200 ff.

59. General Solomon Lovell was born at Abington on June 1, 1732, and died at Weymouth on September 9, 1801. He lived on Neck Street near its junction with Green Street, North Weymouth, in the Captain Enoch Lovell house (*History of Weymouth, Massachusetts* [Boston, 1923], III, 399-400; see also *Massachusetts Soldiers and Sailors of the Revolutionary War,* IX, 1010; and Gilbert Nash, *The Original Journal of General Solomon Lovell, Kept During the Penobscot Expedition, 1779: With a Sketch of His Life* [Boston, 1881]).

60. Beale Cushing was probably Bela Cushing, who was born in Weymouth on January 9, 1772, and died there on October 2, 1840. Apparently he was the natural son of Bela Cushing, which would explain why he was living with Captain and Mrs. Whitman, who never had children of their own (*History of Weymouth,* III, 183, 185; IV, 755).

61. By "the scarlet bird," Margaret probably meant the scarlet tanager, and by "the fire-hang-bird," the oriole.

62. Margaret's reference to monkeys in America here (and once again later in her journal) is difficult to explain. Perhaps she was confusing monkeys with opossums or some other animal.

63. The Bob Lincoln is the bobolink, a shortened form of Bob o' Lincoln; the red linnet, the Virginia nightingale, is the cardinal.

64. Probably the junco.

65. At a meeting of the Selectmen of Boston on January 5, 1785, "Application made for Mr. Haislet [Hazlitt] holding Lectures in Faneuil Hall twice a Week—The Selectmen having considered said Application, declined giving thier [*sic*] consent thereon; they having declined applications of a similar nature" (*A Report of the Record*

*Commissioners of the City of Boston, Containing the Selectmen's Minutes from 1776 through 1786* [Boston, 1894], pp. 257-258).

The *American Herald,* on January 10, 1785, carried the following notice: "In compliance with the wishes of some respectable friends, we learn that the Reverend Mr. Hazlitt will deliver a course of Lectures, at the Church in Middle-street, on the evidences of the truth of the Christian religion.

"The first Lecture will commence to-morrow precisely at half an hour after three in the afternoon. The second Lecture will commence Thursday next at the same hour. The remaining Lectures, will be continued, every Tuesday and Wednesday afternoon until the whole be completed.

"Excepting the pains that will be taken to level the evidences to every capacity, little new can be expected by those who have already particularly applied themselves to this subject. Others, it is presumed, may be benefitted [*sic*], by being furnished with arguments, to support the most important question that can be canvassed by the human mind. Christianity, genuine, glorious Christianity, rather courts, than avoids, the attacks of the unbeliever. It rests upon a basis, which cannot be shaken. The more it is tried, the more firmly will it establish itself in our hearts, and the more fully will it approve itself to every rational being."

The *Massachusetts Centinel,* on January 19, 1785, said: "The Reverend Mr. Hazlitt is now delivering a course of Lectures on the 'Evidences of the truth of the Christian religion.' This learned and ingenious gentleman, by a happy arrangement, and insinuating stile, blends instruction with amusement. Those of a Deistical turn of mind would, we doubt not, reap much benefit from an attendance on these lectures, as the perspicuity of his arguments must strike conviction into the most obdurate hearts." On February 15, 1785, the same paper noted that "Mr. Hazlitt will continue his Lectures on the Evidences of the Truth of the Christian Religion, on Monday Evening next, exactly at six o'clock. His last lecture was on miracles." See also the *Salem Gazette* for January 11, 1785; and the Boston *Exchange Advertiser* for January 13, 1785.

66. On February 24, 1785, the Rev. John Eliot wrote to the Rev. Jeremy Belknap: "We have not set up Paddy [Hazlitt] for a lecturer, but he hath set himself up. He plagued Brother Lathrop till he obtained consent for his meetinghouse [the Second Church in Boston]. His lectures are poorly attended. No wonder; he spins out the subject, proposes to have 30 lectures. They are good solid discourses, but not adequate to the expectations of them who wish to serve him. I wish

he was in Ireland" (Eliot to Belknap, February 24, 1785, "The Belknap Papers," *Collections* of the MHS, Sixth Series, IV [1891], 285).

67. The Blake family held real estate in almost every section of Milton. Among the most prominent members of the family were Ziba, Amariah, and Edward Blake (*The History of Milton, Mass., 1640 to 1887*, ed. A. K. Teele [n. p., n. d.], p. 559). It is now impossible to determine which family of Blakes the Rev. Mr. Hazlitt and John visited.

68. Dr. Cotton Tufts recorded in his diary for 1784 that "Mr. Hazlot," i.e., Mr. Hazlitt, preached in Weymouth on December 5 and 12 ("Diaries of Rev. William Smith and Dr. Cotton Tufts, 1738-1784," *Proceedings* of the MHS, Third Series, II [1909], 478).

69. Ebenezer Gay, born in Dedham, August 15, 1696, took his A. B. at Harvard in 1714. He was ordained in Hingham in 1718, and was settled there from 1717 until his death on March 18, 1787. He gave the Election Sermon in 1745; Convention Sermon in 1746; and the Dudleian Lecture in 1759. In 1785 he received an honorary S. T. D. from Harvard. A close friend of Charles Chauncy, Gay participated in the ordinations of Jonathan Mayhew and his successor, Simeon Howard, at the West Church in Boston.

70. This anecdote about the Rev. Mr. Gay appeared in an article entitled "Particulars of Dr. Chauncey," *Monthly Repository*, IX (April, 1814), 232-234. Signed W. H., this article must have been by the Rev. William Hazlitt.

71. Joshua Barker, son of Captain Francis and Hannah (Thaxter) Barker, was born in Hingham on March 24, 1753, and graduated from Harvard in 1772. He studied medicine with Dr. Danforth, of Boston, and then settled as a physician in Hingham. He married Susanna, daughter of Benjamin Thaxter, in 1779. They had two children, a son who died in infancy, and Susan, who married the Rev. Samuel Willard. Dr. Barker died in Hingham on April 2, 1800 (*History of the Town of Hingham, Massachusetts* [n. p., 1893], I, 308).

72. Major-General Benjamin Lincoln was born in Hingham on January 24, 1733. He served as Secretary of War, one of the commissioners to make a treaty with the Penobscot Indians, and as commander of the militia raised to suppress Shays' Rebellion in 1786-1787. He was a member of the American Academy of Arts and Sciences, and a member of the Massachusetts Historical Society. He was president of the Society of the Cincinnati in Massachusetts from its organization until his death. In 1780 he received an honorary M. A. from Harvard. He died on May 9, 1810 (*History of the Town of Hingham*, I, 303-306; and Bradford Adams Whittemore, *Memorials of the Massachusetts Society of the Cincinnati* [Boston, 1964], pp. 364-366).

73. Mrs. Derby was born Sarah Langlee (or Langley) on April 18, 1714. According to the *History of the Town of Hingham,* I, 115, she was "possessed of great beauty, and without the advantages of early education. She was doubtless illiterate, but her lack of education has been exaggerated. It has been said that she could not write her own name. This is not true, for she wrote many letters and signed her own name to them . . . . It seems sufficiently evident, however, that it was her beauty which attracted the attention of Dr. Ezekiel Hersey,—a graduate of Harvard College in 1728, and an eminent physician in his native town of Hingham, where he practised his profession for many years,—for she was married to him July 30, 1738. Dr. Hersey died December 9, 1770, and his wife survived him. We can well believe that she was comely, for, although she had reached the age of fifty-seven, another admirer presented himself, and she was married to Richard Derby, of Salem, October 16, 1771. Mr. Derby died November 9, 1783, his wife surviving him. Mrs. Derby died in Hingham June 17, 1790, aged seventy-six, and was buried in Dr. Gay's tomb in the cemetery back of the meeting-house of the First Parish." Margaret was twenty years off in her statement that Mrs. Derby was ninety years old.

74. Daniel Shute was born in Malden on July 19, 1722, and graduated from Harvard in 1743. He was ordained in South Hingham on December 10, 1746, and was settled in Hingham (Third Parish) from 1746 to 1802. He died in Hingham on August 30, 1802 (*History of the Town of Hingham,* I, 43-44).

Daniel Shute, the only son of the Rev. Daniel and Mary Cushing Shute, was born in Hingham on January 30, 1756, and graduated from Harvard in 1775. During the Revolution he served as surgeon in the Continental Army. In 1783 he located as a physician in Weymouth, but the following year established himself in Hingham. He died August 19, 1829 (*History of the Town of Hingham,* I, 320).

75. Charles Chauncy was born in Boston on January 1, 1704/5, and graduated from Harvard in 1721. He was ordained in Boston on October 25, 1727, and was settled in Boston (First Church) from 1727 to 1787. In 1784 he published *The Mystery Hid from Ages, or The Salvation of All Men* and *The Benevolence of the Deity Fairly and Impartially Considered.* He died in Boston on February 10, 1787.

76. Born in Norwich, Connecticut, on May 6, 1739, John Lathrop graduated from the College of New Jersey in 1763. He was ordained in Boston on May 18, 1768, and was settled in Boston (Second Church) from 1768 until his death on January 4, 1816. He preached at the ordination of William Bentley.

77. James Freeman was born in Charlestown, Massachusetts, on April 22, 1759, and graduated from Harvard in 1777. Ordained in

Boston on November 18, 1787, he was settled in Boston (King's Chapel) from 1782 to 1835. He died in Newton on November 14, 1835.

78. John Clarke was born in Portsmouth, New Hampshire, on April 13, 1755, and graduated from Harvard in 1774. He was ordained over the First Church in Boston on July 8, 1778, as colleague of the Rev. Dr. Chauncy, and died April 2, 1798.

79. John Eliot was born in Boston on May 31, 1754, and graduated from Harvard in 1772. He was ordained in Boston on November 3, 1779, and was settled in Boston (New North) from 1779 until his death on February 14, 1813. He was a close friend of Jeremy Belknap, who married his cousin Ruth Eliot.

80. Born in Dedham, Massachusetts, on June 11, 1752, Oliver Everett graduated from Harvard in 1779. He was ordained in Boston on January 2, 1782, and was settled over the New South Church in Boston. The father of Edward Everett, orator, statesman, and educator, Oliver Everett died in Dorchester on December 19, 1802.

81. Simeon Howard was born in Bridgewater, Massachusetts, on April 29, 1733, and graduated from Harvard in 1758. Ordained in Boston on May 6, 1767, he was settled in Boston (West Church) from 1767 to 1804. He died on August 13, 1804.

82. Kirk Boott (died 1817), of Derby, England, established himself as a merchant in Boston soon after the end of the Revolutionary War. An advertisement of Kirk Boott's Store, No. 4, Butler's Row, appeared in the *Independent Chronicle, and the Universal Advertiser* as early as December 25, 1783. A long letter from Boott published in the January 15, 1784, issue of the same newspaper indicates that he had recently arrived in Boston. An advertisement in the May 13, 1784, number of this newspaper shows that Boott had acquired a partner, for the firm was now called Boott and Pratt's Store. On November 16, 1787, Kirk Boott, his wife, Mary, and daughter Frances were naturalized by a special Act of the General Court.

83. William Pratt apparently came from England to Boston in May, 1784. The *Boston Directory* for 1789, p. 7, lists "Boot and Pratt, merchants, No. 55, State-street, dwelling-house Brattle-square." The directory for 1796 lists "Boot and Pratt, merchants, No. 30, State-street." In 1798 Boott and Pratt contributed $3,000 to build the *Boston,* a frigate of seven hundred tons (Samuel Adams Drake, *Old Landmarks and Historic Personages of Boston* [new and revised ed.; Boston, 1900], pp. 195-196). In the year 1800 Ralph Haskins went out as supercargo in the *Atahualpa* owned by Messrs. Theodore Lyman, Kirk Boott, and William Pratt, who were involved in the Northwest Coast trade (*The Memorial History of Boston,* ed. Justin Winsor [Boston, 1881], IV, 210, n. 2). In 1810 Boott and Pratt became Kirk Boott and Son (Alfred Gilman,

"Sketch of the Life of Kirk Boott," *Contributions of the Old Residents' Historical Association, Lowell, Mass.,* II [November, 1880], 3).

84. Gregory must have been associated with Potter and Gregory, who advertised in the Boston *Independent Chronicle, and the Universal Advertiser* of May 13, 1784, that they had just arrived from London. The *Boston Directory* for 1789 lists "John Gregory, merchant, No. 54, State-street." The directory for 1796 lists "John Gregory, merchant, No. 6, Kilby street, house Hanover street."

85. Sharp may have been William Sharp, but further identification has not been possible.

86. In the spring of 1785 James Lewis precipitated a great hullaba-loo against British merchants in Boston when he advertised goods from London "Cheaper than ever before in this Place" (the *Independent Chronicle,* March 24, 1785). The Boston merchants held meetings and passed resolutions intended to protect American interests. The Rev. Mr. Hazlitt came to James Lewis's defense against the scurrilous invectives which appeared in the public prints. In the *American Herald* of April 11, 1785, he published a letter signed "The Stranger's Friend" in which he gave information about James Lewis. "He was born at Maidstone, in Kent, in England, and is the youngest of six sons, descended from as respectable parents as any in that country. His father was, from his childhood, the classmate and bosom friend of Dr. Price, and was beloved and highly venerated by him as long as he lived. He was, at the same time, admired and honoured, by all his numerous acquaintance, as the gentleman, the scholar, and the rational, upright, and ingenious divine. From his earliest years he cherished the love of liberty. From the first bickerings, which led to the late contest, he signalized himself as one of the most strenuous assertors of American liberty. Such was his zeal in this cause, that to be born in America, was always a sufficient recommendatory qualification to his friendship, and that, when his health had so far declined that he could not be conveyed in any other manner than in a litter, without being in an agony of pain, he chearfully [*sic*] took a journey of fifty miles, to give his suffrage for those candidates to serve in parliament, who were the known and avowed advocates of America.

"The present Mr. Lewis, the youngest son of his most excellent father, was taught to cherish the love of liberty ever since he could pronounce the term. He, and all his family, have been the uniform friends of liberty, of impartial, universal liberty, and have particularly exerted themselves as the friends of all the friends of the American resistance and revolution. The sums which they have expended, to relieve, support, and redeem the American prisoners in England, shall be nameless. The unprovoked insults, and numerous traductory libels, which have been published against one of them, can scarcely be considered a suitable return for the repeated generous exertions of all the others, in vindicating the cause and the people of this country."

87. *The Minutes of the Common Council of the City of New York, 1784-1831* (New York, 1917) contains references in 1803-1806 to a petition of George Lewis that a debt due his brother James Lewis deceased be paid. See III, 198, 208; IV, 23, 285. The List of Subscribers for Hazlitt's *Sermons for the Use of Families* in 1808 contained the name of George Lewis, New York.

88. On June 26, 1785, Hazlitt preached in Salem for the Rev. William Bentley of the East Church. He preached for Bentley on other occasions too, and he also preached in Salem for the Rev. Thomas Barnard, Jr., of the North Church, and the Rev. John Prince of the First Church (*The Diary of William Bentley, D. D.: Pastor of the East Church, Salem, Massachusetts* [Salem, 1905-14], I, xv, 21; and Joseph B. Felt, *Annals of Salem* [2nd ed.; Salem, 1845-49], II, 605). Apparently Margaret inadvertently substituted the name Barnes for that of either Bentley or Barnard.

89. Hazlitt visited Elias Hasket Derby (1739-1799), son of Richard Derby (1712-1783) by his first wife, Mary, and therefore stepson of the old lady at Hingham, Richard Derby's second wife, Sarah Langley Hersey Derby.

90. Elias Hasket Derby was the founder of the East India business, the basis of Salem's wealth, but he was also a pioneer in American trade with Russia. In 1784 he sent the ship *Light Horse* to Cronstadt, the port of St. Petersburg. Some time later Elias Hasket Derby, Jr., one of eight children and oldest of five sons, sailed to the Baltic, toured Europe, and then returned to Salem to enter on a mercantile career. However, efforts to find a published account of his travels, or of those of his brothers, have been unsuccessful. For more about the Derby family, see Robert E. Peabody, *Merchant Venturers of Old Salem: A History of the Commercial Voyages of a New England Family to the Indies and Elsewhere in the XVIII Century* (Boston, 1912), pp. 53, 78; and Perley Derby, "Genealogy of the Derby Family," *Historical Collections of the Essex Institute*, III (August, 1861), 162-163, and III (October, December, 1861), 201-204.

91. John Hazlitt executed likenesses in Hingham of the Rev. Dr. Ebenezer Gay, General Benjamin Lincoln, Colonel Nathan Rice, Dr. Joshua Barker, and others (Henry T. Tuckerman, *Book of the Artists: American Artist Life* [New York, 1867], p. 54).

92. According to Samuel Deane, *History of Scituate, Massachusetts from Its First Settlement to 1831* (Boston, 1831), p. 188, Hazlitt preached in Scituate in 1784.

93. Hazlitt probably met the former prisoners of war in Marshfield because many Marshfield men served in the navy and some of those captured by the British were committed to English prisons (Lysander Salmon Richards, *History of Marshfield* [Plymouth, Mass., 1901-05], II, 78, 117).

94. Dr. Gay died on March 18, 1787.

95. The town visited by Hazlitt was Truro. In *Truro—Cape Cod or Land Marks and Sea Marks* (Boston, 1883), p. 242, Shebnah Rich writes: "During the two years while Mr. Upham [the Rev. Caleb Upham] was unable to preach, and before the ordination of Mr. Damon, the baptisms were recorded by Revds. Levi Whitman of Wellfleet and Samuel Parker of Provincetown. July 17, 1785, there are several baptisms recorded in a bold off-hand, over the signature of Reverend William Hazlett, a Briton.

"As this was soon after the war, the inference is that Reverend William Hazlett was a chaplain of an English man-of-war, and occasionally preached and did pastoral duty for Mr. Upham."

96. See the Introduction.

97. Hazlitt republished Priestley's *Appeal to the Serious and Candid Professors of Christianity,* and *The Triumph of Truth; Being an Account of the Trial of Mr. E. Elwall,* and *A General View of the Arguments for the Unity of God* in Philadelphia in 1784. Although Hazlitt wrote much himself in Boston, there is no evidence that he republished Priestley's works in that city. It may be well to note, however, that on May 2, 1785, the Rev. William Bentley, of Salem, recorded in his diary: "Received of Hazlet, 6 Priestley's Appeal and 6 Views, 6 Dialogues, of Feskwick. 3 Friendly Dialogues bet. Athan. and Unit. . . . Received as a personal present a Volume of Hints and Essays by a Layman and An Appeal to Common Sense" (*The Diary of William Bentley, D. D.,* I, 19). The Dialogues of Feskwick and the Friendly Dialogues mentioned by Bentley, as well as the works which were a personal present, Mr. Hazlitt had probably received from the Rev. Theophilus Lindsey (Letter from Lindsey to Hazlitt, January 21, 1785, "The Hazlitt Papers," *Christian Reformer,* V [August, 1838], 507).

98. In *The History of Augusta* (Augusta, Maine, 1870), pp. 196-197, 203, James W. North gives the following account of Hazlitt's visit to Hallowell: "At a town meeting held September 6th [1785] the committee raised to procure preaching was directed to endeavor to hire the Reverend Seth Noble, who had preached a number of sabbaths, to continue his services in this town until the middle of March next. The endeavors of the committee were successful, and Mr. Noble preached sixteen sabbaths, for which the town paid him £26 10s. The doctrines however of Mr. Noble were not acceptable to Capt. Henry Sewall [1752-

1845], who absented himself from his meetings and met Sundays for worship with a number of persons at Benjamin Pettingill's house. . . .

"Notwithstanding the engagement with Mr. Noble, when the Reverend William Hazlitt appeared, a short time after, with a letter from Samuel Vaughan of Boston to the committee of the town, recommending him and proposing that the town should employ him, a meeting was called for November 29th, at which the letter was read, and Joseph North, Henry Sewall and Daniel Cony were chosen a committee to return the thanks of the town to Mr. Vaughan for his very generous offer and proposal to the town respecting Mr. Hazlitt. The same committee was desired to request Mr. Hazlitt to continue his services for two months. He officiated fourteen Sabbaths, for which he was paid £21. Sewall heard him preach in the forenoon of November 13th, and declared him an Armenian [*sic*], and believed him an Arian, and said, from such doctrines I turned away, and met with a few brethren at Esq. Pettingill's in the afternoon. . . .

"The action of the town in relation to Mr. Hazlitt . . . seems to have created a ferment which resulted, December 20th, in a call for a meeting for the twenty-sixth of the same month, to see if the town will reconsider all the votes passed at the last meeting, and to see if they will hire Mr. Hazlitt to preach on probation for settlement. . . .

"This meeting assembled at the meeting-house and chose Col. North moderator, when the article to reconsider the votes of the former meeting was dismissed. It was then voted to hire Mr. Hazlitt upon probation. . . .

"The names of the Reverend Seth Noble and Reverend William Hazlitt were presented to the town at the meeting April 1st [1786], as candidates for settlement in the work of the ministry, and were both rejected. The town voted to pay the former £9 for the six Sundays he had preached, and the latter seventy dollars for fourteen days' preaching including Thanksgiving, as already noticed."

That Hazlitt had gone to Hallowell with a prospect of a settlement there and the promise of a fairly comfortable position appears from a letter of March 15, 1786, from the Rev. John Palmer, of Islington, to Hazlitt, in which Palmer wrote: "At all adventures, the income, from Mr. V——'s [Vaughan's] generosity and the contributions of the people, amounting to above 400 dollars per annum, and reckoning a dollar at what I take to be its common value, or about four shillings and sixpence, is a pretty beginning, and, indeed, as you need not be told, much better a provision than is made for most ministers in country situations here. That it is a very healthy spot is an important additional circumstance. And when with this I connect the excellence of the soil and its consequent fertility, supposing hands to cultivate it, the value of education, etc., my hopes rise, that you will soon be in a condition far more advantageous than you have yet known in America; at the same time, you will not be precluded from the view of a better settlement, should such offer at Boston or elsewhere" ("The Hazlitt Papers," *Christian Reformer,* V [November, 1838], 759).

99. This was *A Thanksgiving Discourse, Preached at Hallowell, 15 Dec., 1785* (Boston, 1786).

100. Apparently Margaret did not know that her father had been rejected as minister for the congregation at Hallowell.

101. Margaret here defines the Bay of Fundy rather liberally.

102. Portland, Maine, was called Falmouth at that time.

103. Perhaps this was "old Aaron Renouf," who was sexton of the Old North Church in Weymouth for more than forty years (*History of Weymouth,* II, 912).

104. In June, 1786, Lucy Cranch wrote to her aunt, Abigail Adams, that the Rev. Mr. Evans and his bride were to live in the Smith house in Weymouth, and in July Lucy's mother, Mary Cranch, gave her sister the same news. However, Mr. Evans changed his mind about taking the church in Weymouth and therefore did not move to Weymouth. In a letter of October 8, 1786, Mary Cranch wrote to Abigail: "He [Mr. Evans] desired to have our House ready for him by July. Mr. Hazzlet who was a very good tenant left it and now we cannot find anybody to take it" (*Microfilms of the Adams Papers,* Part IV, "Letters Received and Other Loose Papers," Reels 368 and 369).

105. In March, 1783, Mr. Silvanus Loud was given permission to set up a hatter's shop at the corner of Mr. David Lovell's lot (*History of Weymouth,* II, 590).

106. Mr. Beales was the tenant who occupied the other part of the house in Weymouth.

107. The *Massachusetts Centinel* for January 7, 1786, reported from Boston: "On Monday last [January 2], about 15 minutes after 7 o'clock, a shock of an Earthquake was very sensibly felt in this town. The shock was preceeded [*sic*] by a noise of about 6 seconds continuation, approaching from the East, similar to that made by heavy thunder, at a distance. We hear that the shock was felt at the same time in Salem, Mistick, Beverly, and several other towns." The *Independent Chronicle, and the Universal Advertiser* for January 26, 1786, also reported the earthquake: "The earthquake, on the morning of the 2d instant, was observed at Andover, by a well-regulated clock, at about 14 minutes after seven. The noise was like the burning of a chimney. The tremulous motion of the earth was very sensibly felt, and was so great as to

jar the windows." Margaret could have easily mistaken the exact month when the quake occurred in recollecting it years later.

108. Dr. Cotton Tufts and his wife, Lucy Quincy Tufts, had one son, Cotton, born on August 4, 1757.

109. Lucy Jones, daughter of Peter and Ann Tufts Jones, was born in Medford, Massachusetts, on September 16, 1768. Her father died on January 19, 1772, and her mother on September 7, 1774. After the death of her mother, she went to live with her uncle, Dr. Tufts (W. H. Whitmore, *Register of Families Settled at the Town of Medford, Mass.* [Boston, 1855], p. 49; *Vital Records of Medford, Massachusetts to the Year 1850* [Boston, 1907], pp. 88, 146, 249, 307; and *Vital Records of Salem, Massachusetts to the End of the Year 1849* [Salem, 1925], V, 364-365). Lucy Jones married the Rev. Joshua Cushman of Winslow on September 13, 1801 (*Vital Records of Weymouth, Massachusetts* [Boston, 1910], p. 105).

110. In referring to parrots and monkeys, perhaps Margaret was extending her description of wild life to include Central and South America.

111. By "tiger cat" Margaret probably meant a wildcat or lynx.

112. The Blue Hills of Milton.

113. Margaret should have called Fort William by its right name, Castle William. This fort on Castle Island later was called Fort Independence (Edward Rowe Snow, *The Islands of Boston Harbor: Their History and Romance, 1626-1935* [Andover, Mass., 1935], pp. 109-151).

114. Bunker Hill, or, actually, Breed's Hill.

115. Susan Butt probably was the same person as Susanna Butts, who married Justinian Holden on July 29, 1797 (*A Volume of Records Relating to the Early History of Boston, Containing Boston Marriages from 1752 to 1809* [Boston, 1903], p. 181).

116. A Miss Martha Butts, of Dorchester, married Captain Elisha Tyler, also of Dorchester, on October 16, 1785 (*A Report of the Record Commissioners of the City of Boston, Containing Dorchester Births, Marriages, and Deaths to the End of 1825* [Boston, 1891], p. 238). It seems reasonable to assume that Susan Butt (Butts) was a sister of Martha Butts Tyler, who died on April 18, 1788.

117. *Dorchester Deaths,* p. 274, lists "A Child of Boston a negro man and Tamar his Wife, Died June the ——— 1792." *Dorchester Births,* p. 212, lists "Charles the Son of Boston Tyler and ——— his Wife, was born 1795." Apparently Boston was the Tylers' Negro servant or slave.

118. Possibly the Hazlitts' neighbor was either Captain John Homans or his son, Captain Thomas Homans.

119. The Rev. John Lathrop married, as his second wife, Elizabeth Sawyer of Wells, Maine, on September 14, 1780. They had five children

all told, but one of them died in infancy and another was not born until after Margaret had left America *(Boston Marriages,* p. 121; and *A Report of the Record Commissioners of the City of Boston, Containing Boston Births from A. D. 1700 to A. D. 1800* [Boston, 1894], pp. 331-334, 337).

120. Betsey was Elizabeth, who was born May 18, 1782, and Sam was Samuel Checkley, who was born August 16, 1783.

In a letter of August 4, 1788, the Rev. John Lathrop wrote from Boston to the Rev. William Hazlitt: *"Your* Betsy, in particular, frequently expresses the tender feelings of her heart, in sincere wishes that she could see her beloved friend, Peggy Hazlitt" ([W. Carew Hazlitt], *The Hazlitts,* p. 378).

121. For information about Messrs. Boott, Pratt, Gregory, and Sharp, see notes 82, 83, 84, and 85 on pages 154-55.

122. In 1846 Kirk Boott's house in Bowdoin Square was enlarged into the Revere House, which enjoyed the distinction of entertaining many of Boston's most distinguished visitors in the nineteenth century (Walter Muir Whitehill, *Boston: A Topographical History* [Cambridge, Mass., 1959], p. 177). However, Boott's Bowdoin Square house probably was built later than 1786.

123. This girl was Frances Boott, who married William Wells on May 3, 1808 *(Boston Marriages,* p. 278). In a letter of July 31, 1790, to his son William, the Rev. Mr. Hazlitt mentioned a letter he had received from America. "On Thursday morning we had a letter from Mr. Booth [elsewhere W. Carew Hazlitt has transcribed the name as Mr. Boatt], written at Boston 24 June, just five weeks before we received it. . . . He says, concerning you, 'I read Billy's letter to Fanny [Frances Boott], and she was delighted with it. She sends her love to him, but Fanny has lost the recollection of her little playfellow. The letter does Billy much credit. He has uncommon powers of mind, and if nothing happens to prevent his receiving a liberal education, he must make a great man.' This compliment, I know, will not make you proud or conceited, but more diligent. He, also, desires his and Mrs. Booth's affectionate regards to Billy" ([W. Carew Hazlitt], *The Hazlitts,* p. 391).

124. Mr. Boott early recognized William Hazlitt's genius, and it is interesting to speculate what kind of career William might have had in America under Mr. Boott's tutelage. Mr. Boott's own children were successful, especially Kirk Boott, Jr., who was the master spirit superintending the construction of Lowell, Massachusetts, as a great industrial center. Perhaps William Hazlitt, too, would have become one of the principal founders of Lowell.

125. This journal apparently has disappeared.

126. The *American Herald* for October 2, 1786, carried the following advertisement: "For London, The Ship Rebecca, Now lying at Long-Wharf, George Folgier, Master, Will positively sail by the Fifteenth Instant. She is a new Ship, and has agreeable accommodations for Passengers. Any Person wanting Passage, in said Ship, may know the Terms, by applying at Hinkley and Kneeland's Office, South Side of the Market. Boston, October 2, 1786."

127. This should probably be Nantasket Road.

128. The noddy is a white-capped dark-brown tern, *Anous stalidus.*

129. Mother Carey's chickens are any of various small petrels, especially the stormy petrel, *Oceanites oceanicus.*

130. By "sea pigeon" the Rev. Mr. Hazlitt probably meant either the black guillemot, *Uria Grylle,* or the gray kittiwake, *Larus canus.*

131. By "hoggletts" Hazlitt probably meant haglets or hacklets, a small species of sea-gull.

132. By "sea hen" Hazlitt probably meant the common guillemot, *Uria troile,* or the great skua, *Stercorarius catarrhactes.*

133. The Scilly Isles are southwest of Land's End, England.

134. A seaport on the Isle of Wight.

135. The Downs is a roadstead in the Strait of Dover between the southeast tip of England and Goodwin Sands.

136. He probably landed on December 14, for the December 16, 1786, issue of the *Daily Universal Register,* of London, reported that the ship *Rebecca,* Captain Folger, from Boston, had arrived at Dover.

137. In a letter of January 18, 1787, from Norwich in England, the Rev. William Hazlitt wrote to his friend James Freeman in Boston: "I am now a candidate, in this city, at one of the first congregations in the kingdom, where I have reason to suppose I may settle if I please. But, I have other applications made to me, and may not be able to determine, this month to come, where I shall fix" (Hazlitt to Freeman, January 18, 1787, MS, Autograph Collection of Simon Gratz, Historical Society of Pennsylvania).

138. After his father's departure for England, William Hazlitt wrote to him on November 12, 1786: "My Dear Papa, . . . I have got a little of my grammar; sometimes I get three pages and sometimes but one. I do not sifer any at all. Mamma Peggy and Jacky are all very well, and I am to" ([W. Carew Hazlitt], *The Hazlitts,* p. 377).

139. A joseph was a long cloak with a cape worn by women.

140. "In 1787 (April 20) a fire in Beach Street destroyed a hundred buildings; and of this number were the Hollis-street Church and sixty dwellings. It called out generous donations; and at this time Lafayette made his generous gift" (Russell H. Conwell, *History of the Great Fire in Boston, November 9 and 10, 1872* [Boston, 1873], p. 43).

The *American Herald* of April 23, 1787, had the following account of the fire: "It is with inexpressible sorrow, we relate, that about sun-set last Friday evening, a fire broke out in a Malt-House, belonging to Mr. William Patten, near the Liberty-Pole, at the south end of this town, and was attended with a destruction, similar to which the inhabi-tants of this town have not experienced, since the year 1760. The wind at N. E. blowing hard, carried the flakes of fire to a great height and distance, by which, the houses being very dry, were set on fire in so many places, as rendered it impossible to direct the exertions of the inhabitants to any point.—The spire of the Reverend Mr. Wight's meet-ing-house, situated at a distanch [*sic*] of near 50 rods from the place where the devastation first began, was observed to be on fire, at the ball just below the vane, in less than 15 minutes—as this could not be extinguished by reason of its height, the fire falling therefrom, and from the houses then in flames, in a short time demolished that large edifice. In the direction of the wind for a space of 20 rods wide, the fire carried havock as far as the building extended, crossing the Main-Street, and destroying the buildings one side from Mr. Knapp's to Mr. Bradford's; and on the other side from Mrs. Inches [*sic*], to Mr. Os-borne's. . . . There were several houses empty, which, with the Meeting-House, shops, barns and out-houses, may be computed at 100 buildings. Providentially no lives were lost. . . ."

141. That is, Castle William.

142. Isaac Smith (1749-1829) was the son of Isaac and Elizabeth Storer Smith, a nephew of the Rev. William Smith, of Weymouth, and a cousin of Abigail Adams. During the Revolution he was a refugee in England, where he became a dissenting minister. He had charge of a dissenting congregation in Sidmouth, Devonshire, from 1776 until he returned to America in 1784. He was ordained among the dissenters in 1778. In 1786 he was appointed chaplain at the Castle, a position he held until he resigned to become librarian at Harvard College. At a later time he was a Preceptor at Dummer Academy in Byfield, Massachusetts.

143. Harvard College was founded in 1636.

144. Yale College in New Haven, Connecticut, was founded in 1701.

145. John Hancock was born in 1737 and died in 1793.

146. The *Boston Gazette, and the Country Journal* for July 9, 1787, reported that the ship *Nonpareil*, Captain Cushing, had cleared the Port of Boston for London.

147. The pilot fish, *Naucrates ductor*, is reputed to act as a pilot or guide to the shark. Actually the pilot fish accompanies the shark in order to feed on scraps left by it and also on the parasites present on the shark's body.

# III

## THE HAZLITTS AFTER THEIR RETURN TO ENGLAND

1. The August 14, 1787, issue of the *Daily Universal Register,* of London, listed the *Nonpareil* among the ships which had arrived at Portsmouth.

2. The wreck of the Halsewell East Indiaman attracted attention in America as well as in England. See the *Independent Ledger, and the American Advertiser,* of Boston, for June 12 and 19, 1786, for "A Circumstantial Narrative of the Loss of the Halsewell East-Indiaman, Capt. Richard Pierce." Perhaps the most complete story of the wreck was the one published in London early in 1786 under the title of *A True and Particular Account of the Loss of the Halsewell (East-Indiaman,) Capt. Richard Pierce, Which Was Unfortunately Cast Away, at Seacombe, in the Isle of Purbeck, on the Coast of Dorsetshire, on Friday Morning, January 6, 1786. Shewing the Paternal Behaviour of Capt. Pierce, Who Preferr'd Perishing with His Daughters, to the Being Preserved without Them.* This book has a frontispiece "Engraved for the Halsewell Indiaman which was lost on the Rocks of Purbeck near Portland with Capt. Pierce his two daughters and crew."

3. That is, the garden at Walworth.

4. David Williams (1738-1816) was a former minister in Frome, Somerset, and in Exeter, who introduced the liturgy used in Liverpool into that society. He afterwards moved to London, where he opened a chapel in Margaret Street, Cavendish Square. He was the founder of the Royal Literary Fund.

5. Margaret does not reveal what their misfortunes were. Perhaps these misfortunes explain why the names of David Lewis and David Williams do not appear in the List of Subscribers for Hazlitt's *Discourses* in 1790.

6. Mrs. Cooper must have been the mother of James Cooper, who, as Margaret has told us earlier, also died in New York.

7. Boydell's at the Shakespeare Gallery, Pall Mall. John Boydell (1719-1804) was an engraver, print publisher, and Lord Mayor of London.

8. As noted in the Introduction, John Hazlitt became acquainted with Sir Joshua Reynolds soon after establishing himself in London. Sir Joshua praised John's work and recommended him to his friends. In 1788 John exhibited at the Royal Academy and continued to exhibit there until 1819. He died at Stockport on May 16, 1837.

9. Mr. Wicksteed, of Shrewsbury, father of John Wicksteed (1774-1837), subscribed to the Rev. Mr. Hazlitt's *Discourses* in 1790. His

grandson, the Rev. Charles Wicksteed, became minister of Mill-Hill Chapel, Leeds.

10. In a letter of August 18, 1813, to the Rev. William Hazlitt at Addlestone, the Rev. Thomas Jenkins, of Whitchurch, wrote that Mr. P. Beck had regretted very much not seeing Hazlitt in his transit through Shrewsbury ("The Hazlitt Papers," *Christian Reformer,* V [August, 1838], 512).

11. The Rev. Joseph Fownes (1715-1789) was minister of the congregation assembling in High Street, Shrewsbury, for forty-one years. He was educated at the Academy at Findern, in Derbyshire, and was minister of a dissenting congregation at Cradley, near Stourbridge, in Worcestershire, before accepting an invitation to Shrewsbury in 1748 ("Presbyterian Meeting-House, Shrewsbury," *Christian Reformer,* III [June, 1847], 324-325).

12. John Rowe (1764-1833) was the sixth child of William Rowe, Esq., of Spencecomb, near Crediton. On the completion of his education he became one of the ministers at High Street, Shrewsbury. After Mr. Fownes died, Rowe became sole pastor and remained in this capacity until 1793, when he found it necessary to require assistance in his public duties. In May, 1798, Rowe removed to Bristol, where he remained until the summer of 1832, when he went to Italy. He died in Sienna on July 2, 1833.

13. Mr. Swanwick was a prominent member of the Rev. Mr. Hazlitt's congregation at Wem, and his son Joseph (1777-1841) was a classmate of William Hazlitt's at Hackney College. Like William Hazlitt, Joseph Swanwick was impressed by Samuel Taylor Coleridge's preaching in 1798 and he was accustomed to speak of Coleridge's pulpit addresses with great admiration: "On one occasion, when preaching in Mr. Hazlitt's pulpit at Wem, on the being of a God, Mr. Coleridge delighted the few who could follow him, by the closeness of his reasoning, the variety of his illustrations, and the exquisite beauty of his language. So completely was the orator carried away by his own eloquence, that dispensing with the ordinary close of the service, a hymn and prayer, he burst from the sermon, which he abruptly terminated, into a fervent address to the Deity. That prayer impressed all present as the most sublime devotional exercise they had ever heard" ("Presbyterian Meeting-House, Shrewsbury," *Christian Reformer,* III [June, 1847], 330 n).

14. Thomas Jenkins (1746-1815) of Whitchurch was a dissenting clergyman, and "really a very well-informed, agreeable, sensible man" ([W. Carew Hazlitt], *The Hazlitts,* p. 124).

15. That is, the Church of England.

16. Margaret's mother died on June 10, 1837.

17. The Rev. John Houghton (1730-1800), a native of Liverpool,

was minister of Platt Chapel, near Manchester, and then in Hyde, Cheshire; afterwards in Nantwich; next in Elland, near Halifax, Yorkshire; and lastly in Wem. He was an excellent teacher of elocution. In 1787 he removed to Norwich with his son Pendlebury, and they opened a classical school there in their joint names. The principal labor devolved on the elder Mr. Houghton, who was esteemed a sound scholar, as he certainly was a severe disciplinarian. Interestingly enough, the Rev. Mr. Hazlitt got the post at Wem left by Mr. Houghton when he went to Norwich with his son Pendlebury, who left Shrewsbury in 1787 to accept an invitation from the Norwich congregation to succeed Mr. Alderson as joint pastor with Dr. Enfield. This was the Norwich position Hazlitt had hoped to get (Edward Taylor, "Continuation of the History of the Presbyterian Congregation at Norwich," *Christian Reformer*, IV [April, 1848], 206-209).

18. Pendlebury Houghton, the only son of the Rev. John Houghton and his wife Mary, the daughter of William Pendlebury, minister of Mill-Hill Chapel in Leeds, was born in 1758. He was educated at Warrington Academy and then settled with the society at Shrewsbury, in 1781, as assistant to Mr. Fownes. In 1787 he went to Norwich, and then served as minister in London and Liverpool (Walter Wilson, *The History and Antiquities of Dissenting Churches and Meeting Houses, in London, Westminster, and Southwark; Including Lives of Their Ministers, from the Rise of Nonconformity to the Present Time* [London, 1808-14], IV, 117). The Rev. Pendlebury Houghton died April 3, 1824.

19. Probably Joseph Swanwick, who "was early placed under the private tuition and the pastoral care of the Rev. Mr. Hazlitt" and possessed "excellent natural endowments" ("Joseph Swanwick, Esq.," *Christian Reformer*, VIII [December, 1841], 784).

20. George Dicken, or George Dickin, as W. Carew Hazlitt spells his name in *The Hazlitts*, was a playmate of William's at Wem.

21. In 1790 Mrs. Tracey was living in Wem according to the List of Subscribers for Hazlitt's *Discourses*.

22. Apparently an English translation of Fénelon's *Télémaque*.

23. An institution for educating Unitarian ministers.

24. Probably Mr. Railton of Liverpool ([W. Carew Hazlitt], *The Hazlitts*, p. 108).

25. James Northcote (1746-1831) was a painter, Royal Academician, and author.

26. "On May 22, 1803, four days after the declaration of war between England and France, Bonaparte ordered that all the British tourists in France should be seized. There appear to have been about one thousand. The seizure of these non-combatants was done professedly as a

reprisal for the British Government having seized French vessels" (R. B. Mowat, *The Diplomacy of Napoleon* [London, 1924], p. 129).

27. Joseph Johnson (1738-1809) published the Rev. Mr. Hazlitt's sermons in 1790 and in 1808. William Hazlitt may have painted Johnson's portrait in 1807 (P. P. Howe, *The Life of William Hazlitt*, with an introduction by Frank Swinnerton [London, 1947], p. 92).

28. In 1805 Johnson published William Hazlitt's *An Essay on the Principles of Human Action*. Two years later, in 1807, he published *An Abridgement of the Light of Nature Pursued, by Abraham Tucker, Esq., Originally Published in Seven Volumes, under the Name of Edward Search, Esq.*, with a preface by William Hazlitt, and *The Eloquence of the British Senate; or, Select Specimens from the Speeches of the Most Distinguished Parliamentary Speakers, from the Beginning of the Reign of Charles I to the Present Time,* with a preface and critical notes by Hazlitt. In 1807 Hazlitt published *A Reply to the Essay on Population, by the Rev. T. R. Malthus.*

29. William Hazlitt married Sarah Stoddart on May 1, 1808, not in 1809 as Margaret says. Contrary to W. Carew Hazlitt's statement in *The Hazlitts*, p. 338, that Sarah Stoddart Hazlitt died in 1842-1843, the *Christian Reformer*, VIII (January, 1841), 54, reports that she died on November 1, 1840, at the age of sixty-six.

30. Sir John Stoddart (1773-1856).

31. The Hazlitts' first child died on July 5, 1809 (P. P. Howe, *The Life of William Hazlitt*, p. 108).

32. The word *with* has been omitted as inappropriate here.

33. *A New and Improved Grammar of the English Tongue, for the Use of Schools, in Which the Genius of our Speech Is Especially Attended to, and the Discoveries of Mr. Horne Tooke and Other Modern Writers on the Formation of Language Are for the First Time Incorporated* was published in November, 1809. The *Life of Holcroft* was finished at this time but not published until 1816.

34. Mr. Baring Wall, M. P. (P. P. Howe, *The Life of William Hazlitt*, p. 332, n. 1).

35. Charles Lamb and his sister, Mary, visited William and Sarah Hazlitt at Winterslow in October, 1809 (P. P. Howe, *The Life of William Hazlitt*, pp. 108-109). For a further account of this visit, see E. J. Moyne, "An Unpublished Letter of William Hazlitt," *PMLA*, LXXVII (June, 1962), 341-342.

36. William Hazlitt lectured at the Russell Institution in London from January through April, 1812. He did not give his lectures at the Surrey Institution until 1818.

37. Here Margaret Hazlitt's journal comes to an end.

# Index

GLH=Grace Loftus Hazlitt (Mrs. William Hazlitt)
JH=John Hazlitt
MH=Margaret Hazlitt
Rev. WH=The Rev. William Hazlitt
WH=William Hazlitt

Accident, aboard the *Nonpareil*, 98. *See also* George and Hannah, orphans

Adams, Abigail. *See* Adams, Mrs. John

Adams, John: ambassador to England, 63, 148n*48*; and Tench Coxe, 139n*1*; in Paris, 142n*15*; and Abigail Smith, 148n*47*

Adams, Mrs. John (Abigail Smith): house of, 63; Hazlitts' claimed relationship to, 63; marriage of, 148n*47*; letters from Mary Cranch to, 148n*47*, 159n*104*; letter from Lucy Cranch to, 159n*104*; and Rev. Isaac Smith, 163n*142*

Adams, John Quincy, 63

Adams family, of Quincy: Hazlitts' claimed relationship to, 148n*49*

Addlestone, England, 12, 165n*10*

Algerine pirates, 95, 98

America: Hazlitt kin in, 4; arrival of Hazlitt family in, 5, 20, 115; departure of Rev. WH from, 9; departure of Hazlitt family from, 9; WH in, 20, 21; WH on, 21, 22; MH in, 22; Catherine Emmet in, 23; MH on, 25; McClelland children in, 32; Col. John Hazlitt in, 32, 33; MH on Crèvecoeur's description of, 46; Capt. Jefferson on, 46; security from robbers in, 76; Rev. WH's land of promise, 115; labors of Rev. WH in, 122; WH's fondness for, 128n*25*; Reuben Harvey and, 137n*60*; mentioned, 14, 41, 95, 100, 118

*American Farmer, The. See Letters from an American Farmer*

American foods: at breakfast, 52, 58; at dinner, 53, 63, 91; in winter, 75; in summer, 75; at tea time, 79; preservation of, 50, 75

*American Herald* (Boston): theological controversy published in, 11; scriptural confutation of Thirty-nine Articles published in, 11; advertisement of JH and Joseph Dunckerley in, 15

American independence, 44, 137 n56

American prisoners of war: illtreatment at Kinsale, Ireland, of, 5, 41; aided by Rev. WH, 5, 41; escape of, 41; concealment of, 41; Rev. WH meets two former, 72, 157n93; Reuben Harvey and, 137n60; Rev. Israel Lewis and, 155n86

American Revolution: Col. John Hazlitt in, 32, 33; histories of, 32, 33, 61, 130n9; Col. John Haslet in, 33, 130n8; Rev. WH on, 38; Rev. Samuel Thomas on, 38; Rev. John Wiche on, 40; Thomas Viny on, 40; Col. William Haslett in, 130n8; Reuben Harvey and, 137n60; Tench Coxe and, 139n1; Daniel Gomez and, 147n38; mentioned, 3, 16, 44, 95

Americans: MH on, 46, 93; British officers on, 48

American scenery: in New Jersey, 47, 49, 57; in Pennsylvania, 52, 56; in Rhode Island, 60, 61; in Massachusetts, 63, 64, 65, 67, 73, 78, 79; mentioned, 19

American trade: with the West Indies, 76; with the East Indies, 156n90; with Russia, 156n90

Animals: Newfoundland dogs, 58; wolves, 74, 77; foxes, 77, 96, 97; bears, 77; tiger cat (wild cat or lynx), 77, 160n111; moose deer, 77; "cat-a-mount," 77

*Antiquary, The,* 26

*Appeal to Common Sense, An,* 157 n97

Arians, 121, 133n32, 157n98

Arminians, 157n98

Armstrong, Gen. John, 117

Athanasian Creed, 10

Atkinson, Capt. George, 52, 143 n19

Atkinson, Mrs. George (Catharine McGinnis), 52, 53, 143n19

Autumn weather: in Massachusetts, 62, 63; difference between English and American, 101, 102

Banbury, England, 35

Bandon, Ireland: Rev. WH's ministry at, 5, 39; Rev. WH's services to American prisoners of war while at, 5, 41, 117; residence of Hazlitt family at, 40-44, 134n44; Presbyterian congregation at, 40, 43, 44, 135n45; ill-treatment of Catholics at, 41, 42, 135n47; a riot at, 43, 136n51; departure of Hazlitt family from, 44; visits at, 45; friends from, in Philadelphia, 53, 54; former prisoners of war thank friends in, 72; Fourteenth Regiment of Light Dragoons in, 136 n50; mentioned, 59

Bannon, Mr., aboard the *Henry,* 46, 138n66

Barker, Dr. Joshua: JH's portrait of, 16, 156n91; and a miniature of Rev. WH, 16; and Rev. WH, 70; and JH, 72; sketch of, 152 n71

Barnard, Rev. Thomas, 121, 156 n88

Barnes, Rev. David, 72, 121, 156 n88

Bath, England: the Hazlitts live near, 12, 23; Mrs. Evans' school at, 37; Rev. David Evans at, 37, 133n28; mentioned, 36

Bath (Springs), Pa., 49, 57, 140n3

Beales, Mr., of Weymouth, Mass., 63, 75, 76, 159n106

Beales, Mrs., of Weymouth, Mass., 75

Beck, Mr., of Shrewsbury, England, 102, 165n10

Belknap, Rev. Jeremy: and Ebenezer Hazard, 146n36; on Rev. WH, 146n36; and Rev. John Eliot, 146n37, 151n66, 154n79

Bentley, Rev. William: and Rev. WH, 12, 156n88, 157n97; adopts

Priestley's Catechism, 12; attacks doctrine of the Trinity, 12; JH's miniature of, 15; character of, 121; and James Winthrop, 128 n*17*; diary of, quoted, 157n*97*; mentioned, 20

"Bereanus." *See* Hazlitt, Rev. William

Bible, the, 24, 122

Biggs family, of Bandon, and the Hazlitt family, 44

Birds: MH on, 61; brant, 63; hummingbirds, 64, 67; bluebirds, 67; scarlet bird (scarlet tanager), 67, 150n*61*; fire-hang-bird (oriole), 67-68, 150n*61*; mocking birds, 68, 96; Bob Lincoln (bobolink), 68, 73, 150n*63*; red linnet, Virginia nightingale (cardinal), 68, 77; kingbird, 68; hawk, 68; snow bird (junco), 68, 150n*64*; swallows, 68; robins, 68, 73; pigeons, 77; turkeys, 77; geese, 77; ducks, 77; teal, 77; parrots, 77, 160n*110*; birds in Southern states, 77; noddies (terns), 85, 86, 162n*128*; owl, 85; gulls, 86, 87; Mother Keary's (Carey's) chickens, 86, 162n*129*; hogglets (haglets or hacklets), 87, 162n*131*

Birmingham Riots, 38, 133n*31*

Black sheep in Rev. WH's Bandon congregation, 44

Blake, Mr., of Milton, Mass., 69, 152n*67*

Blue Mountains (Blue Hills of Milton, Mass.), 78, 160n*112*

Book of Common Prayer, 11, 116

Boot. *See* Boott

Booth, Mr. *See* Boott, Kirk

Boott (Boot), Frances (Fanny): in Boston, 81, 161n*123*; naturalization of, 154n*82*; marriage of, 161 n*123*; playmate of WH, 161n*123*

Boott (Boot), Kirk: and WH, 21; on WH's powers of mind, 21, 161n*123*; wishes to bring up WH as a merchant, 21, 81; and Rev. WH, 71, 81, 82; and Hazlitt family, 71, 95; and MH, 81, 89, 90, 91; children of, 81; and JH, 81; sketch of, 81, 154n*82*; and William Pratt, 154n*82-83*;

house of, 161n*122*; letter to Rev. WH from, 161n*123*

Boott (Boot), Mrs. Kirk (Mary): and MH, 80, 81, 90; and the Hazlitt family, 81, 95; and Rev. WH, 88; sketch of, 91; naturalization of, 154n*82*; and WH, 161 n*123*

Boston (a Negro servant). *See* Tyler, Boston

Boston, bay of: view of, 65, 78; description of, 92; mentioned, 82

Boston, Mass.: Rev. WH preaches at, 6, 56, 120; Rev. WH lectures at, 6, 68, 150n*65*, 151n*66*; JH paints at, 15; arrival of Hazlitt family at, 61; their lodgings at, 61; friends of Rev. WH at, 71, 153n*75-77*, 154n*78-81*; English merchants at, 71, 80, 81, 154 n*82-83*, 155n*84-86*; Rev. WH and JH at, 73; earthquake felt at, 75, 159n*107*; MH's visits to, 79, 80, 89, 90, 91, 94; fires in, 80, 91, 92; Rev. WH's visits to, 81; departure of Rev. WH from, 82; description of, 92, 93; departure of Mrs. Hazlitt and her children from, 95; state of things in 1783 at, 114; Rev. WH's arrival in, 115; selectmen of, 150n*65*; controversy over English merchants at, 155n*86*; mentioned, 20, 21, 24, 53, 62, 65, 70, 74, 75, 78, 86

—Beach Street, 162n*140*

—Beacon Hill, 93

—Bowdoin Square, 161n*122*

—Brattle Street Church, 6, 56, 57, 146n*36-37*, 148n*47*

—Common, 93

—Faneuil Hall, 150n*65*

—First Church, 153n*75*, 154n*78*

—Hollis-Street Church, 162n*140*

—King's Chapel, 9, 11, 113, 114, 153n*77*

—Liberty-Pole, 162n*140*

—Long Wharf, 82, 162n*126*

—New North Church, 154n*79*

—New South Church, 154n*80*

—North Square, 15

—Paul Revere House, 15

—Revere House, hotel, 161n*122*
—Second Church, 150n*65*, 151n*66*, 153n*76*
—South Street, 92
—State House, 93
—State Street, 61, 147n*44*
—Trinity Church, 10
—West Church, 152n*69*, 154n*81*
Boston (Bostonian) Association of Ministers: meeting of, 10, 115; Rev. WH and, 10, 115; Rev. James Freeman and, 114; members of, 114; and Priestley's writings, 114
*Boston Magazine*, 10
Boydell's shop, London, 101, 164n7
Braintree, Mass.: the Hazlitt family at, 62; Rev. WH at, 69
Brazier (Brasier), Anne. *See* Hazlitt, 3rd Mrs. James
Brewer, George, playmate of WH, 20, 52
Brewer, Mrs. Jonathan (Margaret Atkinson), 52, 143n*19*, 143n*20*
Bristol, England: Rev. WH preaches as a candidate at, 36; rejected at, 37; Mr. and Mrs. Smyth of, 37; Joseph Smith of, 133n*25*; Puritans from, 135n*45*; Rev. John Rowe in, 165n*12*; mentioned, 36, 79
Bristol, Pa., 49, 57, 140n*3*
British officers in America: and treaty of peace, 47; and Americans, 47, 48
British soldiers in Ireland: cruel treatment of American prisoners of war by, 5, 41; unbridled licence of, 41; cruel treatment of Roman Catholics by, 41, 42, 135n*47*; assassination of Rev. WH threatened by, 42; attack on civilians by, 43, 136n*51*
British troops in America: Gomez family driven out of New York by, 52; devastation of Newport, R. I., by, 60; at the battle of Bunker Hill, 65, 78, 150n*56*; landing near Weymouth by, 66
Bunker Hill, battle of, 65, 78, 150 n*56*, 160n*114*
Burlington, N. J.: the Hazlitt family at, 5, 49, 57; the New

Jersey Assembly meets at, 5, 49; Rev. WH preaches at, 5, 49; Governor's mansion at, 49, 140 n*5*
Bush, Mr. Justice, of Philadelphia, 120
Butt, Susan, 79, 90, 160n*115*
Butts, Martha. *See* Tyler, Mrs. Elisha
Butts, Susanna. *See* Butt, Susan

Calvin, John, 55, 69
Calvinism, 55, 121
Camberwell, England, 100, 101
Cambridge, Mass.: college at, 92; ferry between Boston and, 93
Cape Cod: visited by Rev. WH and WH, 73, 157n*95*; description of, 73; cod fishery carried on by people of, 77-78; whaling and sealing carried on by people of, 78; sand and fish at, 128n*25*; mentioned, 83, 84. *See also* Truro, Mass.
Card games: palm loo, 90; whist, 90
Carlisle, Pa.: Rev. WH preaches at, 6, 51, 117; refuses to subscribe to confession of faith at, 51, 117, 118; departs too hastily from, 118
Carson, Dr. John: and Rev. WH, 51, 120; proposes publication of Rev. WH's sermons, 119; sketch of, 142n*14*
Cashel, Rock of, 31, 32, 130n*4*
Castlebar, Ireland, 33
Castle William, Boston Harbor: view of, 78; lighthouse at, 78, 82, 83; defense of Boston Bay by, 92; garrison at, 92; chaplain at, 92; on Castle Island, 160n*113*
Centreville, Md.: Rev. WH preaches at, 6, 54, 144n*26*; rebuffed at, 6, 144n*26*; description of, 54; people of, 54; Joseph Haslett at, 130n*8*, 144n*26*
Charleston (Charlestown), S. C.: Rev. WH declines settlement at, 56; heat in, 56
Chauncy, Rev. Charles: meeting of Boston Association of Ministers at the home of, 10,

115; and Rev. WH, 71, 115, 152 n70; sketch of, 71, 153n75; *The Benevolence of the Deity Fairly and Impartially Considered*, 71, 153n75; *The Mystery Hid from the Ages, or The Salvation of All Men*, 71, 153n75; member of the Boston Association of Ministers, 114; and Rev. John Clarke, 154n78

Cherokee chiefs, 62

Chess, 90

Chester, England, 39

Child prodigies, MH on, 45

Christ: twofold nature of, 10, 116; doctrines of, 55

Christie, William, 113

Christmas: at the Bootts' home in Boston, 81, 90; in Wem, 104; mentioned, 72

Church buildings in America, 69

Church of England, 33, 104

Cincinnati, Society of the: and Rev. WH, 50, 51; meetings of the State Society of Pennsylvania, 140n8; meeting of the General Society, 140n8, 141n9; and Gen. Benjamin Lincoln, 152 n72

Civil Wars of 1642-1646 and 1648-1651, 31, 32, 130n3

Clarke, Rev. John, 71, 114, 154n78

Clarke, Dr. Samuel, 11

Climate: in Maryland, 54; in South Carolina, 56; in Massachusetts, 62

Clugston, Rev. Mr., of Bandon, 134n43

Clugston, Mrs., of Bandon, 40

Cobbett (Cobbet), William, 57

Cobh, Ireland. *See* Cove, Ireland

Coleraine, Ireland, 123, 148n49

Coleridge, Samuel Taylor: and JH, 20; Joseph Swanwick's impression of, 165n13; preaches in Rev. WH's pulpit at Wem, 165 n13

Collins, Bet, 71

Columbia (Columbo, Calumba) root, 55, 145n28

Combe Down, near Bath, England, 23

Common Hall, University of Penn-

sylvania: Rev. WH lectures at, 6, 118, 145n30

Congregationalism, 9

Conscience, liberty of. *See* Liberty of conscience

Continental Congress, 47, 121, 130 n8, 142n15

Conversation: life and spirit of, in Cork, 44

Cooper, Mrs., of Maidstone, 101, 164n6

Cooper, James, 71, 72, 164n6

Cooper, Rev. Samuel: contrasted with Rev. WH, 146n36; church of, 146n37, 148n47

Copley (Copely), John Singleton: *Esau and Jacob*, by, 63, 64, 149 n52; in England, 64; early paintings of, 149n52

Cork, County of, 5

Cork, Ireland: Hazlitt family at, 44, 45; Rev. Samuel Perrot of, 44, 137n58; Bradshaw Popham of, 44; Reuben Harvey of, 45, 137n60; mentioned, 39, 40

Cottam, William, 105-106

Coulson, Miss, of Peterborough, 34, 132n19

Court of Inquiry: Miss Rolt testifies at, 43; and Rev. WH, 43, 136n49, 148n47; results of, 43, 136n50

Cove, Ireland: Hazlitt family at, 45; description of, 45; departure of Hazlitt family from, 45, 46; name of, 138n61. *See also* Cobh, Ireland; Queenstown, Ireland

Cowes, Isle of Wight, 88

Coxe (Cox), Tench: and Rev. WH, 48, 120, 139n1; sketch of, 139n1; *A View of the United States of America*, 139n1; and the Hazlitt family of New Jersey, 139n1

Cranch, Lucy: letter to Abigail Adams, 159n104

Cranch, Mary Smith. *See* Cranch, Mrs. Richard

Cranch, Richard, 62, 148n46

Cranch, Mrs. Richard (Mary Smith): Hazlitts' claimed relationship to, 62; brant provided by, 63; marriage of, 148n46-47;

letters to Abigail Adams, 148 n*47*, 159n*104*

Crediton, England: residence of the Rev. WH and his wife and daughter at, 12; death of Rev. WH at, 12, 23; death and burial of GLH at, 15; settlement of the Rev. John Johns at, 23; 129n*1*; dedication of MH's journal signed at, 30; mentioned, 165n*12*

Crèvecoeur, Michel Guillaume Jean de (J. Hector St. John). *See Letters from an American Farmer*

Cromwell, Oliver, 103

Cushing, Capt., of the *Nonpareil,* 94, 95

Cushing, Beale (Bela): playmate of WH, 20, 66; and Capt. Abiah Whitman, 66; and his Jew's-harp, 66; sketch of, 150n*60*

Customs: inspection at Dublin, 39-40; and smugglers, 99

Cuzeeno, Mrs., of Boston, 96

Dana, Rev. Edmund, 51, 142n*15*

Dana, Francis, 51, 142n*15*

Darby, Elias Hasket. *See* Derby, Elias Hasket

Davidson, James: and Rev. WH, 51, 80, 120; and GLH, 54; sketch of, 142n*17*

Davidson, Mrs. James (Margaret Linn), 51, 142n*17*

Davidson, Robert: and Dr. John Ewing, 51; *Geography Epitomized; or, A Tour Round the World,* 51, 142n*17*; sketch of, 142n*17*

Davies, Patty, 90

*Death of Clorinda, The* (Lana), WH's copy of, 108

De la Motte, Mr., aboard the *Henry,* 46

Derby, Madam (Sarah Langley Hersey Derby). *See* Derby, 2nd Mrs. Richard

Derby (Darby), Elias Hasket: and Rev. WH, 72, 156n*89*; character of, 72, 121; and Russian trade, 72, 156n*90*; and East India trade, 156n*90*

Derby, Elias Hasket, Jr., 156n*90*

Derby, Richard, 153n*73*, 156n*89*

Derby, 1st Mrs. Richard (Mary), 156n*89*

Derby, 2nd Mrs. Richard (Sarah Langley Hersey): and WH, 21, 70, 72; and Rev. WH, 70, 72; sketch of, 70, 153n*73*; and MH, 70, 72; and GLH, 72; and Elias Hasket Derby, 156n*89*

Derby, England, 81, 154n*82*

Derry, Ireland. *See* Londonderry, Ireland

Devonshire, England, 12, 92, 129 n*1*, 163n*142*

*Dialogues of Feskwick,* 157n*97*

Dicken (Dickin), George: in Liverpool, 106; playmate of WH, 166n*20*

Dickinson College: founding of, 6, 51; Dr. John Ewing and, 6, 118; Rev. WH and, 6, 51, 118; Dr. Benjamin Rush and, 6; Rev. Robert Davidson and, 142n*17*

Dissenters: and the Rev. James Hazlitt, 33; and the death of Queen Anne, 36; mentioned, 43, 144n*26*

Dissenting congregations in England and Ireland: at Wisbeach, 5, 34, 132n*20*; at Marshfield, 5, 36; at Maidstone, 5, 37, 39; at Bandon, 5, 39, 40, 43, 44, 135 n*45*; at Wem, 12, 104; at Crediton, 23, 129n*1*; at Bristol, 36-37; at Shrewsbury, 103; at Whitchurch, 104

Divine Unity, doctrine of, 56

Doctors' Commons, 115

Dolphins, 97

Dorchester, Mass.: residence of Hazlitt family at Lower Dorchester, 6, 61; residence of Hazlitt family at Upper Dorchester, 6, 78-94 *passim*; Rev. WH preaches at, 6, 120; JH paints at, 15; WH at, 21; departure of Hazlitt family from Lower Dorchester, 62; description of Upper Dorchester, 78, 89; view from Upper Dorchester, 78; neighbors of the Hazlitts in Upper Dorchester, 79, 89, 90, 160n*115-116*, 160n*118*; departure of Hazlitt family from Upper Dorchester, 90, 94; mentioned, 83, 87, 88, 92

Dorchester Heights: seen from Weymouth, 65; fortified by Americans, 149n55

Dover, England, 88, 89, 162n136

Dover, Strait of, 88, 162n135

Downs, the, 88, 162n135

Drawing school, in Boston, 15

Dress: of ladies in Ireland, 44; of Lucy Jones, 76; of Susan Butt, 90, 162n139

Dublin, Ireland: Rev. James Hazlitt in, 33; arrival of Hazlitt family at, 39, 40; their stay in, 40

—Barracks, 40

—Barrack Street, 134n41

—Basin, 40, 134n41

—Eustace Street Chapel, 38, 134 n34

—St. Mary's Church, 33, 131n11

—St. Paul's Church, 131n11

—St. Stephen's Green, 40, 134n41

Duffield, Dr. George, 117

Dunckerley, Joseph, 15

Earl, Mr., of St. Paul's Parish, Md., 54, 118

Earle, Richard Tilghman, 54, 118, 145n27

Earthquakes: felt in Philadelphia (1783), 55, 145n29; felt in Weymouth (1786), 75; felt in Boston, Salem, Mystic, and Beverly (1786), 159n107

East Indiamen: in English Channel, 99; and smugglers, 99. *See also Halsewell* (East Indiaman)

East Indies, American trade with, 156n90

Eddystone Lighthouse, 87

Edinburgh, University of: Rev. John Johns at, 129n1; Dr. John Vize at, 136n54; Dr. Benjamin Rush at, 141n13; Dr. John Carson at, 142n14

Education in America: MH on, 92, 93

"Elakistoteros." *See* Parker, Rev. Samuel

Eliot, Rev. John: and Rev. WH,

10, 71, 115; member of Boston Association of Ministers, 114; and Rev. Jeremy Belknap, 146 n37, 151n66, 154n79; on Rev. WH, 146n37, 151n66; sketch of, 154n79

Elwall, trial of: Priestley's work on, republished by Rev. WH, 73, 157n97

Ely, Isle of, 5, 34

Emmet, Catherine, 23, 136n52

Emmet, Christopher Temple, 23

Emmet, Robert, 23, 136n52

Emmet, Thomas Addis, 136n52

Enderwick, Mrs., of Boston, 60

England: Rev. WH in, 5, 33, 89; Rev. WH sails for, 9, 73, 81; epidemic in, 37; Americans' regard for, 78; English merchants' nostalgia for, 81; contrasted with America, 81, 82, 101-102; Rev. WH approaches, 87, 88; WH prefers America to, 128n25; mentioned, 12, 19, 20, 21, 53, 79, 80, 83, 92, 95, 100, 115, 122

English "ceremonial unsociality": WH on, 22

English Channel, 86, 88, 99

English scenery: at Marshfield, 36; at Tenterden, 38; at Winterslow, 110; mentioned, 19

Episcopal bishops in America: and Rev. James Freeman, 10, 11, 114

Episcopal churches in America: King's Chapel, in Boston, 9, 73, 114, 116; in Philadelphia, 50, 140n7; in Massachusetts, 69; Rev. Samuel Parker and, 114, 115; in Maryland, 118; mentioned, 10

Erin, 32

*Esau and Jacob,* painting by Copley, 63

Establishment, the, 115, 122

Evans, Rev. David, 37, 133n27, 133 n28

Evans, Mrs. David, 37

Everett (Everrit), Rev. Oliver: and Rev. WH, 71; member of Boston Association of Ministers, 114; sketch of, 154n80

Ewing, Dr. John: recommends

Rev. WH, 6, 117; friendship with Rev. WH, 51, 80, 118, 120; and GLH, 54; recommends Rev. WH's lectures, 119; sketch of, 142n*16*

Fagg's Manor, Pa., Presbyterian church of, 141n*10*
Falmouth, Maine. *See* Portland, Maine
Fires: supposed ship fire in Boston, 80; Boston fire of 1787, 91-92, 162n*140*
First Unitarian Church in Boston: Rev. WH and formation of, 9-11, 115-116
Fish: mackerel, 47; black fish, 60; codfish, 77, 87, 98; sturgeon, halibut, turbot, sole, 77; pilot fish and sharks, 97, 163n*147*; tautog or black sea bass, 147n*40*
Fishing: for mackerel, 47; in New England seas, 77; off the Newfoundland Banks, 98; mentioned, 52
*Fish Stealers by Moonlight,* a print, 101
Fleming, Rev. Caleb: and Rev. WH, 38; sketch of, 133n*30*
Flowers: violets, 45; apricot blossoms, 49
Folger (Folgier), Capt. George, 82, 83, 84, 86, 162n*126*, 162n*136*
Fort Independence, Boston Harbor, 160n*113*
Fort William. *See* Castle William, Boston Harbor
Fourteenth Regiment of Light Dragoons, in Ireland, 135n*48*, 136n*50*
Fourth of July. *See* Independence Day
Fowl, wild and tame, in America, 77
Fownes, Rev. Joseph, 102, 165n*11*
France: coast of, 88; WH in, 108; Francis Dana and John Adams in, 142n*15*; Abigail Adams in, 148n*47*; detention of British tourists in, 166n*26*
Franklin, Benjamin: and Rev. WH, 5; and Thomas Viny, 5, 133n*33*; house of son of, 49; and

Reuben Harvey, 137n*60*, 138 n*63*; and Crèvecoeur's *American Farmer,* 138n*63*; son of, 140n*5*
Franklin, Sir William, 49, 140n*5*
Freeman, Rev. James: early career of, 9-10, 113-114; friendship with Rev. WH, 10, 71, 115, 116; reformation of liturgy by, 11, 73, 116; ordination of, 11, 113, 114, 116; letters to Rev. Theophilus Lindsey from, 12; and Rev. William Bentley, 12; and WH, 21, 128n*25*; and Boston Association of Ministers, 114; letter to Rev. WH from, 128 n*25-26*; and MH, 128n*26*; sketch of, 153n*77*; letter from Rev. WH to, 162n*137*
Freeme, Mr., of Marshfield, England, 36
French Revolution, 103
*Friendly Dialogues,* 157n*97*
Fundy, Bay of: Rev. WH escapes drowning in, 74, 159n*101*

Gamble, Cornet John, 42, 135n*48*
Gardens: in Ireland, 40, 45; in America, 64; in England, 100
Gay, Rev. Ebenezer: ministry in Hingham, Mass., of, 9, 120, 121; JH's portrait of, 16, 156n*91*; sketch of, 70, 152n*69*; anecdote concerning, 70, 152n*70*; death of, 73, 81; and Charles Chauncy, Jonathan Mayhew, and Simeon Howard, 152n*69*
George and Hannah, orphans: fate of, 98; sailors' superstition concerning George's fate, 98
Germantown (German Town), Pa.: Rev. WH asked to take a school at, 53; uninfected by yellow fever, 53, 144n*23*; MH regrets her family's not settling at, 53
Gilles, Capt., aboard the *Henry,* 46, 47
Glasgow, University of: Rev. WH at, 4, 5, 33, 132n*14*; certificates of Rev. WH's attendance at, 33, 130n*5*; Rev. John Haslet at, 130 n*8*; Rev. James Hazlitt at, 131

n*10*; financial assistance given Rev. WH at, 132n*14*
Gloucestershire, England, 5, 15, 36
Godwin, Mr. (grandfather of William Godwin), 34
Godwin, Rev. John, 34, 132n*20*
Godwin, Mrs. John (Anna Hull), 35, 132n*20*
Godwin, William: and JH, 20; circle of, 20; grandfather of, 34; *Political Justice*, 34, 132n*20*; and MH, 34; and Grace Loftus, 34, 35; father of, 34, 132n*20*; *Caleb Williams*, 35, 132n*20*; mother of, 35, 132n*20*; sketch of, 132n*20*
Gomez, Benjamin, 52, 143n*18*
Gomez, Daniel (son of Moses D. Gomez), 52, 59, 147n*38*
Gomez, Deborah, 52
Gomez, Deborah De Leon, 52, 143 n*18*
Gomez, Esther (wife of Moses D. Gomez), 52, 143n*18*
Gomez, Esther (niece of Moses D. Gomez), 52, 143n*18*
Gomez, Isaac (nephew of Moses D. Gomez), 52, 143n*18*
Gomez, Isaac, Jr. (son of Moses D. Gomez), 52, 143n*18*
Gomez, Mattathis (Matthias), 52, 143n*18*
Gomez, Moses Daniel, 52, 143n*18*
Gomez family, of New York: and Hazlitt family, 52, 59; history of, 52, 143n*18*; in New York, 52, 59, 143n*18*
Gordon, Dr. William: in Jamaica Plain, 61; *History of the Rise, Progress, and Establishment of the Independence of the United States of America*, 61, 147n*43*; publishes his *History* in England, 61, 81, 147n*43*; sketch of, 147n*43*
Gray, Mrs., of Boston, 61. *See also* Gray, Catherine
Gray, Catherine, 147n*44*. *See also* Gray, Mrs., of Boston
Gregory, Mrs., of New York, 48
Gregory, John: and Rev. WH, 71; and Hazlitt family, 71, 95; and Kirk Boott and his family,

80, 81; present to a young lady from, 96; sketch of, 155n*84*

Hackney College: WH at, 107; WH's departure from, 107, 108; Joseph Swanwick at, 165n*13*
Hair dressing: in America, 90; in Ireland and England, 96
Haislet, Mr. *See* Hazlitt, Rev. William
Half way house: Rev. WH at, 86; farce of the, 98
Hallowell, Maine: Rev. WH preaches at, 9, 74, 120, 157n*98*; rejected at, 9, 157n*98*; description of, 73, 74, 157n*98*; people at, 74
*Halsewell* (East-Indiaman): wreck of, 99, 164n2; prints showing wreck of, 100; china and tea boards showing wreck of, 100. *See also* East Indiamen
Hancock, John: wife of, 63; house of, 93; and Rev. WH, 93; birth and death of, 163n*145*
Hancock, Mrs. John (Dorothy Quincy): Hazlitts' claimed relationship to, 63, 93, 149n*51*; and Rev. WH, 93
Hartford College, 93. *See also* Yale College
Harvard College: MH on, 92-93; graduates of, 142n*15*, 152n*69*, 152n*71-72*, 153n*73-75*, 153n77, 154n*78-81*; Rev. Isaac Smith librarian at, 163n*142*; founding of, 163n*143*
Harvey, Reuben: friend to Americans, 45; and Hazlitt family, 45; sketch of, 137n*60*; assists American prisoners of war in Ireland, 137n*60*; correspondence with Washington and Franklin, 137 n*60*, 138n*63*
Harvey, Mrs. Reuben (Elizabeth Wheddon), 137n*60*
Haslet (Hazlitt), Mrs. Harriet (supposed wife of Col. John Haslet), 148n*49*
Haslet (Haslett, Hazlitt), Col. John: Rev. WH's relationship to, 33, 130n8, 130n9; sketch of, 33, 130n8; daughter of, 51, 141

n*11*; minister at Bandon, 135 n*45*; W. C. Hazlitt on, 148n*49*
Haslet, Mrs. John (Jemima Molleston Brinckle), 148n*49*
Haslet (Hazlet, Hazlitt), Polly, 51, 141n*11*
Haslett, Joseph, of Straw, County Derry, 130n*8*
Haslett, Dr. Joseph (son of Joseph Haslett, of Straw): Rev. WH's relationship to, 130n*8*; sketch of, 130n*8*; and St. Paul's Church, Centreville, Md., 144n*26*
Haslett, Joseph (son of Dr. Joseph Haslett), 144n*26*
Haslett, William (son of Joseph Haslett, of Straw), 130n*8*
Haslett, William, Jr., of Fagg's Manor, Pa., 141n*10*
Haslett family, of Fagg's Manor, Pa., and Rev. WH's family, 51, 141n*10*
Hazard, Ebenezer: and Rev. Jeremy Belknap, 146n*36*
Hazlett, Mr. *See* Hazlitt, Rev. William
Hazlett, James (son of Robert Hazlett, of New Jersey), 139n*1*
Hazlett, Robert, of New Jersey, 139n*1*
Hazlett, Samuel (son of Robert Hazlett, of New Jersey), 139n*1*
Hazlett family of New Jersey: and Tench Coxe, 139n*1*; and Rebecca Coxe, 139n*1*; and Rev. WH's family, 139n*1*
Hazlitt, Elizabeth (MH's aunt). *See* McClelland, Mrs. Robert
Hazlitt, Esther (MH's sister), 50, 54, 57
Hazlitt, Grace Loftus (MH's mother). *See* Hazlitt, Mrs. William (Grace Loftus)
Hazlitt, Harriet (MH's sister), 44, 50, 57
Hazlitt, Rev. James (MH's uncle): education of, 33, 131n*10*; ministry of, 33, 131n*10*, 131n*11*; in Dublin, 33; in Castlebar, 33; as a magistrate, 33; marriages of, 33, 131n*13*; children of, 33, 131 n*13*; visited by Hazlitt family, 33, 40; *Eight Sermons upon Different Subjects*, 131n*10*; story of his elopement with Anne Brazier, 131n*12*; later career of, 131 n*12*
Hazlitt, 1st Mrs. James (Margaret Moffet), 131n*13*
Hazlitt, 2nd Mrs. James (Margaret Sherlock), 131n*13*
Hazlitt, 3rd Mrs. James (Anne Brazier), 131n*12*, 131n*13*
Hazlitt, James (MH's cousin, son of Rev. James Hazlitt), 131n*13*
Hazlitt, Jane or Jennie (MH's aunt), 131n*12*
Hazlitt, John (MH's grandfather), of Shronell: poverty of, 31, 123; character of, 32, 123; mentioned, 4
Hazlitt, Col. John (MH's uncle): in America, 32; serves in Revolution under Washington, 32, 33, 130n*9*; death of, 32
Hazlitt, John (MH's brother): portrait of his father by, 13; birth of, 15, 133n*26*; in America, 15; his painting, 15; plan for a drawing school in Boston, 15; miniatures of the Rev. William Bentley, Rev. WH, and WH, 15; picture of MH, 15; his painting for Samuel Vaughan, 16, 89; portraits done in Hingham, 16, 72, 156n*91*; painted panels attributed to, 16, 19; return to England, 19; appearance of, 19; wins praise from Sir Joshua Reynolds, 19, 164n*8*; exhibits at the Royal Academy, 19, 164n*8*; in the Godwin circle, 19, 20; marriage of, 20; character of, 20; death of, 20, 24, 164n*8*; fondness for his brother William, 20; miniature of WH by, 20, 21; miniature of MH by, 22; delights and disappointments on journey from Dublin to Cork, 40; in Bandon, 40; trusted with secret of escaped prisoners, 41; in Cork, 44; and seasickness, 47; in New York, 48; sees George Washington in Philadelphia, 51, 141n*9*; goes on an outing, 52; rides alone from Philadelphia

to Centreville, Md., 55; visits Gomez family in New York, 59; rides around Newport, R. I., 60; in Providence, R. I., 60, 61; in Weymouth, Mass., 63; and painting of Esau and Jacob, 63; childish exploits of, 65; accompanies father to Boston, 68; spends much time in Milton, 69, 152n*67*; cuts ice in wash house, 69; and Kirk Boott, 81; teaches WH Latin grammar, 89, 162n*138*; gives Susan Butt a picture of MH done in crayons, 90; pleasant evenings in America of, 90; tries to assist friends during Boston fire of 1787, 92, 162n*140*; presents a bird from America to a young lady in England, 96; views Portsmouth, 99; begins career as a miniature painter in London, 102, 164n*8*; miniature of Governor John Winthrop by, 128n*17*; miniature of Mrs. Harriet Haslet (Hazlitt) by, 148n*49*

Hazlitt, Mrs. John (Mary Pierce), 20

Hazlitt, John (MH's cousin, son of Rev. James Hazlitt), 33, 131 n*13*

Hazlitt, Kilner (MH's cousin, son of Rev. James Hazlitt), 33, 131 n*13*

Hazlitt, Loftus (MH's brother), 37

Hazlitt, Margaret (MH's grandmother), of Shronell: character of, 32; burial of, 123; mentioned, 4

Hazlitt, Margaret (Peggy): journal of, 3, 4, 14, 15; purpose in writing journal, 4; JH's portrait of, 15; pictures of her brother William in America, 20; birth of, 22, 39, 134n*39*; talents of, 22, 24, 128n*26*, 148n*47*; JH's miniature of, 22; appearance of, 22; character of, 22, 23, 24; undiversified life of, 22; in America, 22; nostalgia for the United States, 22; devotion to her brothers and her parents, 23; friendship with Catherine Emmet, 23, 136n*52*; friendship with Rev. and Mrs.

John Johns, 23, 129n*1*; death of, 24, 129n*31*; Rev. John Johns' tribute to, 24; religious sentiments of, 24; complaints about life in Wem, 25; pleasant recollections of America, 25; style and veracity of her journal, 25, 27; history of her journal, 25-26; dedication of her journal to the Rev. and Mrs. Johns, 25, 26, 30, 129n*1*; addresses her recollections to her nephew William, 31; begins her recollections, 31; and William Godwin, 34, 35; and her grandparents, Thomas and Grace Pentlow Loftus, 34, 35, 36; regard for recollections, 36; regrets father's not being chosen at Bristol, 37; visit to Maidstone, 37, 133n*29*; visit to Tenterden, 38; trip from Maidstone to Holyhead, 39; on sight of Welsh peasants, 39; and Penmaenmawr, 39, 134n*40*; amusement at Holyhead, 39; voyage to Dublin, 39; recollections of Dublin, 39, 40, 134n*41*; delights and disappointments on journey from Dublin to Cork, 40; in Bandon, 40; trusted with secret of escaped prisoners, 41; hears father insulted by British officers, 42; friends at Bandon, 43, 44, 136n*53*, 137n*55*; and Mrs. Vize, 43, 44, 136n*54*; and Miss Rolt, 44; attends fashionable parties in Cork, 44, 45; at Reuben Harvey's, 45; in Cove, 45; on the *American Farmer*, 46; arrival in New York, 47, 48; catches and eats mackerel, 47; cooks for the whole family, 48; in Burlington, N. J., 49; recollections of Philadelphia, 50; narrow escape from a snake, 52, 53; on earthquakes, 55, 75, 159 n*107*; wishes father had settled in Pittsburgh, Pa., 56; regrets leaving Philadelphia, 57; and a Newfoundland dog, 58; and a gentleman named Shakespeare, 58; in New York, 59; admires Long Island Sound, 59; admires beauty of Narragansett Bay, 60; in Providence, R. I., 60, 61; on Rev. William Gordon, 61; her interest in the fate of fellow travelers, 61; in Boston, 61; and Indians, 61, 62; walks from Braintree to Weymouth, 62; her description of house in Weymouth, 63, 64; delighted with a painting of Esau and Jacob, 63; childish exploits of, 65; and Capt. Whitman, 65, 150n57; loves the roaring of the sea, 66; rambles about Weymouth, 67; reads for amusement, 67; on birds, 67, 68; and Madam Derby of Hingham, 70, 153n73; on Elias Hasket Derby and his sons, 72, 156n89-90; and Mr. Beales, 75, 159n106; and Lucy Jones, 76; sees pineapples in Philadelphia market, 76; on animals in America, 77; and Florida, 77; interest in trees, 78; in Upper Dorchester, 78; friends there, 79, 160n115-116, 160n118; prepares tea party for Rev. and Mrs. John Lathrop, 79; visits at Dr. Lathrop's in Boston, 79, 80, 160n119; receives advice from father, 79; feels at ease with the Lathrops, 80; and Lathrop children, 80, 161n120; and Mrs. Lathrop, 80; visits the Bootts in Boston, 80, 81, 161n122; invited by the Bootts to visit America for a year or two after return to England, 81; attentive to her mother, 82; quotes from her father's journal, 82-88 *passim*; birthday of, 88; regrets leaving friends in America, 90; spends Christmas at Kirk Boott's, 90, 91; plays cards at Kirk Boott's, 90; dressed like a woman, 90, 91; and the excitement at the Bootts', 91; on Boston, 92; on education in America, 92, 93; nostalgia for places formerly visited, 94; departure from America, 94, 95; voyage to England, 95, 97-99; pleasures on the ocean, 97; arrival in Portsmouth, 99; attends to William in London, 101; delighted with a print from Boydell's shop, 101, 164n7; likes the people in Shrewsbury, 102; in Wem, 102, 103; describes house in Wem, 102; and Rev. and Mrs. Jenkins, 104; taught by WH, 106, 107; and people in Wem, 107; on WH as portrait painter, 108, 109; at Winterslow, 109, 110; on WH's writings, 109, 110, 167n28, 167n33; on WH's paintings, 110; rambles at Winterslow with Charles and Mary Lamb, 110, 167n35; on WH's lectures, 110, 167n36; friendship with Mary Lamb and Sarah Stoddart Hazlitt, 129n32

Hazlitt, Samuel (MH's cousin, son of Rev. James Hazlitt), 131n13

Hazlitt, Sarah Stoddart (MH's sister-in-law). *See* Hazlitt, Mrs. William (Sarah Stoddart)

Hazlitt, Thomas (MH's brother), 50

Hazlitt (Haislet, Hazlett, Hazlot, Hazzlet), Rev. William (MH's father): visit to North America of, 3; anniversary of the birth of, 3-4, 31; devotion to liberty and truth of, 4, 13, 31, 32, 43; a founder of Unitarianism, 4, 9, 12, 24, 56, 116, 120, 122; birth of, 4, 31, 130n2; education of, 4, 32, 33, 130n5, 132n14; religious sentiments of, 4-5, 6, 25; settlement with the Presbyterian congregation in Wisbeach, 5, 34, 132n18; marriage of, 5, 34, 132 n18; settlement in Marshfield, 5, 36; settlement in Maidstone, 5, 37, 39; friendships enjoyed during stay in Maidstone, 5, 38, 133n30; publication, under the pseudonyms of "Rationalis" and "Philalethes," of articles and sermons, 5; charge of a congregation in Bandon, 5, 40; assists American prisoners of war at Kinsale, 5, 41, 117, 148n47; arrival in New York, 5, 47, 48; preaches before the Jersey Assembly, 5, 49, 116, 140n*4*; preaches Unitarianism in Philadelphia, New London, and Carlisle, Pa., 5-6, 51, 116, 117, 141 n*10*; recommended for presidency of Dickinson College, 6; rebuffed as a dissenter in Centreville, Md., 6, 144n*26*; lectures on the Evidences of the Christian religion at the University of Pennsylvania, 6, 55, 118, 145 n*30*; republishes Priestley's Unitarian tracts, 6, 9, 73, 119, 157 n*97*; preaches at Brattle Street Church in Boston, 6, 56, 57, 146 n*36-37*; preaches to many other congregations in and near Boston, 6, 9; lectures in Boston, 6, 68, 150n*65*, 151n*66*; rejected as minister at Hallowell, Maine, 9, 157n*98*, 159n*100*; return to England, 9, 21, 162n*136*; lays foundation of Unitarianism in America, 9, 120, 122; influence on Rev. James Freeman in reforming liturgy and accepting lay ordination, 10-11, 115-116; publishes, under the pseudonyms of "Philalethes" and "A New Testament Christian," letters, articles, and a scriptural confutation of the Thirty-nine Articles, in support of Freeman's cause, 10-11, 116; influence on Rev. William Bentley, 12; Socinianism of, 12; settlement at Wem, 12, 165n*17*; retirement of, 12; death of, 12, 23, 130n2; accomplishments of, 12-13; later publications of, 13; influence on WH, 13, 14; JH's and WH's portraits of, 13; appearance of, 13; character of, 14, 146n*36-37*, 148n*47*; religious and political beliefs, 14; JH's miniature of, 15, 16; called the first Apostle of Unitarianism in Boston by Rev. John Johns, 24; parentage of, 31, 32; childhood and youth at Shronell, 31, 32; attitude toward his mother, 32; attitude toward his brother James, 33; in London, 33; officiates as a chaplain, 34, 132n*16*; acquaintance with people in Bath and Bristol, 36, 133n*25*; preaches to Lewin's Mead congregation, 36; rejected because of heresy, 37; esteemed by congregation in Maidstone, 37; nearest and most beloved friends of, 38, 133n*32-33*, 134 n*34*; and Benjamin Franklin, 38; enjoys friendship of members of his congregation in Maidstone, 38, 39, 134n*36-37*; removes to Bandon, near Cork, in Ireland, 39; friendships at Bandon, 40, 43, 136n*53-54*, 137 n*55*; correspondence with Maidstone friends, 40; gives offense by his freedom in writing and speaking, 41, 137n*56*; conceals escaped prisoners, 41, 148n*47*; and abuse of Catholics by British officers, 41, 42, 135n*47*; affidavits and papers of, 42; threatened with assassination, 42, 148n*47*; reports English officers to War Office, 42, 135n*48*; intercedes for officers at Court of Inquiry, 43, 136n*49*; in Cork, 44, 45; arrival in New York, 47, 48; Capt. Jefferson apologizes to, 47; and Tench Coxe, 48, 139n*1*; rents a house in Philadelphia, 49; grief at deaths of two children, 50; dines with Society of the Cincinnati, 50-51, 140n*8*; sees George Washington, 51, 141 n*9*; meets some of his kindred in New London, 51, 141n*10*; friends in Philadelphia, 51, 141 n*13*, 142n*14-17*; and Moses Daniel Gomez, 52, 143n*18*; and Samuel Vaughan, 53, 144n*22*; and Stephen Kingston and Joseph Wheeler, 53, 54, 144n*24-25*; faints in the pulpit of St. Paul's Church, Centreville, Md., 54, 144n*26*; cared for by Earl family, 54, 145n*27*; weak from yellow fever, 55; overlooked as founder of Unitarianism in America, 56, 145n*31*; invited to settle in Charleston, S. C. and Pittsburgh, Pa., 56, 145n*32-33*,

146n34-35; in Weymouth, Mass.,
62-78 *passim*; walks to Hingham,
65; walks from Weymouth to
Boston to lecture, 68; in Milton,
69, 152n67; cuts ice in wash
house, 69; preaches in Hingham,
69, 70, 148n47; his friends in
Hingham, 70, 152n71-72, 153
n73-74; his friends in Boston,
71, 153n75-77, 154n78-83, 155
n84-85; and James Lewis, 71,
155n86; preaches at Salem, 72,
127n10, 156n88; visits Elias
Hasket Derby, 72, 156n89-90;
takes WH into pulpit with him,
72; preaches at Scituate, 72,
148n47, 156n92; meets former
prisoners of war at Kinsale in
Marshfield, 72, 157n93; assists
Rev. Ebenezer Gay in Hingham,
72, 156n69; visits Cape Cod, 73,
157n95; assists Rev. James Freeman prepare a liturgy for King's
Chapel, 73; preaches a thanksgiving sermon at Hallowell,
Maine, 74, 157n98, 159n99;
escapes drowning in the Bay of
Fundy, 74, 159n101; gives MH
advice, 79; his American correspondents, 80; last summer in
America of, 81; his preference
for Hingham, 82; departure
from America, 82, 162n126; his
journal, quoted, 82-88 *passim*;
voyage to England of, 82-88; his
concern for his family, 83, 84,
87, 88; remembers MH's birthday, 88; arrival in Dover, 88, 89,
162n136; in London, 89; many
sincere friends in America, 94;
meets family in London, 100;
and David Lewis and David
Williams, 100, 101, 164n4-5;
takes his children to see a panorama, 101; takes MH to Boydell's shop, 101, 164n7; in Wem,
102; and Rev. John Rowe and
Rev. Thomas Jenkins, 103, 165
n12, 165n14; takes charge of a
school, 105; educates WH, 105;
disappointed by WH's giving up
study for the ministry, 107; his
account of the state of rational

religion in America, published
under the pseudonym of "An
Old Unitarian," in which he
refers to himself as Bereanus,
113-123; his suffering for his
attachment to American cause,
115; in the southern states, 115;
attends meeting of the Boston
Association of Ministers, 115;
and Dr. Benjamin Rush, 120;
gets cool reception in England,
122; on Unitarians and Unitarianism, 122, 123; contrasted
to Rev. Samuel Cooper, 146n36;
applies for use of Faneuil Hall,
150n65; his lectures in Boston
advertised, 150n65; his lectures
criticized by Rev. John Eliot,
151n66; uses pseudonym "A
Stranger's Friend" to defend
James Lewis against scurrilous
invectives in the newspapers,
155n86; prospects for settlement
in Hallowell, Maine, 157n98;
letter to WH, quoting a letter
from Kirk Boott, 161n123; letter
to Rev. James Freeman from,
162n137; a candidate for settlement in Norwich, England,
162n137; his sermons published,
167n27
—"Account of the State of
Rational Religion in America,
An," 113-123, 127n4; "Anecdote
of Sterne," 13; *Discourse on the
Apostle Paul's Mystery of Godliness Being Made Manifest in
the Flesh, A*, 9, 122, 128n13;
*Discourses for the Use of Fami-
lies*, 13, 134n36-37, 136n53-54,
137n55, 144n24-25, 164n5, 164n9,
166n21; *Essay on the Justice of
God, An*, 5; "Evidences of the
Truth of the Christian Religion," 6, 55, 68, 118, 150n65, 151
n66; *Human Authority, in Matters of Faith, Repugnant to
Christianity*, 5; "Man of Honour, The," 13; "Particulars of
Dr. Chauncey," 152n70; *Sermons
for the Use of Families*, 13, 156
n87; *Thanksgiving Discourse,
Preached at Hallowell, 15 December, 1785, A*, 9, 159n99

Hazlitt, Mrs. William (Grace Loftus): recollections of, 3; loved by grandson William, 4, 34; marriage of, 5, 34, 132n*18*; appearance of, 14, 34, 37, 38; JH's portrait of, 14; and the captain of the *Henry*, 14, 47, 138n*64*; health of, 14, 15, 47, 48, 100, 101; character of, 14, 15, 148n*47*; death of, 15, 24, 26, 132 n*17*, 165n*16*; resemblance of JH to, 19; parentage of, 34, 35, 36; and the Godwin family, 34, 35; residence in Marshfield, 36, 37; and the Smyths of Bristol, 37, 133n*25*; beloved by the people in Maidstone, 37, 38; friendships in Maidstone, 38, 133n*30*; in Bandon, 40; response to threats of assassination of Rev. WH, 42; gets news from Court of Inquiry, 42-43; in Cork, 44; arrival in New York, 47, 48; in New York, 48; wishes to settle in Burlington, N.J., 49; trial of deaths of children in Philadelphia, 50; attends wedding of Col. John Haslet's daughter, 51, 141n*11*; notified of Rev. WH's illness in Centreville, 54, 55; Bath and Bristol, Pa., bring back pleasing recollections of England to, 57; at Perth Amboy, 57, 58; visits Gomez family in New York, 59; in Providence, R. I., 60, 61; in Weymouth, Mass., 62-78 *passim*; and Mrs. Whitman, 66, 150n*57*; and Madam Derby, 72; and Sam Lathrop, 80, 161n*120*; offers of assistance from American friends to, 94; arrival in Portsmouth, 99, 164n*1*; in Walworth, 100; in Wem, 102; and Rev. and Mrs. Thomas Jenkins, 104; birth of, 132n*17*

Hazlitt, William (MH's brother): earliest years of, 3; influence of Rev. WH on, 13, 14; portrait of Rev. WH by, 13; tributes to his father by, 13; JH's miniature of, 15, 20, 21; birth of, 20, 39, 134n*39*; in

America, 20; memories of the United States, 20; American playmates of, 20; appearance as a child, 20-21; childhood at Weymouth, 21; studies at Upper Dorchester, 21, 162n*138*; genius recognized early, 21, 148n*47*, 161n*123-124*; and Kirk Boott, who wants to bring him up as a merchant, 21, 161n*124*; senses family's disillusionment with the United States, 21; first letter to Rev. WH from, 21, 162n*138*; his letter to Rev. WH from Liverpool, 21-22, 128n*25*; longing for America of, 22, 128n*25*; later career of, 22; in Cork, 44; at sea, 46, 47; in New York, 48, 59; and George Brewer, in Philadelphia, 52; at Perth Amboy, 58; and Maria weep aboard grounded sloop, 58-59; in Providence, R. I., 60; childhood at Weymouth, Mass., 62, 64; protected from the sun by a pear tree, 64; accompanies Rev. WH to Hingham, 65; brings home a dead black snake and tortoises, 65, 66; and Beale Cushing, 66, 150n*60*; Madam Derby, of Hingham, dotes on, 70; accompanies father to Salem, 72; accompanies father to Cape Cod, 73, 157n*95*; on barren and dreary look of Cape Cod, 73; loses a shoe with a silver buckle, 73; and Kirk Boott's offer to bring him up as a merchant, 81; taught Latin grammar by JH, 89, 162n*138*; intense application to studies later almost costs him his life, 89; arrival in Portsmouth, 99; and the garden at Walworth, 100; rambles about the streets in London, 101; affection for Wem of, 103, 106; taught by father, 105; overexertion in his studies brings on a fit, 105; saved from drowning, 105, 106; spends summer vacation in Liverpool, 106; studies French, 106; teaches MH, 106-107; enters Hackney College,

107; gives up studying for the ministry, 107; leaves Hackney College, 107; interest in painting, 107; relationship with brother, 107, 108; begins *Essay on the Principles of Human Action*, 108; paints portraits in Liverpool and Manchester, 108; copies paintings at the Louvre, 108; publishes his first metaphysical work, 109, 167n28; literary pursuits of, 109, 167n28, 167n33; marriage of, 109, 110, 167n29; residence at Winterslow of, 109; grief on the death of first-born child, 109, 167n31; paints at Winterslow, 109, 110; and Charles and Mary Lamb, 110, 167n35; removes family to London, 110; lectures at the Surrey Institution, 110; death of, 129n30; letter from Rev. WH to, 161n123; and Fanny Boott, 161n123; Kirk Boott on, 161 n123; a possible career in America for, 161n124; and Joseph Johnson, 167n27; lectures at the Russell Institution, 167n36

—*Abridgement of the Light of Nature Pursued, An,* 167n28; *Eloquence of the British Senate, The,* 167n28; *Essay on the Principles of Human Action, An,* 108, 167n28; *Memoirs of the Late Thomas Holcroft,* 109, 167 n33; *New and Improved Grammar of the English Tongue, A,* 109, 167n33; "Personal Character, On," 133n23; *Reply to the Essay on Population, A,* 109, 167 n28

Hazlitt, Mrs. William (Sarah Stoddart): marriage of, 109, 110, 167 n29; at Winterslow, 109; close relationship with MH, 129n32; death of, 167n29

Hazlitt, William (MH's nephew): MH's journal written for information and instruction of, 3, 4, 25; irony of MH's never giving the journal to, 25; *Literary Remains,* 25; journal addressed to, 31; MH's speculations concerning, 37; MH's direct address to, 57, 108; sketch of, 130n1; mentioned, 39

Hazlitt, William Carew (MH's great-nephew): on Rev. WH and WH, 13; on GLH and the captain of the *Henry,* 14, 138 n64; on Rev. WH and GLH and on GLH's health, 14, 15; on MH's artistic potential, 22; MH's journal shown to, 26; extracts from MH's journal published by, 26; *Four Generations of a Literary Family,* 26, 128n15, 148n49; *The Hazlitts: An Account of Their Origin and Descent,* 26, 128n15-16, 128n24-26, 129n27, 129n31, 130n5, 131n12-13, 132n15, 132n18, 132n21, 133 n29, 136n49, 138n64, 148n49, 161 n120, 161n123, 162n138, 166n20, 166n24; errors in transcription of and notes to MH's journal by, 27; on John Hazlitt, of Shronell, 123; *Memoirs of William Hazlitt, with Portions of His Correspondence,* 123, 127 n12; gives wrong date for death of MH, 129n31; on Rev. James Hazlitt, 131n12, 131n13; on date of Rev. WH and GLH's wedding, 132n18; on the Pentlows of Oxfordshire, 132n21; on MH's claims of a relationship between the Hazlitt family and the Adams and Quincy families, 148n49; on George Dicken, 166 n20; gives wrong date for death of Sarah Stoddart Hazlitt, 167 n29

Hazlitt family, of Shronell (*See* Appendix II for a genealogical chart of the Hazlitt family): papers of, 3, 25, 31; origin and history of, 3, 4, 31, 32; experiences in Ireland and England of, 3, 31-46 *passim*; visit to America of, 3; collateral branches of, 4, 130n8, 139n1, 141n10; and the Johns family, 23, 24; former opulence of, 31; poverty of, 31; departure from Maidstone, 39; in Dublin, 39,

40; in Bandon, 40; in Cork, 45; in Cove, 45; in New York, 48, 59; in Philadelphia, 49-57; in Providence, 60, 61; in Boston, 61; in Dorchester, 61, 78-94 *passim*; in Weymouth, 62-78; in London, 100, 101; in Wem, 102-107; described by Mary Cranch, 148n*47*

Hazlot, Mr. *See* Hazlitt, Rev. William

Hazzlet, Mr. *See* Hazlitt, Rev. William

Henley-on-Thames, England, 35

*Henry,* ship: Hazlitt family sails to America aboard, 45, 46, 47, 138n*64*; brings news of impending treaty of peace, 47, 139n*68*; arrival in New York reported, 138n*66*

Heresy: Rev. WH's, 14, 36-37; preaching against, 117, 120; circular letter on, 119

Hersey, Dr. Ezekiel, 153n*73*

High churchism, in Boston, 114

Highlands of Never Sunk, 47, 138 n*67*

High Street Congregation, Shrewsbury, 102, 165n*11*, 165n*12*, 166 n*18*

Hingham, Mass.: Rev. WH preaches at, 9, 69, 70, 72, 120, 148n*47*; JH paints at, 15, 16, 72; painted panels at, 16, 19; WH at, 20, 21, 72; road to, 65; Rev. WH's friends at, 70; aged members of congregation at, 71; large membership of congregation at, 71; Rev. WH's visits to, 81; Rev. WH's preference for, 82; historical sketch of congregation at, 120, 121. *See also* Old Meetinghouse, or "Old Ship" Church, Hingham

Hingham Historical Society, 19

*Hints and Essays by a Layman,* 157n*97*

Hodgson, Mr., of Liverpool, 107

Holcroft, Thomas: and JH, 20; WH's life of, 109, 167n*33*

Holyhead, Wales, 39, 134n*40*

Homans, Capt., of Upper Dorchester, 79, 160n*118*

Honour (the Hazlitts' Irish maid): runs away, 22, 47, 48 140n*2*

Houghton, Rev. John, 105, 165n*17*

Houghton, Rev. Pendlebury, 105, 165n*17*, 166n*18*

Howard, Rev. Simeon: and Rev. WH, 71; and Rev. Ebenezer Gay and Rev. Jonathan Mayhew, 152 n*69*; sketch of, 154n*81*

Hull, Mr. (William Godwin's grandfather), 35

Hull, England, 34

Hunter, Rev. Joseph: on JH, 20

*Hyppolito de Medici* (Titian). *See Ippolito de' Medici* (Titian)

Independence Day: departure of GLH and her children from Boston on, 95, 97

*Independent Chronicle* (Boston): advertisement of JH and Joseph Dunckerley in, 15

Indian corn, 76, 79

Indians: in Lower Dorchester, 61, 62; in Philadelphia, 62

Inns: in Marshfield, 37; in Holyhead, 39; in Dublin, 39; in Burlington, N.J., 57; in Perth Amboy, 57; in Boston, 61; in Portsmouth, England, 99; in London, 100; in Shrewsbury, 102; close to the Wrekin, 102

*Ippolito de' Medici* (Titian), WH's copy of, 108

Ireland: the Hazlitt family in, 5, 39-45, 148n*47*; their departure from, 5, 45, 46; British army in, 41-43; appeal for independence of, 137n*57*; mentioned, 4, 31, 51

Irish, the: in Ireland, 22, 23, 37, 135n*47*; in Philadelphia, 50

Irvine, Gen. William, 120

Jacobson, James, 38, 39, 134n*37*

Jacobson, James (son of James and Ann Bond Jacobson), 39, 134n*38*

Jacobson, Samuel, 38, 134n*37*

Jamaica Plain, Mass.: Rev. WH preaches at, 6, 120; MH on, 61; Rev. William Gordon at, 61, 147n*43*

Jefferson, Capt. Henry: and GLH,

14, 47, 138n*64*; and Hazlitt family, 46; and Rev. WH and Capt. Gilles, 47; arrival of his ship in New York reported, 138n*66*

Jeffries, Capt. *See* Jefferson, Capt. Henry

Jenkins, Rev. Thomas: and Hazlitt family, 103; sketch of, 104, 165n*14*; letter to Rev. WH from, 165n*10*

Jenkins, Mrs. Thomas, 104

Jersey Assembly. *See* New Jersey, Assembly of

Jersey woods: first seen by Hazlitt family, 47; Hazlitt family travels through, 49, 57

Jesuit, a suspected. *See* Shakespeare, Mr., at Perth Amboy

Jews, 52, 59, 66

Jew's-harp, 66

Job, book of, pamphlet on, 38, 39

Jocelyn, Sir Conyers. *See* Joscelyn, Sir Giles

Johnny cakes, 66

Johns, Rev. John: and MH and GLH, 23, 129n*1*; settlement in Crediton, 23, 129n*1*; marriage of, 23, 129n*1*; and the Liverpool Domestic Mission Society, 23, 24, 129n*1*; tribute to MH, 24; MH's dedication of her journal to, 25, 26, 30, 129n*1*; death of, 26, 129n*1*; children of, 26; sketch of, 129n*1*

Johns, Mrs. John (Caroline Reynell): marriage of, 23, 129n*1*; MH's dedication of her journal to, 25, 26, 30, 129n*1*; emigration to Australia of, 26; children of, 26

Johnson, Joseph, 109, 167n*27*, 167 n*28*

Jones, Lucy, 76, 160n*109*

Joscelyn, Sir Giles, 34, 132n*16*

Journal of Margaret Hazlitt: style of, 25; accuracy of, 25; dedication of, 25, 26; history of, 25-26; description of, 26; textual and annotation policy in, 27

Journal of Rev. William Hazlitt: cited by MH, 82-88 *passim*; disappearance of, 161n*125*

Kegs, battle of the, 65, 149n*55*

Keighley (Keily), Cornet Joseph, 42, 135n*48*

Kennebec River: a new settlement on, 73; Rev. WH on way to, 121; Priestley's *Appeal* found at, 122; mentioned, 56

Kent, England, 5, 37

Kilkenny, Ireland, 40, 134n*42*

King, Lt. John, 42, 135n*48*

King-Oak Hill, 65

King's Chapel: wardens of, 9; proprietors of, 11

Kingston, Stephen, in Philadelphia, 53, 144n*24*

Kingston family, of Bandon, 43, 53, 144n*24*

Kinsale, Ireland: American prisoners of war confined at, 5, 41, 127n*1*, 135n*46*

Kippis, Rev. Andrew: and Rev. WH, 5, 38; sketch of, 133n*30*; hymn book edited by, 135n*45*

Lamb, Charles: and JH, 20; praises miniature of MH, 22; at Winterslow, 110, 167n*35*

Lamb, Mary: at Winterslow, 110, 167n*35*; and MH, 129n*32*

Lathrop, Elizabeth (Betsey), 80, 161n*120*

Lathrop, Rev. John: and Rev. WH, 71, 80, 151n*66*; visit to the Tylers of, 79; and MH, 79, 89; member of Boston Association of Ministers, 114; sketch of, 153 n*76*; and Rev. William Bentley, 153n*76*; wife and children of, 160n*119*, 161n*120*; letter to Rev. WH from, 161n*120*

Lathrop, Mrs. John (Elizabeth Checkley Sawyer): visit to the Tylers of, 79; and MH, 79, 91; sketch of, 79, 80; children of, 160n*119*, 161n*120*

Lathrop, Samuel Checkley, 80, 161 n*120*

Leavitt, Elisha, 16

*Letters from an American Farmer:* MH on, 46; Benjamin Franklin recommends, 138n*63*; WH's liking for, 138n*63*

Lewin's Mead congregation, Bristol, 36
Lewis, David: and Hazlitt family, 39, 89, 100; and Rev. WH, 89, 101; misfortunes of, 101, 164n5; and JH, 102
Lewis, George, 38, 134n36, 156n87
Lewis, Rev. Israel: sketch of, 134 n36; classmate and friend of Dr. Price, 155n86; love of liberty of, 155n86; assistance given to American prisoners of war in England by, 155n86
Lewis, Israel, of Hampstead, 38, 134n36
Lewis, Mrs. Israel, 38, 101, 134n36
Lewis, James: and Hazlitt family, 71, 134n36; career of, 71; death of, 72, 101; and Boston merchants, 155n86; defended by Rev. WH, 155n86; sketch of, 155n86; debt due, 156n87
Lewis, Leyson, 38, 134n36
Liberty: civil and religious, 21, 155n86; of conscience, 93
Lincoln, Gen. Benjamin: JH's portrait of, 16, 156n91; and Rev. WH, 70, 120; sketch of, 152n72
Lindsey, Rev. Theophilus: revised Prayer Book of, 11, 73; and Rev. James Freeman, 12; and Rev. WH, 38, 157n97; sketch of, 133 n30
Linn (Lynn), Dr. John Blair: Dr. Priestley's antagonist, 119
Linn (Lynn), Rev. William: preaches against heresy of Rev. WH, 117; opposes circular letter on heresy, 119; wisdom of arguments of, 120
Little, Nina Fletcher, 16
Liturgy, King's Chapel, 11, 73, 116
Liverpool, England: WH writes from, 21; Rev. John Johns at, 23, 24, 129n1; MH dies at, 24; Mrs. Tracey at, 106; WH at, 106; WH paints at, 108; Rev. John Houghton of, 165n17; Rev. Pendlebury Houghton at, 166 n18; Mr. Railton of, 166n24
Liverpool Domestic Mission Society, 23-24, 129n1
Loftus, Mr. (great-grandfather of

MH): and the grandfather of William Godwin, 34; settles in Wisbeach, 34; watch made by, 34
Loftus, Grace. *See* Hazlitt, Mrs. William (Grace Loftus)
Loftus, Thomas (grandfather of MH): character of, 34; death of, 34; appearance of, 34; marriage of, 35, 36; children of, 36; mentioned, 5, 125
Loftus, Thomas (uncle of MH): and Miss Coulson, 34, 132n19; and GLH, 36; mother's death at home of, 100; and WH, 133n23
Loftus, Mrs. Thomas (Grace Pentlow): marriage of, 35, 36; fear of two trees cut into shape of giants, 35; and her father, 35; character and appearance of, 35, 36; children of, 36; in Marshfield, 37; visits Hazlitt family in London, 100; visited by GLH, 100; death of, 100; mentioned, 125
Loftus family, of Wisbeach: genealogical chart of, 125
London, England: JH in, 19, 102; MH visits at, 22; Rev. WH in, 33, 89, 100; Hazlitt family in, 39, 89, 100, 101; Dr. Gordon publishes in, 61, 81; departure of Hazlitt family from, 102; WH and family in, 110; mentioned, 76, 96, 99
—Essex Street Chapel, 73
—Margaret Street Chapel, 164n4
—Percy Street, 100, 101
—St. Anne's Church, Soho, 129n30
—Shakespeare Gallery, Pall Mall, 164n7
Londonderry, Ireland, 123, 130n8
Lovell, Gen. Solomon, 66, 150n59
Lovell family, of Weymouth, 66
Lower Dorchester. *See* Dorchester, Mass.
Lynn. *See* Linn

McClelland, Jane, 32
McClelland, Robert, 32, 130n7
McClelland, Mrs. Robert (Elizabeth Hazlitt), 32, 130n7
Mahometans, 52

Maidstone, England: Rev. WH's
ministry at, 5, 37, 38, 39; WH
born at, 20, 39; MH born at, 22,
39; Loftus Hazlitt dies at, 37;
visited by MH, 37, 133n29; Mr.
Wiche of, 38, 133n32; James
Lewis of, 71, 101; Lewis family
of, 134n36; Dr. Milner and the
Jacobson brothers of, 134n37;
mentioned, 38
Malthus, Thomas Robert, 109, 167
n28
Manchester, England: WH paints
at, 108
Marshfield, England: Rev. WH's
ministry at, 5, 36; JH born at,
15, 37; residence of Hazlitt family at, 36, 37; Rev. WH's hearers
at, 36; description of, 36; Loftus
Hazlitt born at, 37; Rev. David
Evans at, 37, 133n27, 133n28;
former ministers at, 133n24
Marshfield, Mass.:    Rev.    WH
preaches at, 6, 120; Rev. WH
meets two former prisoners of
war in Kinsale at, 72, 157n93;
Dr. David Barnes of, 121
Maryland: Rev. WH preaches in,
54, 56, 116, 118, 144n26; climate
of, 56. See also St. Paul's
Church, Centreville, Md.; St.
Paul's Parish, Centreville, Md.
Massachusetts: and Unitarianism,
122; Francis Dana's services to,
142n15; mentioned, 9
Mather, Rev. Cotton, 61, 147n45
Mather, Rev. Samuel, member of
Boston Association of Ministers,
114
Millar, Mr., of Nova Scotia: sketch
of, 95-96; and Hazlitt family, 99
Milner, Dr. Thomas, 38, 134n37
Milton, Mass.: Hazlitts pass
through, 62; Rev. WH at, 69,
152n67; JH at, 69, 152n67
Miniatures, by John Hazlitt: of
Rev. William Bentley, 15; of
Rev. WH, 15, 16; of WH, 15,
20, 21; of MH, 22; of Gov. John
Winthrop, 128n17; of Mrs. Har-
riet Haslet (Hazlitt), 148n49
Mitchell (Mitchel) family, of Phil-
adelphia, 52, 144n21

Monkeys, MH on, 67-68, 77, 150
n62, 160n110
*Monthly Repository*, 13, 113, 127
n4

Nantasket Road. *See* Nantucket
Road
Nantucket Island: cod fishery
carried on by people of, 77;
whaling and sealing carried on
by people of, 78
Nantucket Road, 82, 162n127
Narragansett Bay: description of,
60, 147n41
Nature: MH on, 32, 47
Negroes, 54, 58, 79, 160n117
Neptune, 98
Never Sunk, Highlands of, 47, 138
n67
New England: Episcopal church
in, 9; winter weather in, 55;
thaws in, 69; and the West In-
dies, 76; fishing in, 77; settle-
ment of, 93; education in, 93;
mentioned, 20
Newfoundland Banks: birds at,
85; fishing at, 98
New Hingham (Third Parish)
Church, 121, 153n74. *See also*
Shute, Rev. Daniel
New Jersey, 5, 47, 49, 57, 116, 138
n67, 139n1, 140n5
New Jersey, Assembly of: Rev.
WH preaches to, 5, 49, 116; published proceedings of, 140n4
New Jersey, College of: graduates
of, 141n13, 142n16, 153n76
New Jersey, woods of. *See* Jersey
woods
New London, Pa.: Rev. WH
preaches at, 6, 51, 117, 141n10;
meets some of his kindred at, 51,
141n10
Newport, R.I.: Hazlitt family at,
59, 60; description of, 60; state
house in, 147n42
"New Testament Christian, A."
*See* Hazlitt, Rev. William
New York: arrival of Hazlitt family at, 5, 47, 48; Mr. Gomez of,
52, 143n18; Hazlitt family visits
at, 59; Gomez family at, 59;
James Lewis and James Cooper

in, 71, 101; George Lewis's petition in, 156n87; mentioned, 22, 23, 26, 58

*Nonpareil*, ship, 95, 163n146, 164 n1

Norman Court, Winterslow, 109, 110

North Carolina, 56, 145n32

Northcote, James, 108, 166n25

Oland, William, 36, 133n24

Old meetinghouse, or "Old Ship" church, Hingham: and Rev. WH, 9, 20, 69, 70, 72, 120; WH at, 20; aged members of, 71; large membership of, 71; Rev. WH's preference for, 82; historical sketch of, 120, 121. *See also* Hingham, Mass.

Old North Church, Weymouth, 159n103

"Old Unitarian, An." *See* Hazlitt, Rev. William

Ordination of ministers: Episcopal ordination denied Rev. James Freeman, 10, 11, 114; lay ordination of Freeman, 11, 113, 116

Orthodoxy: and Rev. WH, 4, 14, 52, 116; benedictions and doxologies of, 10; confessions of faith of, 51; persecuting zeal of, 57, 115, 117

Osburne, Mr., of Marshfield, England, 36

Oxford, England, 35

Oxfordshire, England, 35

Packet, for Rhode Island, 59

Paddy. *See* Hazlitt, Rev. William

Painted panels, Hingham, sometimes attributed to JH, 16, 19

Painting: JH's practice in, 13, 15, 19, 20, 21, 22, 72, 89, 128n17, 148 n49; WH's practice in, 13; WH's enthusiasm for, 107; WH's attempts at, 107, 108, 109, 110

Palmer, Rev. John: and Rev. WH, 38; sketch of, 133n30; letter to Rev. WH from, 157n98

Paris, France: WH in, 108; Francis Dana and John Adams in, 142n15

Parker, Rev. Samuel: uses pseudonym "Elakistoteros," 10, 11; Rev. WH's controversy with, 10, 11; opposition to Rev. James Freeman of, 114, 115

Paul Revere House, 15

Peirce, Capt., of the *Halsewell* East Indiaman, 99, 164n2

Penmaenmawr, 39, 134n40

Penn, William, 57

Pennsylvania (Pensilvania): winter weather in, 55; Quakers in, 69; Rev. WH (Bereanus) in, 116

Pennsylvania, University of (formerly College of Philadelphia): Rev. WH lectures at, 6, 55, 68, 118, 145n30; Dr. Benjamin Rush of, 141n13; Dr. John Carson and, 142n14; Dr. John Ewing and, 142n16; James Davidson and, 142n17; Robert Davidson and, 142n17

Pentlow, Miss (half-sister of Grace Pentlow Loftus): frightened by a bat, 35; inheritance of, 35

Pentlow, Mr. (grandfather of GLH): sketch of, 35

Pentlow, Grace. *See* Loftus, Mrs. Thomas

Pentlow, Thomas, 132n21

Pentlow family, of Oxfordshire, 132n21

Perrot, Rev. Samuel, 44, 137n58

Perrot, Rev. Thomas, 137n58

Perth Amboy, N. J.: Hazlitts go to, 49, 57; inn at, 57, 58

Peterborough, England: Rev. WH and Grace Loftus marry at, 34; GLH's mother dies at, 100

Petty, Sir William, 2nd Earl of Shelburne, and 1st Marquis of Lansdowne, 43, 136n49, 148n47

Philadelphia, College of. *See* Pennsylvania, University of

Philadelphia, Pa.: residence of Hazlitt family at, 5, 49-57 *passim*; departure of Rev. WH from, 6; description of Hazlitts' house in Union Street, 49-50; description of, 50, 57, 140n6; George Washington at, 51, 141 n9; Hazlitt relatives at, 51; friends of the Hazlitts at, 51, 53,

120; the Hazlitts' neighbors in, 51, 52, 143n*18-20*, 144n*21*; weather at, 52; earthquake felt in, 55; departure of Hazlitt family from, 57; Indian chiefs at, 62; pineapples in market at, 76; Rev. WH preaches at, 116; churches in, 140n7; Gomez family in, 143n*18*; mentioned, 20, 49, 56, 68, 80, 122
—Christ Church, 141n*9*, 143n*19*
—City Tavern, 140n*8*
—First Presbyterian Church, 6, 141n*11*, 142n*16-17*
—St. Peter's Church, 51, 141n*9*
—Strawberry Alley, 49
—Swedes' Church (Gloria Dei), 143n*19*
—Union Street, 49, 51, 52
"Philalethes." *See* Hazlitt, Rev. William
Pierce, Mary. *See* Hazlitt, Mrs. John
Pittsburgh, Pa.: Rev. WH declines invitation from, 56, 146 n*35*; description of, 56, 146n*34*; MH on, 56, 145n*33*; Presbyterian church in, 145n*33*; lack of morality and order in, 146n*34*
Plymouth, England: Rev. WH sees 87; Rev. John Johns born and educated at, 129n*1*
Popham, Bradshaw, 44, 137n*55*, 137n*59*
Popham family, of Bandon, 44
Porpoises: sight of, 97; sailors' belief concerning, 97
Porter, Mr., of Philadelphia, 120
Portland (formerly Falmouth), Maine: Rev. WH in, 74; cat-a-mount appears near, 77; Rev. WH near, 121
Portraits, by John Hazlitt: of Rev. WH, 13; of MH, 15, 90; of Rev. Ebenezer Gay, 16, 156n*91*; of Gen. Benjamin Lincoln, 16, 156 n*91*; of Col. Nathan Rice, 16, 156n*91*; of Dr. Joshua Barker, 16, 156n*91*
Portsmouth, England: arrival of Hazlitt family at, 99, 164n*1*; description of, 99
Powis, Mr., aboard *Nonpareil*, 96

Pratt, William: and Rev. WH, 71; and Kirk Boott and his family, 80, 81; and MH, 91; sketch of, 154n*83*
Presbyterian congregations in America: in New London, Pa., 6, 117; in Carlisle, Pa., 6, 117, 142n*17*; in Fagg's Manor, Pa., 141n*10*; in Philadelphia, 50, 140n7; in Weymouth, 69; in Pittsburgh, Pa., 145n*33*, 146n*35*
Presbyterianism: in Massachusetts, 69; in South Carolina, 145n*32*; in Pittsburgh, Pa., 145n*33*, 146 n*35*
Presbyterian Synod of New York and Philadelphia: meets in Philadelphia, 119; and Priestley's *Appeal* published by Rev. WH, 119
Price, Dr. Richard: and Rev. WH, 5, 38, 115; sketch of, 133n*30*; and Lord Shelburne, 136n*49*; and Rev. Israel Lewis, 155n*86*
Priestley, Dr. Joseph: and Rev. WH, 5, 38; his *Theological Repository*, 5; his Catechism, 12; and Unitarianism in America, 56, 145n*31*; republishing of many of his Unitarian tracts, 73; *Triumph of Truth; Being an Account of the Trial of Mr. E. Elwall*, republished by WH, 73, 157n*97*; his writings studied, 114; and Dr. John Blair Linn, 119; *Appeal to the Serious and Candid Professors of Christianity*, 122, 157n*97*; sketch of, 133 n*30*; burning of the house of, 133n*31*; *A General View of the Arguments for the Unity of God*, 157n*97*
—Unitarian tracts: Rev. WH republishes, 6, 9, 73, 119, 157n*97*; and meeting of Presbyterian Synod of New York and Philadelphia, 119; copies sold, 120; found at Kennebec, 122
Prince, Rev. John, 156n*88*
Princeton (Prince Town), battle of, 33, 130n*8*, 130n*9*, 148n*49*
Providence (of God), 53, 83, 93, 94, 162n*140*

Providence, R. I.: Rev. WH preaches at, 6, 120; Hazlitt family at, 60; lodgings at, 60; ball at, 60, 61; location of, 147n*41*

Quakers: in Cork, 45; meetings of, 49; in Philadelphia, 50, 140 n7; in Massachusetts, 69
Queenstown, Ireland. *See* Cove, Ireland
Quincy, Dorothy. *See* Hancock, Mrs. John
Quincy, Lucy. *See* Tufts, Mrs. Cotton
Quincy family: Hazlitts' claimed relationship to, 62, 63, 76, 93, 148n*49*

Ram Island, 87
Rathcormac, Ireland, 40
"Rationalis." *See* Hazlitt, Rev. William
Rational religion: and Rev. WH, 4; Rev. WH's account of, in America, 113-123
*Rebecca,* a ship, 82, 162n*126*, 162 n*136*
Rebellion of 1798, 43, 136n*52*
Rebels: in Ireland, 33, 41, 137 n*56*; in America, 48
Reed, Mr., of Marshfield, England, 36
Renouf, Aaron. *See* Uncle Aron
Reynolds, Sir Joshua, 19, 164n*8*
Rhode Island: packet from New York to, 59; Hazlitt family in, 59-61
Rice, Col. Nathan: JH's portrait of, 16, 156n*91*
Rock of Cashel, 31-32, 130n*4*
Rolt, Miss, of Bandon: and Rev. WH, 42; testifies at Court of Inquiry, 43; friendship with Hazlitt family, 44; and MH, 44; as a teacher, 44
Roman Catholics: ill-treatment of, by British officers, 41-42, 135 n*47*; in Philadelphia, 50; in Massachusetts, 69; churches of, in Philadelphia, 140n7
Rowe, Rev. John: and Hazlitt family, 102, 103; MH on, 103; sketch of, 165n*12*

Royal Academy, 19, 164n*8*
Rum: from West Indies, 76; stills in Boston, 92; bottle of, at half way house, 98
Rush, Dr. Benjamin: and Dr. John Ewing, 6, 120; and Rev. WH, 6, 51, 120; sketch of, 141n*13*
Rush, Jacob. *See* Bush, Mr. Justice, of Philadelphia
Russell Institution, 167n*36*
Russia: Elias Hasket Derby and, 72; Francis Dana in, 142n*15*; American trade with, 156n*90*; Cronstadt, 156n*90*; St. Petersburg, 156n*90*

St. Asaph, Wales, 39
St. Paul's Church, Centreville, Md.: Dr. Joseph Haslett active in, 130n*8*, 144n*26*; and Rev. WH, 144n*26*; vestryman of, 145 n*27*. *See also* Hazlitt, Rev. William; Maryland
St. Paul's Parish, Centreville, Md.: Rev. WH denied admission into, 144n*26*. *See also* Hazlitt, Rev. William; Maryland
Salem, Mass.: Rev. WH preaches at, 9, 72, 120, 127n*10*, 156n*88*; JH paints at, 15; WH at, 20, 72; Rev. WH visits Elias Hasket Derby at, 72; Rev. WH's visits to, 81; Rev. WH on churches at, 121; earthquake felt at, 159n*107*; mentioned, 12
—East Church, 12, 20, 121, 156n*88*
—First Church, 121, 156n*88*
—North Church, 121, 127n*10*, 156 n*88*
*Salem Gazette:* advertisement of JH in, 15
Salisbury, England, 110
Sandy Hook, 58
Sawyer, Elizabeth Checkley. *See* Lathrop, Mrs. John
School keeping: proposed to Rev. WH, in Burlington, N. J., 49; in Germantown, Pa., 53; in London, 100; takes charge of a school in Wem, 105
Schuylkill River, 50, 51, 52, 140n6, 140n*8*

Scilly Isles, 87, 162n*133*
Scituate, Mass.: Rev. WH preaches at, 6, 72, 120, 148n*47*, 156n*92*
Scripture, 55
Selectmen of Boston, 150n*65*
Shakespeare, Mr., at Perth Amboy: appearance of, 58
Shakespeare, William, 58
Shapland, Mr., of Marshfield, England, 36, 133n*24*
Sharp, Mr.: and Rev. WH, 71, 155n*85*; and Kirk Boott and his family, 80; return to England of, 81; marriage of, 81
Shelburne, Lord. *See* Petty, Sir William
Shrewsbury, England: the Hazlitt family at, 102; Rev. WH at, 102, 165n*10*; Rev. Joseph Fownes at, 102, 165n*11*; Rev. John Rowe at, 102, 165n*12*; Rev. Pendlebury Houghton at, 165n*17*, 166 n*18*; mentioned, 103
Shrone Hill (Shronell), Ireland: the Hazlitts of, 4, 123; Rev. WH born at, 4, 130n*2*
Shropshire (Salop), 12, 51, 81, 102
Shute, Rev. Daniel: and Rev. WH, 70, 71; sketch of, 121, 153 n*74*. *See also* New Hingham (Third Parish) Church
Shute, Dr. Daniel (son of Rev. Daniel Shute), 70, 153n*74*
Sidmouth, England: Rev. Isaac Smith settled at, 92, 163n*142*
Smith (Smyth), Rev. Isaac: chaplain at Castle William, 92, 163 n*142*; sketch of, 92, 163n*142*; member of Boston Association of Ministers, 114; refugee in England, 163n*142*
Smith, Joseph, 133n*25*. *See also* Smyth, Mr. and Mrs., of Bristol
Smith (Smyth), Rev. William, 64, 148n*46*, 148n*47*
Smith, Mrs. William (Elizabeth Quincy), 148n*46*, 148n*47*
Smith family, of Weymouth, Mass., 148n*47*
Smyth, Mr. and Mrs., of Bristol, 37. *See also* Smith, Joseph
Smyth, Rev. Isaac. *See* Smith, Rev. Isaac

Smyth, Rev. William. *See* Smith, Rev. William
Snakes: black snake, 21, 65; a deadly snake, 52-53; in America, 77; in the southern states, 77; rattlesnakes, 78, 96
Socinianism, 12, 133n*32*
South Carolina: need for Presbyterian ministers in, 145n*32*
Southern states: and the West Indies, 76; nature's gifts in, 77
Sproat (Sprout), Dr. James, 119
Stockport, England, 20, 164n*8*
Stoddart, Sir John, 20, 109, 167n*30*
Stoddart, Sarah. *See* Hazlitt, Mrs. William
Storms at sea: on voyage from Cove to New York, 46; in Bay of Fundy, 74; on Rev. WH's crossing from Boston to Dover, 83-89 *passim*; on voyage from Boston to Portsmouth, 97
"Stranger's Friend, The." *See* Hazlitt, Rev. William
Stuart, House of, 120
Summer weather: in Pennsylvania, 52; in Maryland and South Carolina, 56; in New York, 58; in Rhode Island, 60; in Massachusetts, 64
Surrey, England, 12
Surrey Institution, 110, 167n*36*
Swanwick, Mr., of Wem, 102, 165 n*13*
Swanwick, Joseph: and Rev. WH, 105, 166n*19*; and WH, 105, 165 n*13*; on Samuel Taylor Coleridge, 165n*13*

Tea drinking: in Marshfield, England, 36; in Braintree, Mass., 62; in Upper Dorchester, 79; in Wem, 104
*Telemachus (Télémaque)*: read by MH and WH, 107, 166n*22*
Tenterden, England: residence of Thomas Viny at, 5, 38, 133n*33*; MH at, 38; description of, 38
Thanksgiving sermon: Rev. WH preaches a, 74, 157n*98*, 159n*99*; custom in New England to preach an annual, 74

Thatcher, Mr., of Portland, Maine, 121, 122

Thaxter family, of Hingham, 16

Thaxter-Lincoln house, Hingham, 16, 19

Thelwall, John, 20

Theological controversy: between Rev. WH and Rev. Samuel Parker, 10-11

*Theological Repository,* 5

Thirty-nine Articles: Rev. James Freeman's refusal to subscribe to, 10, 114; scriptural confutation of, 11, 116

Thomas, Rev. Samuel: friendship with Rev. WH, 38; death of, 38; on the American Revolution, 38; and Hazlitt family, 40; health of, 40; sketch of, 134n*34*

Thomas, Mrs. Samuel, 40

Thorny down, Winterslow, 110

Thursday Lecture, in Boston, and Rev. WH, 120

Tipperary, County of, 4, 130n*4*

Tipperary, town of, 31, 123

Tories: feud with Whigs, 41; mentioned, 16

Towns in America: in New Jersey, 49; Maryland, 54; Massachusetts, 61, 89, 90; Maine, 73, 74; contrasted with Wem, 89, 90

Tracey, Miss, of Liverpool, 106

Tracey, Mrs., of Liverpool, 106, 107, 166n*21*

*Transfiguration* (Raphael), WH's copy of, 108

Treaty of peace, between Great Britain and the United States, 47, 139n*68*

Trees: MH on, 61, 78; in southern states, 77; elm, 78

Trench farms, near Wem, 103

Trenton, battle of, 33

Trinitarianism: deletion of passages in Book of Common Prayer savoring of, 11, 116; doxology of, 12; Jews and Mahometans and, 52; Rev. WH disavows belief in, 127n*10*

Truro, Mass.: visit of Rev. WH and WH to, 157n*95. See also* Cape Cod

Truth: Rev. WH's teaching of, 31; spread of, in the United States, 122

Tufts, Dr. Cotton: house of, 65, 78; family of, 76; diary of, cited, 152n*68*; and Lucy Jones, 160 n*109*

Tufts, Mrs. Cotton (Lucy Quincy): Hazlitts' claimed relationship to, 63, 76, 149n*50*

Tufts, Cotton (son of Dr. Cotton Tufts), 76, 160n*108*

Turkeys: JH's painting of, 16, 89; description of, 77, 89

Tyler, Boston (a Negro servant), 79, 160n*117*

Tyler, Capt. Elisha, 160n*116*

Tyler, Mrs. Elisha (Martha Butts), 79, 160n*116*

Uncle Aron (perhaps Aaron Renouf): his cottage blown down, 74, 159n*103*; sketch of, 74, 75

Unitarianism: and Rev. WH, 4, 5, 9, 12, 56, 116; in America, 9, 11, 12, 113; Apostle of, in Boston, 24; Mr. Gomez on, 52; doctrine of, 55, 56; and Dr. Priestley, 56, 145n*31*; in Salem, Mass., 121; subject of conversation in America, 121; in Massachusetts, 122; Rev. WH on spread of, 122; in England, 122, 123; in Ireland, 135n*45*

Unitarian liturgy: at King's Chapel, 11, 12, 116; difficulties concerning, 118

Unitarian ministers: in Salem, Mass., 121; neglect of the old, 122

Unitarian ministry, training for, 122

Unitarian New College. *See* Hackney College

Unitarians: reap fruits of Rev. WH's labors in America, 53; afraid to avow sentiments in America, 55-56; evil reports circulated against, 115; treatment of Rev. WH by, 122; Rev. WH's criticism of, 122, 123

United States, the: conditions in, 3; WH's memories of, 20; lack of civil and religious liberty in, 21; MH's memories of, 22, 25;

tour of, 59; oldest college in, 92-93; T. A. Emmet family in, 136 n52; and treaty of peace with Britain, 139n68; mentioned, 23 University of Delaware Library, 26 Upper Dorchester. *See* Dorchester, Mass.

Vaughan, John, in Philadelphia, 53, 144n22
Vaughan, Samuel (1720-1802): JH paints a picture for, 16, 89; and Hazlitt family, 53; and Rev. WH, 53, 144n22; and English ladies, 53
Vaughan, Mrs. Samuel (Sarah Hallowell), 53, 144n22
Vaughan, Samuel (son of Samuel and Sarah Vaughan): and Hazlitt family, 53; in Philadelphia, 53, 144n22; in Boston, 53; and Rev. WH, 73; generosity to Rev. WH, 157n98
Vaughan family: in Philadelphia, 53, 144n22; return to England, 53; and Rev. WH, 120
Vegetables: kind grown in Ireland, 45; thirteen different sorts at dinner in America, 79
Vehicles: stage-waggons, 49, 57; coaches, 61; one-horse chaise, 62, 79; tandems and gigs, 62, 102; stage, 99
Viny, Thomas: and Rev. WH, 5, 38; and Benjamin Franklin, 5, 38; correspondence with Rev. WH, 40; on the American Revolution, 40; sketch of, 133n33
Vize, Mrs., of Bandon, 43, 44, 136 n54
Vize, Dr. John, 43, 136n54
Volunteer Corps, 44, 137n57

Wales, Mr., of Dorchester, 79
Wales, 39, 40
Wall, Baring, 109-110, 167n34
Walworth, England: Hazlitt family at, 100; garden at, 100, 164 n3; common at, 101
Washington, George: and Col. John Hazlitt, 32, 130n9; seen by Rev. WH and JH in Philadelphia, 51, 141n9; songs about, 62;

and Reuben Harvey, 137n60; and Society of the Cincinnati, 141n9; and the Episcopal Church, 141n9
Welsh, the, 39
Wem, England: Rev. WH's settlement at, 12; residence of Hazlitt family at, 12; 102-107; departure of the Hazlitt family from, 12; contrast between Hazlitts' American abodes and, 25, 82, 89-90; the Bootts visit at, 81; arrival of the Hazlitt family at, 102; the Hazlitts' house in, 102, 103; WH's attitude toward, 103; description of, 103; Mrs. Tracey at, 106, 107; MH on people in, 107; Mr. Swanwick of, 165n13; Samuel Taylor Coleridge at, 165n13; Rev. John Houghton at, 165n17; mentioned, 21
West, Benjamin, 64, 149n53
Western, Sophia, 76
West Indian hurricane, violence of, 85
West Indies: American trade with, 76; Mrs. Tracey from, 106
Westminster Catechism, 12
Weymouth, Mass.: residence of Hazlitt family at, 6, 19, 21, 62-78 *passim*; Rev. WH preaches at, 6, 69, 120, 148n47, 152n68; JH paints at, 15; WH at, 20, 21; description of the Hazlitts' house at, 63, 64; description of, 64, 65; house of prayer at, 65; Cotton Tufts' house at, 65; the Whitmans' house at, 65; actions of British regulars near, 66; Gen. Lovell's house at, 66, 150n59; inconveniences of, 75; MH's recollections of, 76; departure of Hazlitt family from, 78, 159 n104; mentioned, 70, 71, 73, 78, 92
Whales, 78, 97
Wheeler, Jonathan, 54, 136n53, 144n25
Wheeler, Joseph, Jr.: stays with Hazlitt family in Philadelphia, 54, 144n25; death of, 54; and Rev. WH, 136n53

Wheeler family, of Bandon, 43
Whiggism, of Rev. WH, 14, 148n47
Whigs: feud with Tories, 41; of the old stamp, 114
Whitchurch, England, 103, 104
Whitman, Capt. Abiah: and WH, 21, 65; house of, 65; example set by, 66; and the Hazlitt family, 78; sketch of, 150n57
Whitman, Mrs. Abiah (Abigail Giles): visited by the Hazlitt women, 66; visits to the Hazlitt family by, 66; tales of the late war told by, 66; marriage of, 150n57
Wiche, Rev. John: friendship with Rev. WH, 38; death of, 38; correspondence with Rev. WH, 40; on the American Revolution, 40; religious views of, 40, 133n32; sketch of, 133n32
Wicklow Mountains, 40
Wicksteed, Mr., of Shrewsbury, 102, 164n9
Wicksteed, John, 164n9
Wight, Isle of: Sharp settles at, 81; Rev. WH passes, 88; MH mentions, 99; panorama of, 101
Willard, Mr., of Hingham, 71
Willard, Dr. Samuel, 152n71
Willard, Susan Barker, 16
Williams, David: and Hazlitt family, 100; and Rev. WH, 100, 101; misfortunes of, 101, 164n5; sketch of, 164n4
Wiltshire, England, 109
Winterslow, England: MH visits at, 22; William and Sarah Hazlitt at, 109; death of their child at, 109; MH at, 109, 110; scenery around, 109, 110; Charles and Mary Lamb at, 110
Winter weather: in Pennsylvania, 55; in New England, 55; in Massachusetts, 68, 69, 74, 75, 89; in Maine, 74
Winthrop, Gov. John, miniature of, 128n17
Wisbeach, England: Rev. WH settled at, 5, 34, 132n18; Loftus family of, 34, 35; Godwin family of, 34, 35, 132n20; mentioned, 100
Withington (Witherington), Ebenezer, 61, 147n45
Withington (Witherington), Mather, 61, 147n45
Wompatuck Club, Hingham, 16, 19
Wreakin (Wrekin), a hill in Shropshire, 102
Wyatt, Mr., mate of the *Nonpareil*, 95

Yale College, 163n144. *See also* Hartford College
Yankees: sharpshooters of, 65; breed of foxes of, 97
Yellow fever: in Philadelphia, 53, 144n23; Germantown uninfected by, 53, 144n23; Rev. WH seized with, 54, 118; remedies for, 54, 55; victims of, in New York, 72
Yorkshire, England, 34

.